OVERCOMING OBSTACLES IN ENVIRONMENTAL POLICYMAKING

SUNY SERIES IN INTERNATIONAL ENVIRONMENTAL
POLICY AND THEORY
SHELDON KAMIENIECKI, EDITOR

Overcoming Obstacles in Environmental Policymaking

Creating Partnerships through Mediation

John K. Gamman

State University of New York Press

Circle design on cover by Andrea Tassencourt

Published by
State University of New York Press, Albany

For information, address State University of New York
Press, State University Plaza, Albany, N.Y., 12246

Production by E. Moore
Marketing by Nancy Farrell

Library of Congress Cataloging-in-Publication Data

Gamman, John K.
    Overcoming obstacles in environmental policymaking : creating
partnerships through mediation / John K. Gamman.
        p. cm. — (SUNY series in international environmental policy
and theory)
    Includes bibliographical references and index.
    ISBN 0-7914-2207-0 (CH : acid-free). — ISBN 0-7914-2208-9 (PB :
acid-free)
    1. Environmental policy—Caribbean Area—Decision making.
2. Natural resources—Caribbean Area—Management. 3. Sustainable
development—Caribbean area. 4. Economic assistance—Caribbean
Area. 5. Environmental mediation—Caribbean Area. I. Title. II. Title:
Overcoming obstacles in environmental policy making.
III. Series.
HC151.Z9E54 1994
363.7'06'09729—dc20   94-2262
                                                           CIP

10 9 8 7 6 5 4 3 2 1

To Richard A. Cooley
Friend, Colleague, Mentor

Contents

Foreword

Islands can provide microcosms where the ecological and developmental concerns that also afflict continental areas may be more easily examined. This is particularly true of islands that are also nation states since they bring with them the burdens of government and politics combined with close socio-cultural relationships between the governors and the governed. On islands environmental limits are, or should be, apparent. Yet island nations most commonly turn to outside agencies to seek answers to internal problems. These agencies may promise aid for environmental conservation, economic development or both. However, it is unfortunately rare for these agencies to be sensitive to either the social and cultural constraints or the ecological imperatives that island peoples must face.

These issues are what John Gamman has examined in his study of St. Kitts, St. Lucia, and Barbados in the Eastern Caribbean. The problems are not new, nor are they confined to islands. Gamman has proposed ways in which solutions may be reached that certainly should be considered in all development agencies. Indeed this book should be required reading for anyone working in the area of international conservation and development.

—Raymond F. Dasmann

PREFACE

Despite the recent surge of interest in the environmental problems of the developing world, there has been little success in finding effective ways to resolve them. The purpose of my research has been to find out why these problems seem so intractable. There is really no precedent for the complexity they contain. The fields of development planning, economic development, political science, community participation, anthropology, and environmental planning all offer valuable insights into the knotty nature of environmental problems, but solutions are harder to come by.

One thing that is becoming increasing clear is that environmental problems cannot be separated from the intricacies of national culture and politics. Any solution to the environmental crisis, one that promotes lasting change in the public policy processes of affected countries and the many agencies that are hooked into international development, has to account for the crucial roles of culture and politics.

If the public policy process is to respond to the environmental crisis in a meaningful way, which will require substantial reforms, an approach has to be found to account for the complex nature of the problem. One way to accomplish this is to apply the theory and practice of the emerging field of negotiation and conflict resolution. A basic premise of conflict resolution is that all of the parties affected by an action should have a voice in an open dialogue to express their interests. Then, out of this sharing of interests, emerges a collaborative effort to solve what is perceived as a common problem. The parties find that they have more in common than they had imagined. Adversarial behavior diminishes, people talk openly, common ground is forged to create an elegant solution that everyone is satisfied with.

If all goes well, the parties may find themselves better off than before. This model of decision making does work, as experience has shown in the United States and Europe, but it remains largely untested in developing countries.

I believe that a collaborative negotiation process can be successfully used to address environmental problems in the developing world. But the differences in political systems and national cultures between developed and developing countries require the United States–based model of negotiation to be modified to accommodate them. Despite the difficulties involved, I believe that a negotiated partnership holds the greatest promise for effectively addressing the complexities facing the global commons.

My goal in writing this book is to examine the reasons why efforts to protect natural resources are failing, and how they can be improved. Advice is offered to policy analysts to enable them to more accurately account for the constraints and opportunities for donor agencies and developing countries that attempt to protect limited natural resources. To accomplish this, I have tried to tell this story from the perspective of people who are involved in international development, in developing countries, donor agencies, and nongovernmental organizations.

In order to write this book I spent considerable time in several countries, visiting with a wide variety of people, taking the time to build personal relationships in order to hear the stories of individuals involved in all aspects of environmental policymaking. It is the collection of these stories that forms the backbone of this book, its assumptions, reflections and recommendations. Yet, I have attempted to build on existing theoretical research that touches on and interconnects the fields of international development, public policy, environmental studies, international conservation and cross cultural communication. Because I have mainly focused on gathering evidence from people actually involved in the cases I describe, I have not been as specific when tying my findings to existing theory. However, I continue to conduct research and practice professionally in this area, and invite individuals conducting similar research to contact me if they have questions about any of the work that appears in this book.

The case study format that I use to tell this story has required me to interpret key events that have occurred in different countries and organizations. Obviously, the cases are told from my vantage point. Experts from the Caribbean and donor agencies have reviewed the cases, and several suggested changes have been made to ensure accuracy. However, any errors that remain are my own.

Acknowledgments

There are several people to whom I am grateful for offering the support, guidance, and inspiration that helped me endure while I completed this work. My greatest debt is to the people of the Caribbean. During my travels in the region there were many obstacles, real and imagined, but when they seemed the greatest, someone was always there to tell me that my work was important to his or her country, that an outside, unbiased voice like mine would help them protect their islands, and that I shouldn't give up. I am glad I listened to their advice, and I only hope this work makes a small contribution to help the islands survive.

My doctoral adviser at the Massachusetts Institute of Technology, Larry Susskind, gave me intellectual guidance, with great patience, and taught me how to ask the right questions. This is much easier said than done, and I am grateful to him for his enduring support and creative insight. H. Jeffrey Leonard has inspired me through the quality of his work and his leadership in international conservation. Lloyd Rodwin has given me the great benefit of his long experience, reminding me that there are many competing values to contend with when promoting my ideas, and his advice is gratefully acknowledged. Lynton Caldwell encouraged me to return to school after several years in the world of consulting. I am indebted to Professor Caldwell for his encouragement and thankful for the opportunities that his lifelong dedication, and that of many others like him, has created for me and my colleagues. I wish to thank Sheldon Kamieniecki of the University of Southern California, who provided valuable encouragement and invaluable support for this work as he reviewed it and helped me rethink it; Clay Morgan, my editor at SUNY Press, who has provided patient guidence throughout this project;

Tobin Freid, who provided research support, which allowed me to update the cases using the best available information and Mystére Sapia, who helped prepare the final manuscript.

I want to acknowledge several people in the Caribbean who have helped me understand the people and politics of the Caribbean; to Ed Towle of the Island Resources Foundation, Yves Renard of the Caribbean Natural Resources Institute, David Staples of Barbados, Victor and Sheila Williams of St. Kitts, and Mervin Williams of St. Lucia, thank you for your insights that have provoked my thinking and refined my work. My appreciation is extended to Dr. Euna Moore of the Centre for Resource Management and Environmental Studies at the University of the West Indies; her support gave me credibility in the region that opened many doors. I want to thank my former colleagues at MIT, especially Scott McCreary, Eileen Babbitt, Rolf Engler, Maria Hortaridis, and Sandy Wellford.

My parents, Allan and Mary Gamman, have supported my endeavors unceasingly; they have kept me going when my task seemed truly overwhelming. My mentor and dear friend Richard Cooley has served as my role model, and in the midst of hardship, has reminded me in his gentle way why I am doing this work. Ray Evans, at Feather River College showed me the intricate beauty of the natural world, strengthening my environmental ethic. I am appreciative of Bob Brauchli's support, which enabled me to initiate a relationship with the White Mountain Apache Tribe, which in turn has showed me the importance of respecting cultural traditions when one is trying to understand the subtleties of humanity's relationship with the environment. To John Jostes, Teresa and Pat Gamman, Elisa Pederson, David Boghossian, Elizabeth Bartle, Bryan Harvey, Lynn Griesemer, Hugh O'Doherty, Ida Koppen, Leila Zaloui, Ed and Ann Gilbride, Ori Seron, Kelley Quinn, Martha Danly, David Hersten, Ron Hunter, Lori Park, Randy Rutsch, Lynn Hottman, Sara Gaar, Bob and Carol Allen, and the gang back in Santa Cruz: Declan and Donna Gallagher, Kevin Gallagher, Louis and Joanna Runeare, Barbara Wright, Jay Leite, and many more, thank you for your friendship and love. Your constant encouragement has allowed me to fulfill a part of my dream.

Funding for my work was provided by the National Institute for Dispute Resolution, the Organization of American States, the Richard D. Irwin Foundation, and the Eastern Caribbean Natural Areas Management Program, and I thank them all.

Abbreviations and Acronyms

AOSIS	The Alliance of Small States
BDD	British Development Division, Overseas Development Administration
B 1, 2, 3, etc.	confidential interview from Barbados case study
CANRI	Caribbean Natural Resources Institute
CARICOM	Caribbean Community and Common Market
CBI	Caribbean Basin Initiative
CCA	Caribbean Conservation Association
CCPU	Coastal Conservation Project Unit
CDB	Caribbean Development Bank
CERMES	Centre for Resource Management and Environmental Studies
CFO	Chief Forestry Officer
DCA	Development Control Authority
DESFIL	Development Strategies for Fragile Lands
ECCM	East Caribbean Common Market
ECLAC	Economic Commission for Latin American and the Caribbean
EIA	Environmental Impact Assessment
EMC	Environmental Management Committee
EPAT	Environmental Policy and Training Project
FAO	Food and Agricultural Organization, United Nations
IDB	Inter-American Development Bank
IMF	International Monetary Fund
MDB	Multilateral Development Bank
NAFTA	North American Free Trade Agreement
NCEPA	National Conservation and Environmental Protection Act

NEPA   National Environmental Policy Act
NGO   Nongovernmental Organization
OAS   Organization for American States
OECS   Organization of Eastern Caribbean States
OECS/NRMP   Organization of Eastern Caribbean States Natural
             Resource Management Project
PPS   Physical Planning Section
PVO   Private Voluntary Organization
RDO/C   Regional Development Office, Caribbean
SDC   Soufriere Development Committee
SK 1,2,3 etc. confidential interview from St. Kitts case study
SL 1,2,3, etc. confidential interview from St. Lucia case study
TCP   Town and Country Planning
UNEP   United Nations Environment Programme
USAID   United States Agency for International Development

Chapter One

ENVIRONMENTAL POLICY IMPLEMENTATION: THE NATURE OF THE PROBLEM AND SOME DIFFICULT QUESTIONS

This book tells a story about the complexities of trying to protect endangered natural resources in developing countries. It describes why efforts originating in nations of the "north" to protect natural resources in the countries of the "south" often fail, and what can be done to improve such efforts. It offers concrete solutions to address the political, economic, and cultural complexities that underlie large-scale environmental problems.

We are all too familiar with the vivid image of giant fires destroying the rainforests of the Amazon, fires that can now be seen by astronauts circling the globe. We have heard the cries of endangered animals such as the panda and the cheetah, archetypes of a simpler and wilder time. We know that polluted water, air, and land is damaging human health and natural ecosystems worldwide. These types of problems, which seem impossible to solve, comprise an environmental crisis of truly global dimensions.

While significant environmental problems exist in all parts of the world, this book deals with solving these problems as they affect the developing world. This is because the puzzle that needs to be unlocked to resolve environmental problems in the developing world is exceedingly complex, due to the interplay of international and national politics, culture, and economics. If this puzzle can be better understood, it will reveal valuable lessons that can be used to address environmental problems in both developed and developing nations.

In response to the environmental crisis that exists in most of the developing world, environmental groups in the United States and Europe have pressured their own governments to force international development assistance agencies, including the World Bank, the U.S. Agency for International Development, and the Inter-American Development Bank, to reform their lending practices to protect limited natural resources. New laws have been adopted, policies written, regulations introduced, and professional experts sent abroad to implement them. Although some successes have occurred, these efforts have generally not worked. As a result, limited natural resources that are under severe pressure to feed fast growing populations, pay off foreign debt, and improve the standard of living continue to be mismanaged.

If this trend continues, there may not be enough natural resources left to provide for the future economic and political stability of developing nations. This in turn could lead to tremendous economic burdens on industrialized nations as international markets for their goods and services shrink or, in the worst cases, are eliminated, requiring cash subsidies from developed countries that are already strapped for capital because of the worldwide recession of the early 1990s.

This dilemma raises a number of questions. Why are limited natural resources being destroyed so quickly, and why are they not managed more effectively? What special interests prevent natural resources from being preserved, despite tens of millions of dollars spent each year by a plethora of environmental groups, and major pro-environmental initiatives of the donor agencies.[1] Can the developed nations effectively promote environmental protection among the nations of the developing world, given the basic cultural, political, and economic differences that divide them?[2] Should industrialized nations exert economic and political pressure on developing countries to protect resources perceived as part of the global commons? The purpose of this book is explore these and other issues.

In the Caribbean, which is the focus of this study, major fisheries are being depleted, fresh water supplies for entire communities polluted, reef systems destroyed, forests illegally cut, and large stretches of coast eroded away because of overdevelopment. Large development projects, funded by the same donor agencies that espouse environmental protection, displace local villages and fail to create the economic opportunities promised. Experts question whether the current rate of development can be sustained in the long run, given the environmental problems that are surfacing. This situation is not unique to the Caribbean; on the contrary, the Caribbean seems to be representative of what has happened, and what can happen, in South America, Asia, Africa, the South Pacific, Eastern Europe, and Eurasia.[3]

The Complexity of Environmental Policy Making

While national and international policies created to stem the tide of environmental destruction in developing countries often fail, I believe that the policy-making process can be improved. I believe that environmental policies targeted for developing nations, especially those policies initiated by donor agencies and environmental groups in industrialized countries, simply do not show an understanding of three key components of the policy-making process, and how these components interact. The components of policy making that need to be better understood are the negative effects of the closed policy-making process, the critical role of local and national culture in decision making in developing countries, and an excessive dependence on United States–style economic growth.

The closed nature of environmental policy making, both within donor agencies that sponsor large-scale development projects and within the governments of countries where projects are built, promotes a distinct anti-environmental bias. Special interest groups influence national political leaders in developing countries and donor agencies' senior officials, who are usually political appointees, to promote economic growth even when it is well known that severe environmental damage will result. This mutually reinforcing behavior between senior officials in donor agencies and national political leaders underlies a system that often promotes foreign investment at any environmental cost.

Environmental protection policies that originate in donor agencies, consulting firms, and environmental organizations in developed countries are grounded in a Eurocentric world view that promotes misconceptions about how individuals and institutions in the developing world think and act. An overemphasis on large-scale, United States–style economic development strategies creates projects that most countries cannot sustain because of the sophisticated technologies and continuous expenditures of capital required to keep them operating. By themselves, these components each have a great impact on the way international environmental policies are created and implemented. If any one factor is not understood it can spell environmental disaster. If all of these factors are not understood, as is often the case, limited natural resources are depleted and destroyed despite well-intended policies and laws that have been adopted to protect them.

In the remainder of this chapter, I will describe in more detail what kind of environmental problems result from failures in the policy-making process. I will then define in more detail what the key components of international environmental policy making are, and how they interact to enforce the pattern of environmental destruction. I will describe why a more open public policy process is needed to protect limited natural resources. Finally, I will explain why I chose the Caribbean as the focus for three case studies of failed environmental policy making, how the problems in the Caribbean apply to all developing countries, and the methods I used to create the case studies that are presented here.

SOME COMMON NATURAL RESOURCE PROBLEMS IN DEVELOPING COUNTRIES

The nature and extent of environmental problems in developing nations is well documented.[4] How shortcomings in the policy-making and policy-implementation process allow these problems to occur is not as well understood. But before the major obstacles to an effective environmental policy-making process are presented, I would like to review some of the major environmental problems that developing countries experience.

Population growth is one root cause of environmental problems in the developing world. World population growth increased to an annual rate of 1.9 percent between 1950 and 1955, compared to .8 percent between 1900 and 1950. The majority of population growth now occurs in developing countries in Latin America (including the Caribbean), Asia, and Africa. These regions accounted for 85 percent of the growth in world population between 1950 and 1985.[5] Although some effects of population growth can be accommodated with scientific innovation such as more efficient agricultural production, the demands on scarce natural resources are always increased when population grows.

Coastal marine ecosystems, which are a major source of protein in the form of fish harvested at ocean fisheries for many developing countries, are being depleted in many regions of the world. Coral reefs, mangrove ecosystems, estuaries, and lagoons, which serve vital roles in the life cycle of many marine species, are all being depleted. Some species are being overfished, while others are permanently displaced by ports, harbors, and industrial facilities. Inadequate waste disposal systems result in polluted near-shore waters, which harms marine life. Sand mining for cement production, and construction of tourist resorts and housing on beaches, result in coastal erosion and destruction of the near-offshore habitat needed to support local fisheries.[6] This trend appears especially serious given that the world fish catch increased from 21 million to 66 million metric tons between 1950 and 1970, an annual growth rate of 6 percent, but then slowed to less than a 1 percent annual increase after 1970, apparently the result of overfishing.[7]

Destruction of tropical forests causes local impacts on soils, water quality, fisheries, and wildlife, and contributes to regional and global problems as well. Slash and burn agriculture, cattle ranches, large mining operations, charcoal production, and programs to resettle communities commonly lead to deforestation. Deforestation leads to at least two major environmental problems. First, destruction of large areas of tropical forests, particularly in South America and Asia and Africa, is causing a loss of biological diversity. Scientists are finding that the ecology of tropical forests is based on a delicate and complex set of relationships among the plants and animals that have evolved in the moist tropical environment. It is not merely the immediate physical destruction of the forest, which causes erosion of thin tropical soils and a permanent loss of fuelwood, that concerns scientists; rather, the loss of biological diversity in tropical forests is the primary concern. Fifty percent of earth's life forms live in tropical forests, and of these 8 to 10 million species, only 1.5 million have been named.[8] According to leading scientists such as E.O. Wilson, this barely tapped biological reservoir may, and almost certainly does, contain cures for cancer, heart disease, and other human maladies—cures that could be refined and sold to the world's population. Thus, the loss of biological diversity represents potential immense long-term economic losses for both developed and developing nations.

The second major environmental problem associated with deforestation is a worsening of the global Greenhouse effect. Burning trees produce carbon, which is dispersed into the earth's upper atmosphere, adding to carbon loading and contributing to global warming. The precise contribution of deforestation in the tropics to the Greenhouse effect is not known, but it is known that carbon loading in the atmosphere is increasing. Other effects of deforestation include alteration of the hydrologic cycle, which has changed rainfall patterns in several areas, changing a moist landscape to one that is arid and barren of water. This in turn affects the ability of regions to support irrigation practices for agriculture, displacing communities, forcing migration to urban megacities that have their own problems resulting from rapid population growth.

Desertification is another major environmental problem in developing countries. Alteration of local microclimates has also been related to desertification. Desertification commonly occurs when local water and soil resources are mismanaged due to overly intensive agriculture practices. Productive land is converted to wasteland due to overcultivation, overgrazing, clearing of forests, and irrigation practices that leave behind deposits of salt and heavy metals that denutrify the soil. In Africa alone an estimated 6.9 square kilometers of the sub-Saharan region, an area twice the size of India, has characteristics that make it ripe for desertification. Large scale irrigation projects that convert large blocks of marginal soils to new farmlands, based on the U.S. and European model of industrial agricultural production, have contributed to this problem.[9] Large-scale agricultural operations also tend to create agricultural industries that produce one type of commodity, such as groundnuts in Africa or bananas and sugar in the Caribbean and South America. This monotype agriculture is generally easier to manage as it requires uniform production techniques, but at the same time it makes countries dependent on single export commodities subject to trade restrictions and international competition, something that the sugar and banana industries constantly face.

Other serious environmental problems typically found in developing countries include pollution of fresh water supplies from poor sanitation practices and disposition of pesticides and fertilizers from agricultural operations. Poor land-use decisions, resulting from a lack of trained planners and clear land-use guidelines, allow landfills and industrial facilities that generate water and land pollution to be located close to urban communities. In addition to land-use practices that degrade limited natural resources, a dependency on particularly large-scale projects can cause substantial environmental damage.

Examples of large projects that can damage natural resources, because of their immense size and physical impact, are the Polonoroeste Project in Brazil, the Sardar Sarovar Dam in India, and the Pak Mun Dam in Thailand. The Polonoroeste Project was initiated in 1982, funded by a $500 million loan from the World Bank to Brazil. The project had several objectives: to pave Highway 364 along Brazil's northern border in the state of Rondônia, which transported 200,000 migrants to the rainforested interior in 1985; the construction of several dams for generating electricity; and promotion of new cattle ranching, mining, and cash-crop farming. Areas that had been slated for environmental protection, based on consultants' reports that fragile soils would not support intensive agriculture, remain unprotected, and are being developed by impoverished migrants. Indigenous Indians in the region have been placed in conflict with newly arrived miners, farmers, and ranchers, and also lack adequate protection.[10]

The Pak Mun Dam in Thailand, to be financed by the World Bank with a $55 million development loan, was slated to start construction in 1993. The dam will flood farmland and destroy fisheries that are used to feed local communities. It has been estimated that 20,000 villagers will be negatively affected or displaced by the dam; in March 1992 a petition signed by 12,000 villagers protesting the dam was presented to Bank officials. In May 1992 800 villagers met near the dam site to protest its construction and to rebuild a religious shrine that had been destroyed by French contractors. Farmers who are being required to resettle away from the construction area refuse to leave, believing that the land in the resettlement area is not suited for cultivation.[11]

The Sardar Sarovar Dam in India is funded by a $450 loan and credits approved by the World Bank in 1985. The dam, under construction, will forcibly displace 90,000 residents of rural communities. Eight basic environmental studies that were to be completed by 1985 as a precondition for the dam have not been completed.[12] While the Bank has established a special Independent Mission to review the project, and has budgeted a $150 credit towards protecting the Narmada River watershed where the dam is located, the projects' sheer size will permanently impact the natural and cultural resources in the region. In short, this type of massive capital improvement projects, which also take the form of highways, airports, pipelines, refineries, and industrial plants, cause their own widespread environmental damage. These projects, which are intended to and often do provide some economic benefits, create a entire new class of environmental problems. The physical environment is degraded or destroyed, boom and bust communities are created that do not provide for sustainable long-term economic growth, cultural traditions and values are lost, and special local knowledge of natural resource trends and conditions, essential to creating environmentally sustainable development strategies, is neglected.

There are several reasons why this pattern of environmentally damaging projects has emerged. Under the best of circumstances, when abundant renewable natural resources, trained personnel, and the political will to develop environmentally sustainable projects are available, such development is still extremely difficult to do. Even if development planners go through all of the steps to design an environmentally sound project, the effort to transform these ideas into concrete action in countries with political systems that tend to be closed, blocking key parties from participating, requires a high degree of innovation and accountability that usually does not exist.

Decision making processes that create and implement both environmental policies and development projects are closed. Leaders in developing countries with a relatively short history of democracy and sovereign government, and top officials in donor agencies who depend on lending money to advance in their careers, collaborate to keep control of decision making. They perceive that they will lose control, power, and prestige if they allow new pro-environmental interests to have a real voice in the development and policy-making process. Hence, environmental laws and policies, and conditions attached to projects to protect natural resources, often remain ineffective and unenforced. Long-term environmental and economic stability is traded for short-term political control and economic gain. As a result, economic development and environmental protection are pitted against one another, instead of being framed at the policy level as two parts of an integrated, sustainable planning and development process.

Because of this single-purpose planning process, which values perceived short-term economic benefits over long-term natural resource management, other critical elements of a sustainable development process are also left out or undervalued. Unorganized interest groups, called stakeholders, such as local non-governmental organizations and resource users and producers, are left out. These parties often possess special knowledge about two key elements of the environmental planning process; the status of local ecosystems, and how they are affected by a range of human actions, and how the local political system operates. Cultural attitudes and traditions that drive human behavior, communication, and interactions with the natural landscape are not understood or seriously considered by decision makers.

To understand the human and institutional shortcomings in environmental decision making, one must first reflect on the benefits of open decision making in a society. What elements of open, more democratic decision making are important? Does a more open environmental decision-making process lead to policies that protect resources? Are public institutions capable of responding to the need for more open decision making? A brief review of democratic theory, and how a democracy attempts to account for different viewpoints, will help start to answer these questions.

DEMOCRATIC DECISION MAKING: INDIVIDUAL AND INSTITUTIONAL BEHAVIOR

The traditional principles of democratic theory are based on the idea that all citizens should participate actively and meaningfully in the decisions their governments make. James Q. Wilson describes three kinds of democratic political systems. The first kind of democratic system is one that serves the "true interests" of the citizens, with their direct participation, or indirect participation through government. This is admittedly a broad definition of democracy. The second kind of democratic system is one that approximates Aristotle's "rule of the many," which occurs if all, or most, citizens directly take part as policy makers or elected officials. The third kind of democratic system is one where political leaders dominate competitive struggles, commonly known as elections, and win the right to represent the citizens, and make decisions on their behalf.[13] While this form of governance, also called representative democracy, is the closest to the contemporary expressions of democracy found in modern societies, several critical factors influence how this method of decision making works, and whose interests are served.

Within representative democracies public policy decisions are made by elected officials, supported by public institutions such as a ministry or office of the executive branch. These public institutions are generally staffed by career civil servants or bureaucrats who are responsible for two key elements of the public policy process, policy design and policy implementation. When a government is initially considering whether to adopt a new policy, career civil servants are often responsible for formulating a set of alternative policies for political leaders to choose from. Then, when the political leaders choose which policy to adopt, civil servants are responsible for designing an administrative mechanism—which can be a new program, project, or set of guidelines—to implement the policy that was chosen. However, public policies are seldom designed and implemented in such a clear and consistent manner. This is because of the relationships within bureaucracies and between the bureaucratic institutions and individuals who run them.

A top layer of officials in the bureaucracies is typically staffed by non-career political appointees. These senior officials typically turn over ever four to six years, depending on the frequency of national or state elections, when their political bosses are elected or re-elected. It is important to understand the significance of this layer of top political appointees. Individuals in these top positions tend to be very influential in policy making, as they have personal access to political leaders. So, while in an ideal world citizens first demand a new policy, and bureaucrats develop a series of policy options and political leaders choose the best one, this rarely happens. Rather, special interest groups, combined with a variety of other influences, exert pressure on political leaders to create policies that will serve their own needs.

Interest groups are only one of the influences on the policy-making process, but they are a significant one. Representatives of interest groups influence policy making at many levels, including how laws are designed, ratified, and implemented. This influence takes many forms, including the appointment of senior officials in bureaucracies, who in turn influence the policy-making process on behalf of their special interest clients, who may have contributed time, staff, and energy to help elect the political leaders who appointed them. These close relationships among special interest groups, political leaders, and political appointees within bureaucracies have been called "subgovernments." But I believe that this special relationship between individuals and institutions of power is more than a subgovernment, and constitutes an interest group of its own.[14] This is especially true of governments that are young and lack democratic traditions, as is often the case with developing countries that have been independent of their former colonial sponsors for a small part of their history. In these countries, the influence of this government interest group is magnified for several reasons.

In most developing countries, national policies are set by a small group of political leaders, supported by their senior civil servants and political appointees. This is especially true in countries that have adopted parliamentary systems of government, most commonly modeled on the British system. Many scholars and practioners who work on environmental policies in developing countries do not seem to understand the significance of the parliamentary system in the policy-making process. The characteristics of the parliamentary system of governance are rarely, if ever, mentioned as a major contributing factor to failed environmental policies.

Within a parliamentary system the prime minister is selected to be the head of the national government by fellow members of parliament. The members of parliament supporting the selection of the prime minister are generally all from the same political party. This is not always true, as on occasion the majority party lacks a real majority, and must join with a minority party, or parties, to form a coalition government. However, coalition governments seem to be much more common in industrialized nations, which tend to have more sophisticated electorates. The prime minister then chooses various fellow members of parliament, who have just elected him or her as head of government, to be members of the cabinet. Together, the prime minister and the cabinet make up the national government, now firmly controlled by the ruling, or majority party. The parties, or party, that is in the minority becomes the opposition party and is basically left out of the national policy-making process, reduced to attacking the initiatives of the majority party.

The power dynamics between the majority party and opposition party affects national policy making in two fundamental ways. First, it creates a basic power imbalance between the parties and the citizens they represent. Members of the majority party are clearly insiders; they are consulted when the government formulates new public policies, and the interest groups that helped put them in power are listened to. Second, a strange sort of equilibrium develops between political leaders of the majority and opposition. The majority proposes new policies and the opposition inevitably attacks them, with their only goal being to cause enough damage to become the majority party in the next national election. If the opposition party does unseat the majority in the next election, many of the policy initiatives created by the majority are arbitrarily thrown out, causing great discontinuity in the national policy-making process.

These fundamental dynamics of a parliamentary system of government are exaggerated by a set of social, economic, and political conditions found in many developing countries. The flow of public information is often controlled by a government news service, such as the Ministry of Communications, in place of a free press. Political newspapers published by the majority and opposition parties may be the only forum in some countries. Frequently there are no regularly scheduled public hearings to solicit public comment on proposed public policies. In many countries there are no government-sponsored public hearings of any kind. These characteristics of decision making are the opposite of what exists in true democracies: a free press, a government that is directly accountable to citizens, and civil servants that are insulated from political retribution if they disagree with the political leadership.

When these conditions persist, affecting all aspects of national policy making and related decisions, governments are not perceived by those they govern as legitimate. Citizens are not allowed to participate in their governments in an active and meaningful way. Rather, the citizenry realizes how political decisions are being made and knows that its interests are not being represented. As a result the governed lose faith in their government and are alienated from it. The pattern of "insiders" and "outsiders" is magnified and becomes a fixture of policy making.

Large institutions such as donor agencies tend to behave in a similar manner. Top jobs are given to political appointees who routinely overrule recommendations from professional staff, preferring choices that promote the financial and political objectives of the institution. Internal deliberations that debate which policy to adopt are closed to the public, or are not officially recorded. The professional staff grows wary, not wanting to risk opposing those above them. As these tendencies are reinforced through repetition, institutions develop a collective memory that in turn creates an internal tradition for the way that decisions are made. Like the countries they often collaborate with to develop natural resources, whether it is a dam project, a highway, an airport, a redevelopment area or an agricultural project, donor agencies also create and maintain a closed decision-making process. Such a closed process virtually eliminates the wide scope of conflict that effective democracies must accommodate.

When both the countries and institutions largely responsible for establishing the policies and projects that develop natural resources employ closed decision making, they cater to traditional interest groups who possess the most political and economic power. This pattern of closed decision making excludes the opinions and interests of non-traditional stakeholders who have a stake in protecting natural resources. These non-traditional stakeholders include resource users who work day to day with the natural environment, such as fishers, farmers, and indigenous communities; environmental professionals within governments and donor agencies; and citizens represented by non-governmental environmental organizations, both foreign and domestic.

This trend of exclusion, which is contrary to the basic tenent of a democratic society, particularly harms efforts to implement new environmental protection policies. This is because environmental policies are among the newest within the policy arena and must compete for political capital and institutional resources with policies that favor economic development. Ministries within governments and departments that are newly created to design and implement environmental policies are at a distinct disadvantage, compared with existing institutions that favor long-standing economic development policies and the interest groups that benefit from them.[15]

I have found, and the case studies that follow will show, that closed decision making within developing countries and donor agencies has led to severe environmental damage in the Caribbean. But this pattern of environmental policy making, and the resulting damage to limited natural resources, is not limited to the Caribbean. The mutually reinforcing behavior of top officials in national governments and donor agencies leads to decisions that prevent natural resources from being protected and properly managed. This is because efforts to make and implement environmental policies fail to account for these major elements of policy making: the combined behavior of national politicians in developing countries and of political appointees and senior officials in donor agencies, which causes key stakeholders to be routinely left out of the decision-making process and leaves control with traditional entrenched interest groups; the culture of decision making in developing countries, which is the inseparable link between politics and the local culture and is rarely understood by outsiders; and the dominance of economic policies and incentives that promote large-scale projects that damage natural resources and dwarf efforts to manage these resources on a sustainable basis.

WHY DEVELOPMENT DECISION MAKING LEADS TO ENVIRONMENTAL DESTRUCTION

There are several reasons why the current trend in international development that stresses large projects, immense amounts of capital, and a Eurocentric planning perspective got started, and why this trend continues. I believe that four basic conditions dominate the process of international development and related environmental policy making and allow this trend to continue. Although the evidence I have gathered to show why environmental destruction is occurring is from the Caribbean, these conditions exist throughout the developing world. The lessons and insights that result apply to the vast majority of developing countries in South America, Asia, Africa, the South Pacific, the Caribbean, Eastern Europe and Eurasia. The first three conditions relate to how national policy making takes place in developing countries.

First, national political leaders often exert near-total control over a closed public policy process. Development decisions are made in private. Stakeholders who have an interest in preserving natural resources and who provide vital services for the society, such as farmers, fishers, herders, foresters, and charcoal producers, are excluded from development decisions. National planning agencies and civil servants are controlled by powerful ministers who believe that environmental planning causes unnecessary delays in the development process.

Civil servants who believe their government has an obligation to reject projects that damage the environment may lose their jobs, and occasionally face even greater risks. A St. Lucian familiar with one development controversy in that country said "Civil servants, when faced with pressure from the political leadership, may bleed inside if they disagree with a development project, but can't speak due to politics, it is too dangerous to their families." Governments respond to the political aspirations of leaders who favor short-term solutions to economic problems and wish to remain in power.

Many developing countries possess unique cultural characteristics that outsiders, such as donor agencies, do not understand. When outside parties attempt to intervene in the political process, which happens when donor agencies introduce new environmental policies as a condition of approval for development projects, they fail to understand the strong influence that culture has on the public policy process. In countries that have a low level of political and economic development, the effects of culture are especially pronounced. The pace of life in countries with tropical climates is slower than it is in continental societies. It takes a long time for new public policies to be accepted, as politicians wish to slowly gauge their effect on the society. People often develop indigenous methods of dealing with political problems, and guard against interference by outside parties, a distrust born of a long history of political and economic dependence resulting from the intervention of more powerful countries.

Political decisions are made based largely on personal relationships, "person to person" communication, ties within political parties, and patronage appointments. As one man who has worked in St. Kitts for several years said, "Outsiders don't understand the tremendous intensity of politics, everything is political. A large part of the culture is political, intense personal communication is part of culture, and most conversations are political." I call the close relationship between politics and culture the "culture of decision making." If outsiders do not understand this phenomenon, they will not be able to work effectively within the political systems of developing countries.

Decisions to develop limited natural resources are based primarily on economic factors. National policies that strongly favor development have been created to respond to persistent high unemployment, balance of payment deficits, and the need for hard currency to buy imported food, oil, and other necessities. The way that governments have responded to these economic problems conflicts with their own environmental policies, effectively canceling them out. For example, in St. Lucia and several other countries, the cabinet offers financial incentives to outside investors, such as repatriation of profits, waivers of duty on construction materials, and subsidies for infrastructure. These incentives are usually given before civil servants have a chance to evaluate the effect of a project on national environmental policies. The incentives constitute an informal political approval, overriding any environmental policies that exist, preventing them from being implemented. As an official in St. Lucia said, "Cabinet approval of concessions does suggest what government wants, and whose wrath will be incurred if a project is denied."

A second way that economic conditions prevent environmental policies from being effective is the lack of financial incentives to protect natural resources. In most instances, countries have not developed a strategy to implement environmental laws and policies, and part of this void is a lack of economic incentives to promote conservation. Donor agencies that possess the financial resources to establish such linkages also are failing with their environmental policies.

Donor agencies have made some progress in making reforms in their lending programs to protect the environment. But this progress has been piecemeal and generally ineffective. This is because there are countervailing forces at work within donor agencies. Environmental professionals are few in number in most donor agencies, compared to the number of economists, policy analysts, financial officers, planners, engineers, and administrators. It is these environmental professionals who develop and suggest to their superiors that new and innovative policies are needed to protect natural resources. At the same time, top agency officials, who are often political appointees, seek to complete projects and maintain the flow of development assistance without delay. The top officials generally prevail, with the result that environmental concerns are not integrated into project design and implementation. These institutional problems are compounded because many environmental management practices are new and somewhat undefined.

The donor agencies have other systemic problems as well. Most donors place a strong emphasis on environmental analysis at the front end of a project, but do not give enough attention to how to protect natural resources when it is being built. Since environmental protection depends on the effective implementation of specific measures to protect natural resources, this means that environmental policies are undercut and resources damaged. In addition, several donors delegate the responsibility for implementing environmental policies to countries where projects are located, where governments often lack the resources and political will to carry out environmental protection policies. National political leaders depend on the prestige that large donor-funded projects bring, and exert tremendous pressure to get them approved and built, even though "Projects may be a white elephant, but they are big and look good," as a senior civil servant said in Barbados. By defining development within the constraints of the single-project cycle, the donors have created a system that is biased against the long-term solutions that are needed to resolve complex environmental problems.

METHODOLOGY

This study employs a cross-national comparative case research approach, using information gathered in three Caribbean countries and from international organizations headquartered in Washington, D.C. Several sources of information were used to create the chain of evidence in the cases, including open ended interviews, public and private reports, newspaper archives, and my own experiences living and working in the region. The evidence was then organized in three ways: an annotated chronology of key events, summaries of the major themes, and lessons that emerged from each case. After the evidence was collated, I refined my major working hypotheses that formed the framework for each chapter.

I encountered some difficulties during the field research, because of the politically sensitive nature of the cases and my participation in policy dialogues that are generally not open to outsiders. All of the cases were extremely controversial, because of the large size of the projects, the political stakes involved, and in two instances substantial opposition to them. I found that it was a major benefit to be in the countries when the controversies were unfolding. Insights into the public policy process were easier to obtain by examining them through the lenses provided by the cases. The specific cases gave meaning to my major themes, such as the role of culture in policy implementation, that would have been very difficult to quantify.

To maintain objectivity, interviews were conducted with people from a variety of backgrounds who represented a wide range of opinions about the relationship of economic development and environmental management. I presented myself as an outside participant-observer, gathering factual data to describe why environmental policies were failing in the three countries. My affiliation as a research associate with the Centre for Resource Management and Environmental Studies at the University of the West Indies, Barbados, gave me the credibility that was required to gain access to the people I interviewed. In most instances this affiliation, combined with my role as an outside observer, was advantageous. It created the legitimacy that was needed for people to share confidential information about how their political systems work.

To gather the information needed to construct the cases, I interviewed seventy-eight people in four countries: Barbados, St. Lucia, St. Kitts, and the United States. Among those interviewed were senior civil servants; appointed and elected politicians; representatives of non-governmental organizations (NGOs); as well as representatives of the three donor agencies involved in the cases, the U.S. Agency for International Development (USAID), the Inter-American Development Bank (IDB), and the Organization of American States (OAS).[16] With follow-up interviews to check facts and keep track of events in the cases as they unfolded, I made more than 100 separate contacts with the seventy-eight parties.

Primary sources in each country received drafts of each chapter, and were asked to check my facts and chronology of key events for accuracy, and to review my basic propositions, such as the relationship of culture to the public policy process. The resulting comments helped me refine the cases. All interviews were kept confidential, and were recorded by taking notes by hand; I did not use a tape recorder, as I felt it would inhibit the subjects. A few people I interviewed were not comfortable with my role as a participant-observer, but this only happened with a few senior civil servants. Ironically, these people invariably referred me to other people, such as recently retired senior civil servants, who proved to be among my most valuable sources of information.[17]

SUMMARY

Limited natural resources are being depleted and destroyed in developing countries at a rapid pace. Efforts by international development assistance agencies, also known as donor agencies, to protect these resources are largely failing. Long-term economic losses for both developing and industrialized nations will occur if this trend continues. Efforts by donor agencies to protect limited natural resources are failing because they do not account for three key factors: the negative effects of the closed policy-making process in both developing countries and donor agencies, the critical role that local and national cultures plays in the "culture of decision making" in developing countries, and the dominance of United States and Eurocentric economic development strategies that cannot be successfully implemented with the shortage of money, staff, and political will in developing countries.

In developing countries, typical environmental problems which are growing worse, include deforestation, overfishing, desertification, pollution of fresh water supplies, and loss of biological diversity. Many environmental problems are also caused by massive development projects, such as dams and highways, funded by donor agencies. In general, environmental policies and laws within both donor agencies and developing countries are not followed because they use a closed decision-making process that favors traditional economic interest groups and leaves out environmental interest groups, including local residents, resource producers, civil servants, and environmental professionals.

This type of closed decision-making process caters to powerful interest groups, including political leaders in the countries and top-level political appointees in the donor agencies that want to maintain the flow of investment funds and keep their careers. This exclusionary approach to decision making contradicts all of the basic tenents of a representative democracy. Public institutions in developing countries reflect the political preferences of elected leaders, enforcing environmental laws on a limited and selective basis. This behavior is reinforced in parliamentary systems of government where the majority party through the prime minister and cabinet ministers exert total control over decision making. Large donor agencies develop traditions of decision making that cause top officials to overrule environmental professionals, creating an atmosphere of distrust. The combination of top-level control in both countries and donor agencies causes recent environmental policies to remain largely unenforced, allowing natural resources that are already limited to be further depleted.

I conducted research in several developing countries in the Caribbean, examining large donor-funded projects, to determine why the environmental laws and policies of both the donors and the countries are not enforced. While doing this work I also conducted extensive research into the environmental policies and activities of major donor agencies. The result is three case studies that examine why a highway was constructed in a pristine wilderness area, how a high-tech fisheries harbor was built in a country that lacks the expertise to run it, and how a proposed national park stayed in private hands when a tourist resort was built in the middle of it.

In chapter 2 I describe the three case studies, explaining key events and circumstances in the countries and donor agencies that created obstacles to protecting natural resources. Chapter 3 examines the influence of interest groups on the development process. Chapter 4 shows how local and national cultures, and the cultural differences between industrialized and developing nations, hamper efforts to create stronger environmental policies. Chapter 5 discusses how economic factors can be integrated with environmental policies to strenghten environmental protection. Chapter 6 focuses on how behavior within donor agencies affects their ability to implement environmental policies. Finally, chapter 7 presents a new model for strengthening the environmental planning and decision-making process, in both developing countries and donor agencies, to improve environmental policies and how they are used.

Chapter Two

An Introduction to the Failures and Complexities of Environmental Policies

The countries of the Eastern Caribbean sit among a series of oceanic islands clustered in the Lesser Antilles, starting 1,200 miles off the southeast coast of the United States and extending in an arc to the north coast of Venezuela. The islands, volcanic in origin, are bordered by the Caribbean Sea to the west and the Atlantic Ocean to the east (see Figure 1). The natural resource endowments of the individual islands vary, tied mainly to regional rainfall patterns. Some countries are in a rain shadow, creating an arid and dry environment. However, most of the islands in the region do possess natural resources, in the form of tropical rainforests, dry woodlands, rivers and streams, offshore fisheries, fertile soils, and wildlife that has evolved to fit the special environmental conditions found on the islands, such as the endangered St. Lucia parrot.

Because the island countries in the region are small in size and physically separate from surrounding land masses, they have a very limited resource base. The amount of fresh water from seasonal rain showers that can be stored in aquifers, streams, catchments, and reservoirs is limited. Forests are limited as they have specialized requirements for moisture and soils that restrict their distribution. Offshore reefs, which provide breeding and feeding habitat for fish,

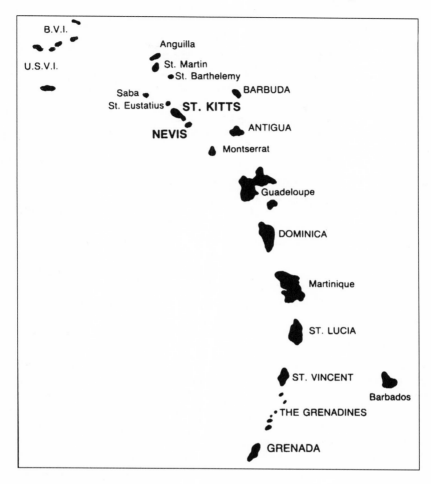

FIGURE 1
Map of the Eastern Caribbean

are geographically limited. Fertile soils suitable for agricultural production also exist only in certain areas. All of these conditions help
explain why islands are insular natural systems with an inherent
scarcity of resources.[1]

The biological uniqueness of these insular islands, coupled
with their biological diversity, constitutes an irreplaceable natural
resource akin to the much larger rainforests of South and Central
America. While limited in size, the natural landscape possesses a

high degree of biological diversity, because of the mixture of high and low elevations, wet and dry microclimates, proximity to both the larger islands of the north and Latin America to the south, and different types of soil. For example, nearly 2,000 species of flowering plants and 243 species of trees were found by J. S. Beard in the Lesser Antilles in the 1940s.[2]

As the population of these countries grows, their development patterns intensify, to provide for the needs of local residents and the expanding tourist industry—in the form of new roads, airports, power plants, and reservoirs—placing increased stress on limited natural resources. Conflicts between different land uses intensify, such as pollution from agricultural pesticides in local streams, a common problem in the region given the heavy emphasis on sugar and banana production. Large-scale industrial projects displace fishing villages and degrade offshore reefs, increasing the demand to import food to feed local people. In many countries in the region, limited natural resources are being degraded by current development practices. In some instances limited natural resources are at risk of being eliminated, a situation that is common in many developing countries.

I selected the Eastern Caribbean as the focus of this book for several reasons. The environmental problems in the three countries I have chosen, St. Kitts, St. Lucia, and Barbados, are well documented. The study sites are easily accessible, so carrying out a research program did not present any major obstacles. These tropical islands all maintain a delicate ecological balance, so the effects of over-development are easily seen. In spite of damage to the environment due to the stress of centuries-old intensive plantation agriculture, many natural resources that are needed to sustain human settlements survive in relative abundance, including fisheries, rich soil, forests, and fresh water. But, as in other developing countries, these resources are under severe pressure to feed a fast-growing population, to pay off foreign debt, and to improve the local standard of living.

All three of the countries I have selected to study are democratic with small public institutions and policy-making processes that are easy to understand.[3] The existence of clear environmental problems, simple public policy processes, and the dilemma posed by the demands of economic growth on limited natural resources make these countries an ideal subject. Despite some differences, the islands are representative of other nations with similar environmental problems, enabling this research to be applied to other developing nations. Most importantly, if national and international agencies are serious about stopping environmental degradation in the developing world, the small size and accessibility of these islands present the best opportunity to do so. If effective solutions cannot be found to the environmental problems in the Eastern Caribbean, there is little hope they can be successfully addressed in other, more complex, societies within the developing world.

Attempts have been made in St. Kitts, St. Lucia, and Barbados to implement new environmental policies to protect natural resources. Unfortunately, these efforts have generally failed, resulting in the degradation of island ecosystems. To understand the extent of this problem, the environmental laws and policies of these countries need to be examined. International foreign assistance agencies have also played a key role in environmental policy making in all three countries. Even though these agencies claim to have a major interest in promoting environmentally sustainable development, in many instances the projects they sponsor fail to do so. To understand why this is true, the environmental policies and procedures of international agencies also need to be examined.

St. Christopher and Nevis

History of Human Settlement and Use of Natural Resources

Discovered by Christopher Columbus in 1493, the two-island country of St. Christopher Nevis became the first permanent British settlement in the West Indies in 1624. It is one of several small islands in the Leeward Group. This island nation, known locally as St. Kitts, became independent in 1983, and has a parliament, headed officially by Queen Elizabeth II who is represented by a governor general. The 46,000 residents of St. Kitts and Nevis live on two islands that measure slightly more than 100 square miles. Its citizens are mainly of African descent, whose ancestors were brought to the region to provide slave labor for sugar plantations. Adult literacy is estimated to be about 90 percent.[4]

The national economy is largely dependent upon sugar, which accounts for over 50 percent of its export revenue. Efforts are under way to strengthen the economy by diversifying the agricultural base and providing new facilities for tourism. Economic problems increased in the 1980s, as indicated by an external debt of $32 million, a 20 percent rate of unemployment, and a current account deficit.[5] Domestic savings have declined continuously since 1978, adding to fiscal difficulties caused by the deteriorating financial performance of the sugar industry.[6]

A large portion of St. Kitts is known as the Southeast Peninsula. This 4,000-acre peninsula is unique in the Lesser Antilles, as its large wilderness areas include a wide variety of marine and terrestrial resources, some of which are in danger of extinction.[7] Within the six square miles of the peninsula, a very small portion of which is developed, are found ten arcuate bays, several coral reefs, salt ponds, sea grass beds, mangroves, wetlands, eleven beaches, and a diverse pattern of wildlife habitats including grasslands, forested hillsides, and valleys. The peninsula remained relatively undisturbed until 1988 when USAID funded a project to build a large, two-lane paved road the entire length of the peninsula. The intent of the project is to attract investors to build tourist resorts, condominiums, golf courses, commercial and recreational facilities, and perhaps a port for cruise ships.

History of Environmental Laws and Policies

National environmental legislation in St. Kitts includes laws to control the use of land, forests, water, beaches, wildlife, and public areas. In most instances, no regulations have be created to implement legislation, and if regulations do exist, they are not enforced. The Town and Country Planning Ordinance was passed in 1949 but has no regulations to implement it. The Land Development (Control) Ordinance, passed in 1966, requires that development plans be approved by the Minister of Development, but there are no regulations to accompany it.[8] As a result, there are no controls over new developments being built on steep hillsides, on fragile soils, or in areas with flooding problems from intense seasonal rainfall.

A Forestry Ordinance was adopted in 1904 with the chief agricultural officer in charge of regulations intended to control clearing, burning, and charcoal production. This legislation does not include provisions to establish and manage forest reserves. Field surveys in 1989 showed that this law remains largely unenforced. The result is clearing and burning of forest areas, which contributes to erosion and siltation of downstream water catchment areas.

The Pesticides Act of 1973 does not have any regulations to implement it, and pesticide misuse and contamination of neighboring lands are growing problems. The Pesticides Board accompanying the act has apparently stopped functioning.[9] Sand mining on beaches is supposed to be regulated by the Beach Control Ordinance. To stop illegal sand mining, which provides beach sand at low cost to make the foundations for new buildings, a quarry was opened up near the Canada Estate in the mid-1980s to protect the nearby beach. However, mining of the beach has continued, degrading the adjacent mangrove habitat in Greatheeds Pond and destabilizing the coastal sand dune system.

Fish that are caught and marketed by local fishermen are a major source of protein for the people of St. Kitts. The Fisheries Act of 1984 allows for the regulation of shellfish such as lobster and conch that are heavily fished and exported to earn foreign exchange. However, both fisheries remain largely unregulated, resulting in a severe decline of the local fishery (SK 13).[10] The Watercourses and Waterworks Act adopted in 1973 established a Water Board to manage fresh water resources. Its responsibility includes pollution abatement. A field survey of the many drainage channels on the island, including a river that drains into the main beach in the capital of Basseterre, shows that water pollution is evident in virtually every settled area.

The existence of these environmental problems was confirmed during a workshop with civil servants responsible for resource management in St. Kitts in 1987. During the workshop, problems documented included the improper dumping of industrial waste in the main harbor in Basseterre, unregulated dumping of garbage in watercourses, uncontrolled construction in coastal areas, destruction of coral reefs, coastal erosion, the failure of beach protection projects, and the removal of mangroves as a result of sand mining.[11]

In 1985 the Parliament passed legislation establishing an Environmental Department with a wide range of duties, including taking over all functions related to environmental management from the Physical Planning Section of the Central Planning Unit.[12] The department has not been funded and has no staff. The responsibility for environmental concerns is scattered among various ministries, so no one office is accountable for them.

After the 1989 national election the cabinet eliminated the ministerial portfolio for the environment, which had been held by the premier of Nevis. This action reflected the low priority given to environmental protection by the national political leadership. The failure of the St. Kitts government to enforce its own environmental legislation was an indication of what would happen when the government decided to intensively develop the island's southeast peninsula.

USAID and the Southeast Peninsula Development Project

In early 1984 representatives of the St. Kitts government asked USAID to provide financial and technical assistance to develop the island's southeast peninsula as a major tourist destination. Since the USAID first became involved with the southeast peninsula project in St. Kitts, one of its stated goals has been to carry out the mandate of the U.S. Congress to preserve the island's natural resources. But the efforts of USAID to protect the environment of the peninsula have not been effective. The fragility of these resources makes them particularly vulnerable. They could easily be destroyed given the lack of a strong national policy to protect them.

Officials within USAID's Regional Development Office in the Caribbean (RDO/C) expressed their concern about the peninsula's natural environment as early as mid-1985: "RDO/C considers the adoption of a land use and environmental policy as essential to guiding the development of the peninsula along an appropriate path."[13]

According to its Congressional mandate, USAID is required to assess the potential adverse environmental effects of its projects by preparing environmental impact assessments to mitigate damage to natural resources. The stated purpose of this procedure is to " . . . permit consideration of alternatives and mitigating features in project design."[14]

In early 1986 an independent consultant completed the environmental assessment. It identified several possible environmental impacts of the project, including coastal erosion, damage to reefs, wetlands, and mangroves; degradation of the marine ecosystem; destruction of wildlife habitat; and disposal of dredge materials. The report contained several recommendations intended to mitigate such environmental damage, including the establishment of special conservation zones, formation of a new Environmental Unit within the government to improve its capability to address environmental problems, and preparation of building guidelines and a Land Use Management Plan.[15]

In July 1986 the Land Use Management Plan was published. It also contained several recommendations to protect the natural resources on the peninsula. Key recommendations included (1) to adopt legislation establishing an advisory board to oversee planning and environmental aspects of the project; (2) to adopt laws for beach control, marine pollution, fisheries management, parks, and protected areas; (3) to establish an Environmental Unit within the Planning Unit. Most importantly, the report stated that "prior to commencement of Southeast Peninsula construction projects, Government needs to provide the necessary legal and administrative framework within which an orderly but creative process of development can take place without causing environmental damage."[16]

In September 1986 the Project Grant and Loan Agreement financing the project was signed by St. Kitts and USAID. In November Parliament approved the Southeast Peninsula Development and Conservation Act establishing a five-member advisory board. The board is appointed by the Minister of Development, and is responsible for reviewing development proposals and conservation guidelines for the peninsula. In response to pressure from USAID, Parliament then passed the National Conservation and Environment Protection Act in April 1987 (SK 12). Major elements of the act included a comprehensive law to replace outdated environmental statutes that were outdated and unclear, and establishment of a national Conservation Commission to implement the law.

Over the next two years, consultants prepared several reports documenting the natural resources on the peninsula, and recommending how the government should preserve them. The road penetrating the peninsula, the largest part of the project, was completed in early 1990. But at the time the road was completed, the government had still not taken several measures to increase its institutional capacity for environmental planning.

By mid-1990 the advisory board was functioning, reviewing development proposals that included 140- and 400-acre residential projects, and a 250-room hotel. Yet, the Conservation Commission still was not appointed, despite repeated assurances from the attorney general that its appointment was imminent (SK 12, 17, 21).[17] The chairman designee of the commission resigned, after saying that the government was not interested in incorporating conservation into the peninsula developments (SK 8). The National Conservation and Environment Protection Act was not implemented, the Environmental Unit still did not exist, and laws for beach control, marine pollution, fisheries, parks, and protected areas remained unenforced.

By late 1993, a water supply had been extended to the peninsula. Scattered houses had been built, and a small bar constructed near Mosquito Bay—all without the required permits, although permits were granted ex post facto. Preparations have been made to develop the Casa Blanca Hotel. The salt pond near Cockleshell Bay has been filled in, vegetation cleared from the beach, and sea grass dredged from the sea floor to accommodate the hotel. Palm trees were transplanted from higher elevation but died when exposed to salt water. A hillside was removed to build a warehouse to house construction equipment and a large parking lot to park heavy equipment. The hotel sits partially finished. Efforts to attract foreign investment to the peninsula, the major goal of the development project, have largely failed (SK 20). The outlook for the natural resources on the peninsula, despite a long and involved program to increase the environmental accountability of the government, is not good.

ST. LUCIA

History of Human Settlement and Use of Natural Resources

The native Carib Indians fought off attempts by English settlers to colonize the island between 1605 and 1641. The island was finally settled by the French in 1650, and changed hands several times between the British and French until it became a British Crown Colony in 1814 under the Treaty of Paris. St. Lucia was one of several trading centers in the Caribbean where commodities such as timber, livestock, and provisions for the sugar industry, including slaves, were traded with European cities and Spanish and French colonies in the region. The French culture has maintained its dominance in St. Lucia, as expressed by a French Patois that is widely used. Most St. Lucians are of African descent, brought to the island to supply labor for the sugar industry in the seventeenth century.[18]

The 145,000 residents of St. Lucia, which measures 238 square miles, depend on income from private remittances by St. Lucians living abroad, and from agricultural export crops, chiefly bananas. Growth of the banana industry stabilized the economy in the 1950s, but uncertainty over the future of banana sales, and the inherent instability in depending on monocultural export crops, has caused the government to aggressively promote tourism as a source of jobs and foreign exchange.

Current economic indicators include an annual growth rate of 1–5 percent, 20–25 percent unemployment, and heavy dependence on imports of manufactured goods, food, machinery, fuels, and chemicals, which are not produced in the country. A $55 million national debt also requires an accumulation of foreign exchange, placing additional importance on the growth of the tourism sector.[19]

St. Lucia is mountainous, with large areas of the interior covered with rainforest and dry forest interspersed with fertile inland agricultural valleys, ringed by beaches, a natural harbor, and bays that possess mangroves, salt ponds, and seagrass beds. The steep terrain and high seasonal rainfall in the interior mountains has made them somewhat inaccessible, allowing substantial portions of the rainforest to remain intact. The St. Lucia parrot, an endangered species, depends on rainforest habitat for its survival, and is a symbol of conservation in the country. Near-offshore reefs support an abundant local fishery which provides much of the protein requirement of the islands residents. Attempts to protect and manage these natural resources have been undertaken with some success.

History of Environmental Laws and Policies

In St. Lucia, legislation exists that is intended to regulate several aspects of natural resource management, but it is only partially enforced. This has resulted in environmentally destructive land-use practices and pollution problems that degrade the island ecosystem. The Forest, Soil, and Water Conservation Ordinance, originally adopted in 1946 and amended in 1983, is intended to regulate forestry activities, promote conservation, and establish forest reserves.[20] The law is accompanied by enforcement powers including fines and criminal prosecution. However, it is estimated that only 10.8 percent of the forested areas on the island are protected. This has led to deforestation on steep slopes cleared for agricultural production, causing erosion and sedimentation problems.[21] A field survey in 1989 showed that forest lands are being cleared for agriculture, grazing, and charcoal production in many parts of the island.

The Water and Sewage Authority Act established an enforcement mechanism to regulate water pollution, but raw sewage is discharged directly into the main harbor in Castries, posing a health hazard. Similarly, the Pesticide Control Act adopted in 1975 established a board empowered with enforcement capabilities, but no regulations have been enacted to control pesticide use.[22] This lack of enforcement has allowed water supplies to be contaminated by toxic chemicals used for agricultural production.

In addition to these regulatory problems, the political leaders of St. Lucia have forestalled several efforts by civil servants to create a comprehensive national policy for the environment. In 1982 a National Environmental Commission was proposed by the chief forestry officer. The purpose of the commission was to establish a government agency to eliminate overlaps and gaps in the jurisdiction of natural resources, and to form a national consensus on the environment. All of the major interest groups from both the public and private sectors were to be represented on the commission. However, the prime minister felt that the commission would delay development projects, so it was never given its official terms of reference by the government (SL 6). As a result, there is no organization within the government to coordinate the resolution of environmental problems. The failure of the national planning authority to perform long-term planning, due to a refusal by the cabinet to authorize the required legislation, has contributed to this problem.[23]

The Pitons Controversy: A National Park or a Resort?

The Pitons controversy involves two competing proposals to develop the same site in the Piton mountains. The first and original project is the establishment of a Pitons National Park, proposed by the OAS. The second and newer project would prevent the establishment of the park. Sponsored by private international investors, developers proposed to develop a large tourist resort on the Jalousie Estate, a 316-acre parcel in the saddle between the Gros and Petit Pitons, two forested peaks on the Caribbean Sea that are the national symbols of St. Lucia. The two proposals were in conflict as the Jalousie Estate would house the park headquarters under the OAS proposal, but would be developed as the tourist resort under the proposal by the private investors. Both projects have involved attempts to implement environmental policies to protect natural resources.

The proposal to privately develop the Jalousie Estate started in 1981 when the cabinet issued an Alien Landholding license to Sir Colin Tennant. This decision also started the Pitons controversy, as when the cabinet issued the license, it reversed its own earlier decision to acquire the site as part of a Pitons National Park. Tennant never did build a resort on the site, and in 1988 he sold it to the Swiss-based M-Group Resorts, who then received a new license from the cabinet. The Development Control Authority (DCA) gave the new developer an Approval in Concept for a tourist resort on the estate shortly after they purchased it.

After it gave conceptual approval for the resort, the DCA required that the developer provide an environmental impact assessment, ostensibly to protect the natural resources of the estate. However, the scope of the assessment was limited to site-planning concerns, and did not include an evaluation of whether or not the Jalousie Estate was an appropriate site for the resort. The assessment was written by a consultant hired by the developer. It was rejected by the DCA as being biased in support of the project. A second assessment was then prepared by a new consultant hired with the assistance of the United Nations Development Program (SL 5). This assessment was accepted by the DCA as adequately addressing a limited range of site-planning concerns.

When the cabinet issued the second Alien Landholding license in 1988 to the Swiss-based M-Group Resorts, it also granted financial concessions (repatriation of profits, duty-free import of construction materials, etc.) and a promise that the government would use public funds to build the major access road needed to serve the project. These decisions by the cabinet placed immense pressure on planning officials to approve the project, even though the environmental assessment process was not finished. In the words of an official familiar with the project, "The development permit itself is not before the cabinet, but (the) cabinet makes its wishes well known with its tacit support, so the choice to not develop the site is no longer feasible for DCA technicians" (SL 5).

When the government granted the Approval in Concept for the resort, plans for the project were not available to the public. The approval was granted without a public hearing, preventing environmental groups or concerned citizens from voicing their concerns. Before the DCA finished reviewing the second environmental assessment, and before it had issued any permits allowing the site to be developed, the developer posted "No Trespassing" signs on the beach and main road, preempting the long-standing public use of the site for fishing, boating, and picnicking. The developer then brought a bulldozer to the beach, proceeded to grade it, and started construction of a jetty as part of a marina to serve resort guests. Meanwhile, the government started to build the access road it had promised the developer, also without the required permits.

At about same time, in early 1989, the Department of Regional Development of the OAS was submitting a formal proposal to the government for the Pitons National Park. The proposal stated that "the proposed development of a large private hotel on the Jalousie Estate is incompatible with the overall concept of the Pitons National Park and could also hamper the conservation or preservation of the unique cultural and natural attractions of the area."[24]

A group of businessmen from the nearby town of Soufriere who had formed the Soufriere Development Committee (SDC) had asked the OAS to prepare the proposal. The main objective of the national park was to provide economic opportunities for this remote part of the island that were compatible with the natural environment. The vision of park planners was to create growth strategy that was environmentally sustainable.

When the park proposal was given to the government, it was not released to the public. The government did not adopt the proposal. In mid-1990 the OAS closed its St. Lucia office. It had not met its objectives to create a national park that would protect the natural resources of the Jalousie Estate and surrounding lands. In mid-1990, the government gave the developer permission to build the resort. Neither the government nor the OAS had met their objectives to protect the fragile natural resources of the Pitons. A second large tourist project, the La Gros Piton Resort Village and Aerial Tramway was proposed in mid-1990, envisioned as carrying 250,000 tourists a year to an eleven-acre resort built on the top of the Gros Piton.[25] In late 1992 the Jalousie Plantation Resort, with 120 cottages and a restaurant, opened for business. Plans are underway to build additional rooms near the beach during a second phase of construction (SL 18). It appears inevitable that the environment of the Pitons will be drastically changed, with the government pursuing an aggressive strategy to intensively develop the area.

BARBADOS

History of Human Settlement and Use of Natural Resources

Barbados was discovered by an English sea captain and claimed in the name of King James in 1624. He found a lush island that was uninhabited and covered by dense forests. The island developed quickly, and by 1640 had a population of 30,000, comprised mainly of immigrant landless farmers tending tobacco and cotton crops. These indentured farmers were bound to English landlords, and were a forerunner to slave laborers imported to provide labor to the sugar industry.

The 270,000 residents of Barbados live on an island measuring 166 square miles with a density of over 1,600 people per square mile, one of the highest population densities in the western hemisphere. Over 90 percent of the population is of African descent, with Europeans, Indians, Asians, and other minority groups. Barbados is known for maintaining cultural and social traditions imbedded in its English colonial heritage as indicated by its political system, the school system, and the great popularity of cricket.

Like other islands in the West Indies, Barbados is heavily dependent on external markets. The economy is based mainly on international tourism and agriculture both of which are highly sensitive to external economic fluctuations. During the 1970s Barbados broadened its economic base through the rapid development of a manufacturing sector, but the international recession of 1980–1981 created serious pressures on the national economy.[26]

Barbados has a smaller natural resource endowment than some other islands in the region. This is mainly due to the long history of human settlement on the island, which resulted in large-scale production that required clearing large forested areas, deforestation for fuel wood, and a high population density, one of the highest in the western hemisphere. Still, the abundance of fresh water, fertile soils, and an ocean fishery provide a substantial base of limited natural resources that require management and protection.

History of Environmental Laws and Policies

Like St. Kitts and St. Lucia, Barbados has many laws intended to protect the environment, but they are generally not enforced, which has resulted in serious damage to natural resources. The Beaches Protection Act of 1890 prohibits removal of sand from the foreshore, while the Fisheries Regulation of 1904 is supposed to regulate the harvesting of sea turtles and sea eggs.[27] Yet the beaches of the south coast were heavily mined to supply construction materials during the building boom of the 1970s, and remain unstable, while sea eggs and sea turtles are becoming scarce because of overexploitation and habitat destruction (B 16).

Legislation exists to establish marine reserves, but coral reefs are harvested to sell souvenirs to tourists, damaged by boat anchors, and degraded by raw sewage and agricultural runoff.[28] The Tree Preservation Act was passed in 1981 but lacks an enforcement mechanism, so trees continue to be illegally harvested, causing deforestation, erosion, and sedimentation that damages water catchment areas.

The Coastal Conservation Project Unit has recommended that a comprehensive Coastal Zone Management Act be passed but the government has taken no action. Government officials have publicly stated that competing uses are depleting limited natural resources, such as reefs and beaches.[29] If poor enforcement, badly written legislation, and a lack of awareness by the public have not contributed enough to Barbados's environmental problems, the political leadership sent a strong message that there will be no improvements in the near future when it replaced the Ministry of Tourism and the Environment with the Ministry of Sport and Tourism in 1987. This action dropped the environment to a sub-cabinet position in the government, reflecting a de-emphasis of the environment by the political leadership.

The Bridgetown Fisheries Harbor

In 1982 the government of Barbados asked the IDB to provide the financial and technical assistance needed to build a large fisheries harbor in the capitol of Bridgetown. The harbor is a large project, especially by island standards. It includes slips for 150 boats, a boat repair facility, an ice plant and fish processing facilities, a vending area, a rum shop, and fuel docks. To build the harbor required massive cutting and filling of coastal land, and construction of a large breakwater to guard against storm surges. The jetty and harbor are next to the Constitution River, which houses several boats and drains a large part of urban Bridgetown.

Between 1982 and 1984 the IDB undertook several steps to evaluate the feasibility of the project, including a Country Programming Paper, and orientation and analysis missions for its Washington, D.C., staff that resulted in a project report. A loan proposal was then prepared and submitted to the Bank's Board of Directors as the last step prior to executing a Project Agreement. The Barbados government and the IDB signed the Project Agreement in late 1984.

While evaluating the feasibility of the harbor, the bank did not examine its potential adverse impact on the natural environment. Possible environmental impacts included depletion of local and regional fish stocks, sedimentation of the harbor mouth and the adjacent river mouth, and degraded water quality in the harbor because of improper waste disposal from live-aboard fishermen.

One of the project's major objectives was to increase the production of the fishing industry. Technical experts from the IDB assumed that the population of flying fish, the mainstay of the Barbadian fishing industry, was sufficient to sustain the increased fishing pressure the harbor would create (B 34, 43, 17, 42),[30] but this judgment was made without any scientific evidence about the status of the fishery. To the contrary, recent studies indicate that fishery resources throughout the Eastern Caribbean are comparatively limited and can be subject to overexploitation with existing fishing technology.[31] In addition, when the government decided to redesign the harbor and extend the large breakwater in 1986, the IDB had the opportunity to assess the effects of the project on coastal resources, but decided to proceed without doing so (B 17, 31).

Several reasons have been given by IDB officials to explain why the environmental impact of the fisheries harbor was not integrated into the evaluation, design or construction of the harbor. One official said that the project simply "Pre-dated the environmental period of the bank" (B 34). Other officials explained that the IDB focuses on analyzing projects, not implementing environmental safeguards, because bank staff in the regional offices are not trained in environmental management (B 35, 42). Whatever the reason, a multimillion-dollar public investment was made without an evaluation of its negative impact on the environment, including the ability of the fishery to sustain it. In recent years, in response to pressure from international environmental groups and the United States Congress, the IDB has initiated reforms to strengthen its capacity to integrate environmental concerns into its projects. However, its main response has been to delegate the implementation of a new environmental impact assessment process to borrowing countries, rather than carrying out this work itself. Most countries lack the political will and technical resources needed to make such a process work and, given the huge economic and political stakes involved, are generally incapable of conducting a full, fair, and impartial analysis of the adverse environmental effects of projects. The combination of these factors makes it unlikely that this approach will result in the effective protection of limited natural resources.

SUMMARY

In all three of the countries, existing environmental laws and policies remain largely unenforced. Difficult economic conditions, magnified by the lack of economic diversification and a pro-development bias by political leaders, routinely cause these laws and policies to be ignored. Although the three development assistance agencies used different approaches to protect limited natural resources, all three failed. The infrastructure to allow the fragile natural environment on the Southeast Peninsula of St. Kitts to be intensively developed is in place, but few economic benefits are being generated. The proposed Pitons National Park has been blocked by construction of the Jalousie Plantation Resort, and the potential growth in nature tourism has disappeared along with it. The Bridgetown Fisheries Harbor is functioning with marginal results amidst a declining regional fishery. There is no evidence that the institutional capacity to manage and protect limited natural resources in any of the countries has improved, and there is no reason to believe this will change.

A major reason why the efforts of development assistance agencies to improve environmental protection in these countries has failed is the role of special interest groups in the political process. Political leaders, along with the senior civil servants who work for them, exert near-total control over the environmental policy process, as has been demonstrated in this chapter. Developers create strategies to influence political leaders in order to obtain favorable decisions that often cause limited natural resources to be degraded or destroyed. Political leaders and senior civil servants form their own pro-development interest group that is very difficult to penetrate. Outside parties, such as environmental organizations and development assistance agencies, often do not understand how these inside parties make decisions. Chapter 3 discusses why this situation exists, and why a more open and accountable policy-making process is needed to protect natural resources.

Chapter Three

INTEREST GROUPS AND THE POLITICS OF EXCLUSION

Close relationships among interest groups within a country, along with a policy-making process that excludes key stakeholders, frequently causes decisions to be made that are environmentally destructive. The failure of environmental policies can be explained by examining how interest groups use their relationships with political leaders to create a closed decision-making process. In turn, this closed decision-making process prevents environmental policies from being implemented.

National political leaders want to maintain their power by supporting large development projects that are environmentally destructive but highly visible to voters. Bureaucrats who might want to enforce policies to protect fragile natural resources are dependent on politicians for their jobs, preventing them from taking action to enforce environmental policies. Political leaders and civil servants often form a coalition within government representing key parties that seek to weaken environmental laws and policies. Such a coalition undermines efforts by development assistance agencies and international environmental organizations to protect limited natural resources.

Stakeholders who are excluded from national policy making are often poorly organized and not even represented by a spokesperson or leader. These stakeholders can be environmental professionals, civil servants, farmers, fishers, environmentalists, or members of indigenous communities, individuals who possess special knowledge of the natural environment and its capacity to provide natural resources that are essential for the survival of a society. If the needs, interests, and special knowledge of these stakeholders are not considered as part of the environmental decision-making process, policies and programs that result are far less likely to be implemented.

Other gaps between individuals in a society also undermine policy making, including the gap between rich and poor and the gap between urban decision makers and rural communities. Collectively, these gaps create a greater need for the involvement in national decision making by underrepresented and loosely organized stakeholders. If greater involvement can be achieved in an orderly and disciplined manner, it can result in environmental policies and programs that are clearer, more durable, and broadly acceptable, policies that promote political and economic stability.

THE IMPORTANCE OF INTEREST-GROUP POLITICS

Interest groups play an important role in the formation and implementation of public policies. They represent their constituents by forming a link between citizens and their government and different political factions within the political leadership. By studying how individual interest groups behave and relate to each other, we can find out how they influence government and its policy-making process.[1]

The emphasis on the importance of interest groups in policy making reflects the theory that society does not consist of a monolithic organization such as the state, but in George Catlin's words is "an aggregate of individuals organized into various groups, sometimes contrary, sometimes mutually inclusive, sometimes overlapping."[2] The importance of interest groups in developing countries, such as the island states of the Eastern Caribbean, often reflects the power of individuals who value political and economic goods more than the health of the natural environment.[3]

The behavior of interest groups offers insight into the reasons there is often a gap between the purpose and the result of national policies. While policy making is often seen as a formal and predictable process, unintended consequences often result. By examining the interplay among interest groups we can explore aspects of the policy-making process that may not be revealed otherwise.[4]

In the context of the Eastern Caribbean it is essential to examine how different interest groups—including the political leadership and agencies of the government—interact, as policy implementation depends largely on the politics within the executing agency.[5] An analysis of the informal linkages among interest groups portrays the evolution and direction of policy change.

SOME CHARACTERISTICS OF INTEREST GROUPS

Governments, public institutions, and the number of interest groups in the Eastern Caribbean are small, so that relatively few individuals exert great influence over the policy-making process. Interest groups themselves are usually small, with no more than a few members. Typically, a single official within a small agency, with close personal ties to a minister or senior civil servant, is the chief representative of an interest group. The role of the individual within an interest group is magnified due to an emphasis on personalism and charisma in the region. The effect of personalism and charisma are amplified, because of the emphasis on informal relationships, oral traditions, and "person-to-person" politics that characterize decision making.[6]

The development of interest groups and their relationship with governments has not been static. As the economies and political systems of countries have matured, the strategy and influence of key interest groups has changed. Bureaucratic elitism and interest group manipulation, dominated by land owners, sugar producers, and general importers, has been augmented by formalized political parties, trade unions, and influential outside groups such as international development assistance agencies and multilateral development banks (MDB).[7] With the increase in international development assistance in the region, the importance of outside interest groups, such as the MDBs, has grown.

Local interest groups influence political leaders and bureaucrats responsible for carrying out environmental policies. These groups include local land owners, the business community, industrial and trade associations, the tourist industry, and private investors. Some interest groups that have a stake in implementing environmental policies are not as influential. These groups include environmentalists, educators, community groups, and resource users, such as fishers and farmers, who depend on the health of the environment for their livelihood.

INTEREST GROUPS AND STAKEHOLDERS

There are some important distinctions between interest groups and stakeholders. Interest groups are existing organizations with an expressed interest in the outcome of a public policy decision. Stakeholders also have, as the name implies, a stake in the outcome of a government decision or policy, but may not be organized into a group.[8] In many developing countries, stakeholders who have an interest in minimizing the adverse environmental effects of development decisions do not have a formal voice in the decision-making process. Stakeholders who have an interest in promoting effective environmental policies are generally newly organized and do not belong to existing interest groups.

When both interest groups and stakeholders are identified and examined, it becomes evident who is included and who is left out of key policy decisions concerning natural resources. The ability of different parties, whether they are organized into groups or not, to strengthen or weaken environmental policies is a result of their underlying interest, who represents them, and their strategy of influence. The issue of who has access to power and how they use that access is also important.

Parties that have an interest in public policy decisions that impact the environment can be divided into two groups, those that are included in development decisions and those that have a stake but are left out. Parties that are typically included in development decisions include the political leadership, private investors and developers, local civil servants, labor unions, and selected members of the local business community.[9]

PARTIES INCLUDED IN DEVELOPMENT DECISIONS

The Political Leadership: An Interest Group Unto Itself?

The national political leadership is headed by the prime minister, who is leader of the majority party and chairman of the cabinet of ministers. The prime minister also holds a major cabinet portfolio, often doubling as premier and minister of finance or planning. The prime minister typically often exercises great personal influence in an informal manner through one-on-one conversations and public oratory, reinforced by charisma and the force of personality.

In recent years in the Eastern Caribbean, since many countries have gained national independence, political parties have become better organized. The emergence of community-based political parties, reinforced by patronage appointments of party members to top government jobs, creates an intense loyalty to the political leadership. The concentration of power among a few political leaders is further accentuated by their tendency to make decisions personally, without bringing outsiders into the policy-making process. Outsiders can be senior civil servants, technical experts from foreign assistance agencies, or members of the public. The prime minister sits atop a network of influence, persuasion, pressure, and obligation, fueled by relative isolation that perpetuates particularistic role play and factionalism based on political ideology, party affiliation, and social class.[10]

The prime minister, cabinet, and top officials such as permanent secretaries have a primary interest in staying in power. They do this by promoting policies that promise to increase economic growth, reduce unemployment, and preserve foreign exchange. The agenda of economic growth is often highlighted by large, highly visible development projects which are approved just before or after national elections. At the same time, political leaders tend to be adverse to new risks that may spell trouble in the next election. New environmental laws and policies whose benefits are hard to calculate are often perceived as increasing the political risk of national leaders. It is easier for this perceived risk to drive national political decisions in countries that have a relatively young and immature tradition of democracy, where power is focused in the hands of a small political majority.

In most of the countries of the Eastern Caribbean, virtually all decisions that affect natural resources are made directly by political leaders with little or no input from the public. The cabinet or a single minister usually initiates and must approve all large development projects. The wide range of decisions made by political leaders is a sign of the ubiquitousness of government as the major stakeholder in these societies.

Private Investors and Developers: Soliciting Informal Approvals

When development projects are proposed and funded by private investors, they usually directly approach the political leadership to "test the waters," instead of first applying for a development permit using formal planning procedures. In this way an informal project approval may be obtained from a member of the cabinet, usually the minister with the portfolio similar to the project (e.g., a resort developer will approach the minister of tourism), prior to submitting the project to the national planning authority. When a project is formally submitted to the planning agency for review, developers benefit from pressure exerted on civil servants by political leaders through party affiliation, patronage-dominated relations, subservient relations, and direct interference.[11] Private investors and political leaders have a complementary objective, namely to bring in foreign exchange that promotes investments and economic growth.

Civil Servants: Good Intentions Blunted by Political Pressure

Civil servants involved in development decisions that impact natural resources work in a central planning unit, physical planning office, or in some specialized area of natural resource management (fisheries, forestry, agriculture, or water quality). An office within the central planning unit, usually either Town and Country Planning or the physical planning section, is the lead agency for evaluating development projects. To understand how civil servants influence the outcome of development projects, it is necessary to review how the planning process typically works.

When a proposed project is reviewed for conformity with planning laws and policies, the chief planner is responsible for informally consulting with technical experts in other agencies (fisheries, forestry, agriculture, water engineering, public works, transportation, coastal management) to determine how a project will impact natural resources. The consultative process used for evaluating projects is informal, and the way that it is used depends on the discretion of the chief planning officer, who reports directly to a permanent secretary and a minister. When planning officials are pressured to approve projects that have received informal approvals from ministers or the cabinet, the input of natural resource managers is usually ignored.

This abuse of the consultative process usually results in developments that damage natural resources. For example, in the late 1980s permission to build the Sierra Hotel on the south coast of Barbados was denied by all government agencies, including the office responsible for managing coastal resources. But the hotel was built because a key minister had a financial interest in the project (B 3). This project resulted in severe beach erosion that affected the new hotel and adjacent properties. Numerous interviews with local officials and subsequent field observations showed that it is not uncommon for projects to be approved in this ad hoc fashion in Barbados, St. Lucia, or St. Kitts.

The general interest of civil servants involved in natural resource management is to carry out government policies in a way that meets their professional standards and protects the resources. This is very difficult for several reasons. Planning agencies operate under the same financial and technical constraints as other ministries and, as a result, their staffs are routinely overworked. The planning authority only makes recommendations; its decisions are not binding, but are referred to the lead minister who reports to the cabinet, which makes the final decision. By placing the responsibility for development decisions, including the enforcement of environmental protection standards, in the political directorate, authority is effectively removed from the civil service.

In addition, the way in which natural resource managers are spread among disparate ministries that have narrowly defined responsibilities for different sectors of public management prevents a coordinated approach to evaluating the environmental effects of development projects. Civil servants are in a double bind; they wish to use their technical training to integrate natural resource management with development planning, but find it politically infeasible to implement environmental policies because of their close personal ties and dependency upon the political leadership for jobs.[12]

Unions and Trade Associations: The Clout of Labor

Unions and trade associations are indirectly involved with the development approval process. In the past several years these groups have increased in size and solidified their place in Eastern Caribbean society. Due to the overwhelming need for foreign exchange and employment, these groups often publicly support large development projects.

A case in point is the National Workers Union in St. Lucia, the largest union in the country, with 5,000 members. The union publicly supported construction of a large tourist resort in the proposed Pitons National Park, in the belief that it would generate local jobs and increase government support to rebuild the west road connecting Castries with Soufriere.[13] Unions and trade associations generally support the ruling political party in its effort to attract foreign investment. They utilize local media and regular meetings of their membership to support projects that provide jobs, which in turn weakens the authority of civil service officials who lack the resources and jurisdiction to respond.[14]

Members of the Business Community: Advocates for Economic Growth

The members of this interest group are individuals and companies in the local business community who profit directly from the economic benefits often credited to development projects. Their interests in a specific project are usually represented directly by themselves, as opposed to representation by a trade association or chamber of commerce. It is common for key members of the business community who also belong to the ruling party to be appointed to influential government advisory boards or commissions, where they can represent their own interests.

The business community often promotes its influence through close ties to political leaders in a variety of ways. For example, politicians are depending more and more on their patrons in the business community to provide money and staff in national election campaigns. It is also common for politicians, both elected and appointed, to own a local business or have a financial interest in one. For example, a member of Parliament may have a local business as a contractor, supplier, or attorney for a developer or investor. When such a politician meets with other political leaders to determine whether a project should be approved, he represents his own business interests as well. This creates a pro-development liaison between political leaders and the business community that values economic development more than environmental protection, and places these individuals in conflict with parties often left out of the policy-making process, parties whose primary interest is the protection of natural resources.

Parties Excluded from Development Decisions

Stakeholders that are left out of the policy-making process when development decisions are made often lack direct and personal access to the political leadership. Many of these stakeholders are unorganized and have no formal representation. This includes local resource users such as farmers, fishers, and small landowners. If these parties are organized, such as in a farming or fishing cooperative, they usually are hesitant to become advocates in the policy-making process, as this behavior will place them in competition with established political leaders.

Other stakeholders that are usually excluded from policy making include those who have recently organized and have not been in existence long enough to build the personal relationships with political leaders needed to affect the policy dialogue. These groups can include environmental groups, regional universities, and research centers based in the country, region, or abroad.

Stakeholders who are unorganized or who have recently formed, such as environmental groups, need to increase their political power to obtain a stronger bargaining position when negotiating with political leaders.[15] Governments in the region have not agreed to share authority with most stakeholders, so these stakeholders have little influence in the public policy process.

The General Method of Exclusion

Individual ministers and the cabinet control the development review process, so there is no opportunity for members of the public to take part in development decisions. Formal public meetings to obtain the feedback of local citizens are not held. A high national official in St. Kitts told me that "the day of St. Kitt's independence was the first and only public meeting sponsored by the government, and we are not planning on another" (SK 3). As the government owns the only radio and television stations on St. Kitts, public dissent is not encouraged.

If the political leadership decided to sponsor public hearings, it is uncertain what effect such hearings would have, given a cultural predeposition against community participation, a perception of powerlessness, a sense of self doubt, and the acceptance of dependency.[16] However, the lack of public participation means that resource users (farmers, fishers, charcoal producers, etc.) who have special knowledge of local environmental conditions are not consulted during the development review process. Local knowledge of the natural environment is hard to find, given the general rejection of land-based manual labor due to its association with slavery. This condition, combined with illiteracy among rural dwellers, who tend to be the resource users, means that it would take a concerted effort to tap the knowledge of these individuals. In general, members of the public who may have an interest in preserving environmental quality are few in number, unorganized, and not consulted.

Local Environmental Groups: The Weakness of Environmental Advocates

Environmental stakeholders are a disparate group, and include individuals who are experts in natural resource management, historians, anthropologists, architectural preservationists, and naturalists. These parties are often organized into small non-governmental organizations by one or two key individuals originally motivated to carry out a specific task, such as the preservation of a particular area, building, or wildlife species.

Pro-environmental groups and individuals have a limited capacity to affect public policy decisions for several reasons. These groups are small in size and lack the staff that would enable them to work on more than a few small projects at once. Most are self supporting and must find a way to support themselves financially, as few organizations have the official support of national governments. Exceptions to this are the National Trusts in St. Lucia and Barbados, which are officially recognized by their governments. However, organizations such as these must be careful to not alienate political leaders by taking sides in environmental disputes, or they can be branded as anti-government or as being aligned with the opposition party. To keep government sponsorship, these quasi-governmental organizations have to remain politically neutral, so they are not able to serve as advocates for the environment in most disputes.

Most environmental groups have been formed in the last few years. They lack the public base of support needed to be effective political organizations, and find it very hard to increase their constituencies. This is due to the public's lack of awareness of environmental concerns, and a perception that environmental protection results in lost economic opportunities. In addition, governments are often skeptical or suspicious about the role of nongovernmental organizations in general.[17]

Environmental stakeholders are usually motivated by a personal environmental ethic, which is difficult to translate into the economic terms that politicians understand.[18] This dilemma will require local NGOs to develop new strategies if they are to make any substantial contribution to protecting the natural resources in the countries of the Eastern Caribbean.

Local Community Organizations: Catalysts for Reform

This group of stakeholders includes educational institutions, small regional foundations specializing in natural resource management, and environmental groups based in the region and the United States. These organizations are providing a valuable contribution to natural resource management in the region by training technicians, developing programs to improve environmental management, and performing field research. However, because governments in the region do not have formal mechanisms to allow these stakeholders to participate in the policy-making process, they generally do not become directly involved in development decisions. The following descriptions are not meant to be exhaustive, but are included to give a general idea of the organizations that are involved in the Eastern Caribbean.

The Centre for Environmental Studies and Natural Resource Management (CERMES) at the University of the West Indies, Barbados, trains students in a new degree program; several graduates of this program are now employed by governments in the region. The Caribbean Conservation Association (CCA), located in Barbados, is the oldest environmental NGO in the region. Seventeen countries belong to the CCA. It sponsors conferences, coordinates training, advises governments, and conducts environmental education programs. The Caribbean Natural Resources Institute (CANRI), formerly the Eastern Caribbean Natural Area Management Program, has offices in St. Lucia and the U.S. Virgin Islands. It coordinates several natural resource management projects in the region, and is helping several countries increase their institutional capacity. The Island Resources Foundation, located in the U.S. Virgin Islands and Washington, D.C., also works with several countries. It provides technical environmental services, works with USAID to prepare national environmental profiles for several countries, has a new program to organize small NGOs throughout the region, and has published many papers on a wide variety of environmental topics.

Two key factors influence the involvement of community organization in the political process. Regional organizations, such as the CCA, cannot become directly involved in local politics out of fear that they will alienate their members in government. It is politically more acceptable to serve a regional coordinating role, and this helps assure a longer life for the organization. In addition, regional organizations lack the credibility within each country to work effectively on local environmental issues. In general, organizations have to have a local institutional presence on an island to have legitimacy, and have to know enough about the political system and culture to be effective.

An additional factor preventing these organizations from being effective is the prevailing view among political leaders in the region that environmental concerns are obstacles to development. If on a given project these groups take a pro-environment stand that political leaders deem too strong, they will lose their access to the government, rendering them ineffective in the future. However, these organizations are collectively helping the region to slowly form an environmental tradition.

ILLUSTRATING THE POLITICS OF EXCLUSION: THE CASE STUDIES

The role of interest groups in the policy-making process, and how they do or do not influence environmental policy implementation, is the subject of the following case studies. The cases describe large development projects in three countries: St. Kitts, St. Lucia, and Barbados. By using the collective evidence from the cases, I will show why attempts to implement environmental policies have failed.

St. Kitts and the Southeast Peninsula Development Project

St. Kitts is governed by a unicameral legislature, the fourteen-member House of Assembly, which has eleven members elected by the public and three that are nominated by the House (two on the advice of the prime minister and one on the advice of the leader of the opposition).[19] The prime minister leads the majority party and heads the cabinet, which consists of five ministers and the attorney general. The legal system is based in English common law. The cabinet is the highest executive body, and is directly responsible for formulating and implementing national policy.

Each government department (e.g., Labor, Finance, Tourism, Agriculture) is headed by a minister. Civil servants within each department report directly to a permanent secretary, who in turn advises the minister who submits recommendations to the full cabinet. The cabinet makes final policy decisions, which are then approved by the House of Assembly. The portfolio for minister of the environment was held by the premier of Nevis—the sister island to St. Kitts, which has its own central government—but this portfolio was dropped in 1988.

A large portion of St. Kitts is known as the Southeast Peninsula. This 4,000-acre peninsula is unique in the Lesser Antilles, as its large wilderness areas include a wide variety of marine and terrestrial resources, some of which are in danger of extinction.[20] Within the six square miles of the peninsula, a very small portion of which is developed, are found ten arcuate bays, several coral reefs, salt ponds, sea grass beds, mangroves, wetlands, eleven beaches, and a diverse pattern of wildlife habitats including grasslands, forested hill-sides, and valleys. The peninsula remained relatively undisturbed until 1988 when USAID funded a project to provide the infrastructure to develop the peninsula. The intent of the project is to attract investors to build tourist resorts, condominiums, golf courses, commercial and recreational facilities, and perhaps a port for cruise ships.

The project elements include a 6.4-mile-long road to provide access to the peninsula, in addition to public utilities (water, power, and communication), to serve future tourist developments including hotels, condominiums, houses, shops, duty-free concessions, marinas, and a possible cruise-ship port. Construction of the road has been funded by USAID. The USAID loan agreement includes a grant for $1.14 million, a loan of $11.40 million, with St. Kitts contributing $4.1 million, for a total package of $16.64 million.

The project has been closely tied to the National Development Plan for St. Kitts. The Five Year Plan for 1986–90 emphasizes the development of the tourism sector to lead national economic growth. The general objectives of increased tourism include generating foreign exchange earnings, providing jobs, and a secondary boost to local manufacturing and agriculture. The plan contains specific objectives, including 800 new hotel rooms, the doubling of the number of tourists from 50,000 to 104,000 annually, and an increase in tourist revenue from $20 million to $50 million.[21]

Prior to the peninsula project, the government had no organized national growth strategy. The Five Year Plan was coordinated with the project, as evidenced by a 1985 study on tourism prepared for USAID, which concludes that "the maximum value of the peninsula lies in its ability to broaden the island of St. Kitts as a tourist destination" as the plan will increase tourist visits, add investor interests in providing a tourist infrastructure, and improve foreign exchange earnings.[22]

St. Lucia and the Pitons Controversy

St. Lucia is a constitutional monarchy. The top executive officer in the state is the governor-general, who is appointed by and represents the British sovereign as head of state. The Parliament consists of a seventeen-member House of Assembly that is elected by universal adult suffrage, while Parliament's eleven-member Senate is composed of members appointed by the prime minister, the leader of the opposition, and the governor-general. The prime minister is the top elected official in the country, leads the majority party, and has to have the support of the House of Assembly. The legal system is based on English common law. The centerpiece of the case study consists of the Gros and Petit Pitons, tall green peaks rising dramatically from the Caribbean Sea. The Pitons are considered the symbols of St. Lucia, as illustrated by their presence in the national flag and their prominent place in the national culture and heritage.

The case involves two competing proposals to develop the 316-acre Jalousie Estate, a former plantation located on the beach between the Gros and Petit Pitons. A variety of proposals have been put forward since 1981 to include the estate as a centerpiece of a proposed Pitons National Park, which would encompass 1,600 acres of surrounding land and include a visitors center to be built on the estate.

Businesspeople and community leaders from the town of Soufriere, near the Pitons, have formed the Soufriere Development Committee, which received assistance from the OAS to prepare a proposal for the acquisition and development of the Pitons National Park. While the centerpiece of the proposed park was the Jalousie Estate and surrounding lands, it included a comprehensive plan to redevelop the coastline of Soufriere to stimulate economic development in the area.

The proposal for the national park included a park headquarters and visitor facilities on the Jalousie Estate, surrounded by a 25-acre botanical garden, a spice- and fruit-tree plantation, a reserve for the protected St. Lucia parrot, a mini-zoo, a small jetty on the beach to service small boats and water taxis, a combination bar/restaurant, a museum, and areas for picnic, camping, and hiking. The park was to serve as a field laboratory for research activities by educational and scientific organizations and the natural sciences. A funding source for the initial $1.63 million needed for land acquisition, roads, and buildings was not included in the park proposal.[23]

The competing proposal to develop a tourist complex on the estate was sponsored by the M-Group, a Swiss-based company, which received an Alien Landholding license from the cabinet to purchase the site and approval from the Development Control Authority to build on it. Plans for the tourist resort called for a $25 million private investment to build about 120 cottages and suites, sporting facilities, a health spa, and docking facilities for yachts.[24] When the cabinet granted the license it also gave the developer financial incentives (duty-free import of construction materials and goods for the hotel, a multi-year tax holiday, and expatriation of profits), and agreed to build the access road to the estate at government expense. Phase 1 of the project, known as the Jalousie Plantation Resort, with 120 cottages and a restaurant, was completed in late 1992. Phase 2 of construction will include many more rooms to be built near the beach.

The natural resources at stake in the Pitons include the beach, prime near-offshore fishing grounds, open space uses on the estate, the vegetation and wildlife within the relatively intact mountain ecosystem, and natural hot springs and mineral baths. The proposed park site also contains important cultural and archaeological resources from past human settlements in the area.

Both the park and the resort proposals were consistent with a national policy to diversify the agriculture-based economy by promoting tourism. The St. Lucia National Plan calls for developing the island as a tourist destination through improved marketing and airline services, to provide foreign exchange, stabilize employment, and benefit local businesses that provide supplies to hotels and resorts. The plan also promotes "harmonization of the growth of tourism with regional development thrusts," which is compatible with the regional growth strategy in the national park proposal. The plan, and statements by the prime minister, reflect a target of 3,000 new hotel rooms in the country by the year 2000. There are currently about 2,000 hotel rooms.[25]

Barbados and the Bridgetown Fisheries Harbor

Barbados has one of the oldest parliamentary democracies in the Western hemisphere. The foundation of its political system was motivated by a desire for self rule. The island gradually gained greater independence into the 1900s, urged on by widespread riots in the late 1930s in the West Indies by residents demanding political independence. A history of strong unionism fostered the development of democracy, promoted by the Barbados Labor Party and the Barbados Workers Union. Barbados remained a colony of Britain under the old representative system, and was granted independence in 1961.[26]

The national government is headed by the governor-general, who serves as the head of state and is appointed by the British sovereign. The top executive officer is the prime minister, who leads the majority party and is chairman of the cabinet of ministers. The prime minister is appointed by the governor-general as the member of the House of Assembly who is capable of commanding the support of a majority of its members. Parliament is a bicameral body, with a Senate and a House of Assembly. The Senate is appointed by the governor-general on the advice of other political leaders, while the House of Assembly is elected by universal adult suffrage. The normal term of office is five years, but the majority party may require elections at any time to seek support for its policies.[27]

The fisheries harbor project originated within the political directorate of the Ministry of Agriculture in 1983. Its facilities include dock space for 150 boats, a boat repair facility, ice plant, processing area, boning and vending facilities, a rum shop and grocery, four fuel docks, and a large jetty constructed of several hundred interconnected cement *dojos* (B 17, 22, 29). The project was financed with a $12.3 million funding package from the IDB. The project agreement also includes technical components to strengthen the institutional capacity of the National Fisheries Division to improve fishing gear technology, processing, and marketing operations. These programs were completed in mid-1990 (B 17, 31, 42).

The Fisheries Harbor Project is consistent with national planning objectives contained in the Barbados Development Plan, 1983–1988. The plan states "the main factors which have tended to inhibit the growth of the [fishing] industry are inefficient marketing and distribution systems and inadequate facilities for servicing and shelter." The plan also contains policies to improve marketing, upgrade the local fleet, and increase the efficiency of fishing operations, so that the industry supplies 75 percent of local protein. Several specific projects are outlined in the plan, including construction of a large fisheries harbor in the capital city of Bridgetown.

The natural resources at stake with the development of the Bridgetown Fisheries Harbor include terrestrial and marine resources, local and regional fisheries, the stability of the interface between the near-offshore marine environment and a major river basin, and overall local water quality.

POLITICAL LEADERS REPRESENT PRO-DEVELOPMENT INTERESTS

Environmentally destructive decisions take place in the Eastern Caribbean because key stakeholders are excluded from the policy-making process. In addition, these decisions can be best be explained by examining the relationships among interest groups that are included in policy making, and the relationships between these groups and political leaders.

Executive authority for creating and implementing public policy in St. Kitts, St. Lucia, and Barbados is held by the prime minister and the cabinet. Members of the cabinet are selected from elected members of Parliament by the prime minister. Both the executive and legislative branches of government are controlled by members of the majority party, which consolidates the control the party has over the policy-making process.

The prime minister, also known as the premier, is the head of state, exerting great influence over the cabinet and civil servants in different ministries, even though the governor-general officially heads the Parliament as the representative of the British sovereign. The prime minister consolidates this influence by appointing ministers to the cabinet who are sympathetic to the prime minister's policies, and by giving top positions in the civil service to loyal party members. As the architects of the national policy-making process, the prime minister, cabinet, and top civil servants work together to promote policies that will help keep them in power and enable them to win the next election.

The national political leadership itself is in some ways a special interest group that maintains relationships with other special interest groups who have a stake in how government policies are carried out. Politicians want to stay in office. Developers want to profit from their investments. A link exists between these private and public interest groups that serves to reinforce both of their objectives.

In all three countries, the political leadership represented pro-development interest groups to support development projects that had environmental problems. In each case, the developers used a different strategy of influence. Certain stakeholders were included in the policy-making process while others were excluded.

St. Lucians describe the Piton mountains as "the breasts of their mother." These twin peaks, towering over the land as they rise from the Caribbean Sea, are widely recognized as the symbols of St. Lucia. They appear on the national flag, and on the logos of countless businesses. Should a resort be built between the Pitons, privatizing an area where a national park is proposed? In the words of St. Lucia writer Derek Walcott, "When the tribe sells the Pitons it has sold its mother, it has turned her into a prostitute."[28]

St.Lucia: The Prime Minister and the Cabinet Represent the Interests of the Developer

In November 1981, the cabinet issued an Alien Landholding license, required of all foreign landowners, to Sir Colin Tennant, enabling him to buy the Jalousie Estate. Tennant planned to develop the 316-acre site, located in the heart of the Piton mountains, as an exclusive tourist resort. By granting the license the cabinet reversed its earlier decision to acquire the estate as the key parcel within the proposed Pitons National Park. However, the developer apparently lacked the funds needed to build the resort, so the site remained undeveloped throughout the 1980s.

A series of events took place from late 1988 to mid-1989 that underscored how the prime minister and cabinet represented the interests of the developer. In late 1988 the cabinet issued a second Alien Landholding license to a new developer, the M-Group, a Swiss-based holding company. Although there is no public record of the meeting at which this decision was made, officials close to the project reported that the cabinet granted substantial economic concessions to the developer such as repatriation of profits, waiver of duties on construction materials and supplies for the resort, and a multi-year tax holiday (SL 15). The cabinet also gave an unusual incentive to the developer by approving public funds to build the main access road to the site.

In January 1988, the DCA gave the developer an approval in concept for a resort project, without a public hearing. It is important to realize that the prime minister holds the portfolios for Planning and Finance. This gives him control over policy decisions involving financial concessions and planning approvals. In the words of one senior civil servant, "When cabinet approves economic concessions for the project it does suggest what the government wants, and whose wrath will be incurred if the project is denied. Cabinet makes its wishes well known. The choice not to develop the site is no longer feasible" (SL 5).

The prime minister took action in March 1988, to show that he was willing to use his authority to represent the interests of developers. He made headlines in local newspapers when he presided over a ground-breaking ceremony for the Windjammer Landing Villa Hotel. This project has 190 individual villas spread over several acres above the Caribbean Sea, and includes a beach with private recreational facilities. It is a large project. At the ceremony, the prime minister joked that "We are all participating in a criminal activity."

He was right, as the DCA had not issued any permits for the project. The civil servants in the DCA were badly embarrassed. They fined the developer and appointed an ad hoc commission to issue conditions under which the project could be built. The villas were completed in 1989 (SL 13).[29] The action of the prime minister showed how far he was willing to go, including flagrantly breaking national laws, to support the interests of private developers.

The prime minister took a similar action that reflected his control over the national planning process when he used the occasion of his annual address to Parliament in April 1988 to publicly support the developers of the proposed resort at the Jalousie Estate. During this widely reported speech he said "Government has indicated its approval to an investment group to proceed with a touristic development on lands between the Pitons, without encroaching upon lands which have been earmarked as a National Park and nature reserve."[30] At the time, the project had not received approval from the DCA.

The response to the prime minister's public support of the project was swift and blunt. Newspapers printed editorials within the week asking how a large resort could possibly be built in the center of the proposed park without degrading it.[31] When the cabinet secretly gave the landholding license and financial concessions for the resort, while taking no action to implement the park proposal, it clearly showed that the government favored the resort.

The Developer's Strategy of Influence.   The developer enlisted the support of other political leaders in addition to the prime minister. In February 1988, the developer presented EC$100,000 to the Soufriere Hospital Committee. The payment was personally delivered to the minister of health, who also holds the portfolio for the Environment. In March the minister of communication and works initiated construction of the access road. In May, after several newspapers published editorials condemning the way that the cabinet secretly approved the resort despite the estates' value as a national park, the minister told a reporter that "Government fully supports the tourism development project, approval has been granted in principle to the Jalousie Plantation Company, the developers, and it's just a matter of time before approval is granted in full for the commencement of construction." Vincent Lewis[32] The same minister threatened to revoke the broadcast license of a local television station planning to televise a public hearing sponsored by the Concerned Persons on the Environment, an environmental group concerned about the negative impact of the resort (SL 4, 8, 13, 15).

It is generally believed that in negotiations with the political leadership to gain support for the project the developers were represented by a local attorney who is also chairman of the M-Group (the developers company) and Director of the St. Lucia Tourist Board. This attorney also obtained the support of the national tourist industry for the resort. In April, when the prime minister used his speech to the Parliament to state his public support for the resort, he also announced that he was increasing the subvention to the Tourist Board by EC$5 million, thereby linking the project to a national effort to increase tourism.

The developer also funded a grassroots organizing effort in the impoverished town of Soufriere near the Pitons. A local mason was hired to circulate a petition in support of the project. In May, the National Workers Union, the largest union in the country, with 5,000 members and over 400 in Soufriere, announced its support for the resort. All of these actions reflect a focused effort by the developer to orchestrate how the political leadership and public were organized to support the project.

St. Kitts: Political Leaders Manipulate the Public Policy Process

In St. Kitts a small group of political leaders, with the advice of influential members of their political party, possesses the power to make public policy decisions that effect the environment. Throughout the decision-making process for the Southeast Peninsula Development Project, the same few people have represented the government. The primary representatives of two main interest groups, the national political leadership and landowners on the peninsula, have been the prime minister, the minister of development and the attorney general. The minister of development and the attorney general have represented the government in its negotiations with USAID over the past several years. In turn, the minister of development represented peninsula landowners in these negotiations (SK 12).[33]

The control that the minister of development exerted over the development process in St. Kitts, and how the implementation of environmental policies is discouraged, can be seen by examining this minister's role in the government. His ministerial portfolio included Agriculture, Lands, and Housing in addition to Development. His responsibilities included overseeing the Central Planning Unit, which reviews development applications for the country. His multiple portfolio made him responsible for the enforcement of most environmental laws. He controlled the Southeast Peninsula Land Development and Conservation Board, an advisory body coordinating all development activities on the peninsula. By holding these positions of authority, this minister was the major force in forming national policies that determine how decisions are made that favor either development or the environment. The way the minister chose to favor pro-development interests can be seen by examining some of his actions.

The minister appointed five members to the Southeast Peninsula advisory board. The board is responsible for making recommendations to the minister to provide for the development, conservation, and management of the peninsula.[34] The minister takes recommendations from the board to the cabinet, which makes all final decisions, which are then ratified by the House of Assembly. However, the individuals appointed by the minister only represent development interests. No member of the board has a background or interest in natural resource management or conservation. Board members include the permanent secretary of tourism, a senator who also is a private electrical contractor, a landowner/hotelier, a private engineer, and the public works engineer. The hotelier is a major landowner on the peninsula and is a founder of the Peoples Action Movement party, the majority party in the country. He is a member of the government's inner circle and wields much political influence (SK 8, 14, 17). He represents the interests of large landowners and the tourist industry, and supports intensive development of the peninsula, including projects he is sponsoring (SK 25). He perceives the role of the board as a "coordinator for developers" (SK 18). This is in contrast with the legal mandate for the board, which is to evaluate development proposals, control pollution, preserve environmental quality, and implement environmental protection plans.[35]

The Failure of National Environmental Policies. USAID required that St. Kitts pass new comprehensive environmental legislation to replace outmoded and ineffective laws, in an attempt to improve the implementation of national environmental policies. The National Conservation and Environment Protection Act (NCEPA) was passed in April 1987. It required the establishment of a National Conservation Commission to oversee environmental management on St. Kitts and Nevis, including the southeast peninsula. The government delayed gazetting (issuing public notice) the act until mid-1989 because of concerns of peninsula landowners that its provisions for public access to the coast would adversely effect their property rights (SK 3).

More importantly, the Conservation Commission was still not operational as of mid-1990. The designated chairman of the Commission resigned to protest the lack of action by the government to implement the act (SK 23). The government's decision not to empower the Conservation Commission appears to be part of a strategy by the minister of development and the cabinet to set a precedent that allows large projects to be built on the peninsula without any political interference (SK 8).

The failure of the government to enforce the NCEPA is consistent with other policy decisions that favor pro-development interest groups. The Land Use Management Plan prepared for the Southeast Peninsula project strongly recommended that a new Environmental Management Unit be established within the Central Planning Unit, but this has not occurred. Virtually all of the environmental laws in St. Kitts remain unenforced.

The authority to control public policy decisions that affect the environment is held within the closed circle of a few top political leaders. The chain of command that controls decisions favoring the use of the peninsula for intensive commercial development starts and ends with the minister of development, the prime minister, and the attorney general, who have thus far favored pro-development policies while refusing to implement policies intended to protect the island's fragile natural resources. Given the obvious lack of enforcement of environmental laws throughout the country, and the lack of political will to mitigate environmental damage that development of the peninsula will bring, the future looks bleak for one of the most important wildlife areas in the Eastern Caribbean.

Barbados: Political Leaders' Strategy of Influence

The development of the Bridgetown Fishing Harbor shows that when large projects, often funded by donor agencies, originate in the political directorate of a country, strategic political interests cause environmental problems to be ignored (B 2).

Expansion of the fishing industry has been a major goal of the Barbados government for fifteen years.[36] To carry out this policy, the minister of agriculture initiated two projects in the early 1980s. The first was a small fishing complex at Ostins on the south coast. The second was a major fishing harbor in the capital city of Bridgetown. This project, also known as the Cheapside harbor after the neighborhood where it is located, was initiated by the ministry in 1983.

When he initiated and successfully completed the project, the minister of agriculture represented his own interests and those of the national political leadership, including the prime minister and the cabinet. The primary interest of the leadership is to stay in power. At the beginning of the project, the minister formed a coordinating committee with representatives from relevant government offices, assigned his permanent secretary of the Special Projects Division to be in charge of it. These actions consolidated the authority of the ministry within the government, giving it the political mandate necessary to build the harbor.

The significance of the project being originated in and coordinated by the political directorate is emphasized by the following observation by a government official: "Projects such as the fishing harbor are often decided by one man, the minister of agriculture in this case, who decides that the project is good, and will be visible, so investigations of concerns like the environment are frowned upon, so bureaucrats don't or can't review them. Projects like this may be a white elephant, but they are big, and look good" (B 22).

In 1983, after the Ministry of Economic Affairs reviewed the project, the government asked the IDB to provide funding for it. The IDB agreed in concept, and after conducting its own economic analysis, the project agreement was signed in November 1984. With the funding now in place, the Ministry of Agriculture had to obtain permission from national planning authorities before construction commenced.

Political Control of the National Planning Agency. In Barbados the planning authority is the Town and Country Planning Department (TCP). In September 1985, the Ministry of Agriculture submitted a site plan to the TCP. It included slips for 150 boats; facilities for boat repairs and for weighing, processing, and storing fish; a fish market; fuel docks; a grocery; a rum shop; and a large jetty to protect against storm surges (B 17, 22, 29).

When the TCP evaluates a project like the harbor, it solicits feedback from other government agencies that have relevant expertise or jurisdiction related to it. This is called the "consultative process." On one hand, this process gives the planning authority considerable flexibility. For example, it theoretically gives natural resource managers the opportunity to have input into the planning process so that potential environmental problems can be identified.

On the other hand, the informality of this approach reduces the accountability of the planning process because the minister who oversees the planning department determines whose input to accept. The result is that planning authorities give up control of the development review process to the political leadership.

As part of the consultative process, the TCP contacted the Coastal Conservation Project Unit (CCPU), the national agency responsible for coastal management. The CCPU happened to be funded by the IDB, the sponsor of the fishing harbor. Officials at the regional office of the IDB asked the government to have the CCPU review the project (B 17). The CCPU had not been asked by the Ministry of Agriculture to help with the design of the harbor (B 20). After reviewing the project, the CCPU staff identified four major areas of environmental concern, including (1) long-term degradation of harbor waters from sewage disposal from live-aboard fishermen; (2) adverse effects of dredging; (3) changes in coastal dynamics caused by the breakwater, which could cause siltation of the harbor mouth or adjacent river mouth; and (4) the impact of increased fishing pressure on limited fish stocks in the region (B 5, 20). No scientific information existed to address any of these concerns.

In January 1986, the TCP approved the site plan for the harbor. The environmental concerns pointed out by the CCPU were not mentioned or included in the conditions of approval (B 22). During the 1988–89 fishing season the catch of the Barbados fishing fleet dropped 40 percent. It is not known if this is a cyclical drop or the result of overfishing (B 29).

The political leadership was the primary pro-development interest group in this case. It wanted to build the harbor without the possible delays that would be caused by researching potential environmental problems, even though the result could be the decline of the regional fishery and sedimentation of the harbor. The manner in which the government pushed this project through the permit process, ignoring environmental concerns, supports the contention that large projects do not receive a thorough environmental evaluation when they are initiated in the political directorate, especially if politicians want the project approved before a national election (B 3, 20).[37]

St.Lucia: Civil Servants Prevented from Implementing Environmental Policies

While national policies are formulated by political leaders, civil servants are often responsible for implementing them. At the same time that civil servants work to implement environmental policies, they are dependent on political leaders for their jobs. The relationship between politicians and civil servants prevents environmental policies from being implemented. The events that took place in St. Lucia show how this happens.

After the cabinet granted an Alien Landholding license to Sir Colin Tennant in 1981, reversing its earlier decision to acquire the Jalousie Estate as part of a national park, a senior planner in the Central Planning Unit wrote the "Proposed Policy of Development at the Pitons, Soufriere." It included several recommendations to the cabinet to protect the natural resources on the estate, stressing its importance to the country. The cabinet refused to adopt the report however, so these recommendations were not implemented, despite the efforts of the Central Planning Unit.

The Chief Forestry Officer (CFO) was the most outspoken environmental advocate in the government. He founded the Environmental Commission, which the prime minister has refused to certify, so it remains an unofficial body. In late 1988, the Ministry of Tourism asked the CFO to attend a meeting of officials who had voiced concern about the environmental impact of the resort project. There the CFO voiced concerns about the protection of the site's prime agricultural lands, and asked the Ministry of Tourism to provide information showing how these lands would be protected if the project was built. The ministry failed to provide the information requested, and excluded the CFO from further discussions about the project (SL 6).[38] Similarly, the Chief Fisheries Officer has an interest in seeing that the prime fishing grounds adjacent to the estate are protected, but has no direct voice in the policy process to present this viewpoint.

When the OAS submitted the formal proposal for a Pitons National Park to the government in March 1988, it had to go through official channels. The report was submitted to the permanent secretary of planning who controlled its distribution. The permanent secretary is also the assistant to the prime minister, who is also minister of planning. When interest groups supporting the inclusion of the Jalousie Estate in a national park wanted to obtain information in the park proposal that summarized how the park would generate more economic benefits than the resort, the report was not available for them to use because its distribution was controlled by the permanent secretary (SL 9).

The frustration of civil servants who want to implement policies intended to protect the environment is summarized by a St. Lucian close to the Pitons controversy: "Civil servants, when faced with pressure from the political leadership, may bleed inside, if they disagree with the development project, but can't speak out due to politics; it is too dangerous to their families" (SL 4).

The hesitancy of senior civil servants to pressure political leaders to implement environmental policies is also the result of a thwarted reform movement they initiated in the 1970s. Individuals who had recently returned to St. Lucia after obtaining graduate degrees abroad started meeting to express their concerns about the process of economic development in the country. When their jobs were threatened they realized that unless they held political office, reform was not possible (SL 8).

St. Kitts: Political Leaders Undermine Environmental Protection

The small size of the government in St. Kitts gives political leaders near-total control over civil servants who could use their jobs to carry out environmental policies to protect the natural resources on the southeast peninsula. There are several ways that the political system exerts control over civil servants, preventing them from being involved in the planning process for the peninsula.

The Physical Planning Section (PPS) of the Central Planning Unit is under the jurisdiction of the minister of development. It has a dual responsibility for evaluating development proposals and examining the possible adverse environmental effects they could cause. But it remains unclear what the role of the PPS is in the development process for the Southeast Peninsula. The PPS is the only agency responsible for environmental planning, but it has no formal liaison with the peninsula advisory board. The Board's staff offered to train planning officials in environmental planning to help build the government's institutional capacity, but were refused by the minister of development (SK 17).

The problems caused by the lack of integration between planning authorities and the board were summarized in a 1988 report: "It is imperative that planning['s] standing, and management and tenure policies with respect to the southeastern peninsula be defined. Given its high touristic potential it could be subject to all sorts of pressures, speculative and expansionist, in the near future."[39] The decision by the minister of development not to integrate the national planning process with the development of the peninsula has prevented civil servants from implementing policies designed to protect the peninsula's natural resources.

Similarly, the government's refusal to create an Environmental Unit and make the National Conservation Commission operational has prevented civil servants from being involved in environmental planning. These policy decisions, combined with the fact that several national environmental laws regulating coastal development, sewage disposal, industrial pollution, garbage disposal, and beach mining are not enforced, has created an atmosphere where civil servants know that politicians do not want them to enforce environmental laws.

The political relationship between ministers and civil servants in St. Kitts also prevents the natural resources of the peninsula from being protected. The policy of the government is to strongly support the peninsula project by attracting investors who will fund various commercial projects. If a discussion were allowed among civil servants about how environmental policies should be enforced on the peninsula, it would lengthen the development process, something that political leaders want to avoid (SK 4). Civil servants are forced to follow the government's policy of not enforcing environmental standards, because of the control exerted by political leaders over every aspect of the development process.

St. Lucia: Environmental Interest Groups Excluded from Development Decisions

During the controversy over the development of a resort on the Jalousie Estate in St. Lucia, environmental interest groups who wanted to preserve the site as part of a new national park were systematically excluded from key public policy decisions. Two key meetings between the M-Group and government officials that resulted in decisions to support the resort project were not open to the public, which prevented pro-environmental groups from attending.

The first meeting was in late 1988 when representatives of the developer met with the cabinet to seek a new Alien Landholding license. This meeting resulted in the cabinet granting financial concessions to the M-Group to encourage development of the resort. The second meeting was in early 1989 when the developer met with the cabinet and the DCA to obtain an official Approval in Concept for the resort. This decision, combined with the cabinet approval, made it unlikely that the detailed site plan for the resort would be rejected.

Environmental interest groups were prevented from participating in any of the decisions that determined the future of the national park. Groups excluded from the decision-making process included civil servants responsible for managing natural resources such as the forest, agricultural lands, and fisheries; the Concerned Persons on the Environment; and individual stakeholders who live and work in the area. As a government official said, "Development review is not public; the developer presents technical information to the cabinet without input from others, so there is a bias for the developer due to the process" (SL 5). The lack of public participation has also prevented park advocates from building a local political base to convince politicians of the need for the park (SL 2, 13).

The Concerned Persons on the Environment was an ad hoc group of professionals and community leaders who started meeting in mid-1988 as a result of the secrecy surrounding the resort project and its conflict with the proposed Pitons National Park. Its members included leaders of the Catholic church, the National Trust, the Naturalists Society, the Soufriere Development Committee, the OAS, the Caribbean Conservation Association, and senior civil servants from several ministries. The Concerned Persons was formed to increase the collective bargaining power of its members. To do this they sponsored unprecedented public meetings in Soufriere and Castries to express concerns over the Pitons controversy. The meetings were widely reported in the local press, but offers from its most influential members to meet with the prime minister were rebuffed (SL 4, 9).

The Catholic church emerged as a major public voice in the Pitons controversy. It opposed the resort to protest the secrecy surrounding the public policy process, and was against privatization of the Pitons, which are recognized as the national symbol of St. Lucia as indicated by their appearance on the national flag.[40] The opposition of the church to the commercial development of the Jalousie Estate is notable, as an estimated 90 percent of St. Lucians are Catholic. However, it is not clear that the Concerned Persons or the Church has had any influence on the government.

Other parties that have an interest in protecting the environment of the Pitons are unorganized stakeholders who use the natural resources in the area for subsistence. This includes several individuals and families who live or work within the boundaries of the proposed park, such as fishers who use the prime offshore reefs, herders, small farmers, squatters, and charcoal producers. These resource users have not been involved in the planning process for the park or the resort. Their interests in maintaining a healthy natural environment are represented indirectly by the Concerned Persons, but they have no direct access to the public policy process, including the prime minister, the cabinet or the DCA.

The closed public policy process in St. Lucia prevented all environmental groups from participating in the decision to use the Jalousie Estate as a private resort or a national park. In early 1990 the government gave its final approval for the resort and the OAS closed its St. Lucia office. The proposal for the Pitons National Park has not been accepted by the government. Soon after the resort was approved, another developer submitted plans for the Gros Piton Resort Village and Aerial Tramway, a resort on eleven acres at the summit of the mountain with a tram to carry 250,000 people a year.[41] Planning authorities are deciding whether to issue an Approval in Concept for it. The privatization of the Pitons is becoming a reality. It seems likely that within a few years the natural environment of the Pitons will be irreversibly changed by several large tourism projects, contrary to the goals of the proposed Pitons National Park.

St. Kitts: Government Control of Information Stifles Environmental Advocacy

Environmental stakeholders in St. Kitts face a similar situation. There are no organized environmental interest groups on St. Kitts. Individuals that depend on the natural resources of the peninsula are few in number. There are a few herders, one charcoal producer, and several squatters. These parties are unorganized, lack any formal representation, and have no voice in the decision-making process. St. Kitts does have small organizations that promote the preservation of historical homes and the famous Brimstone Hill Fortress, as well as a horticultural society, but they have not been involved with the peninsula project. The Historical and Conservation Society in the neighboring island of Nevis has not been directly involved with the project.

There are several reasons why there are no environmental interest groups in St. Kitts. There is a general lack of awareness among the citizens about the need to protect the environment. The low level of political and economic development on the island has discouraged such a group from forming, as it would be perceived as antidevelopment and anti-government. The government controls the flow of information in the society.[42] The only two regular newspapers on the island are published by the majority and opposition political parties. The only radio station on St. Kitts (ZIZ Radio) is run by the government news agency. The Public Information Officer decides what issues to air on the radio and what stories to send to regional newspapers. Differences of opinion between the few individuals involved in policy making, including both civil servants and politicians, are deemed confidential, and people refrain from "airing their dirty laundry in public" (SK 4).

Since no organized environmental interest groups exist in St. Kitts, and the flow of information is controlled by the government, environmental issues are not part of the public policy debate. The result is a total lack of political pressure on the political leadership to protect the fragile natural resources on the southeast peninsula.

Barbados: Emerging Advocacy for the Environment

Barbados does not have a tradition of supporting local environmental interest groups. Historically the public has not been concerned about the environment, and there was no public debate about the environmental consequences of the fishing harbor. However, a public dialogue about environmental problems is starting to occur (B 30, 33).

There are two environmental groups in the country, the Barbados Environmental Association (BEA) and the National Trust. The BEA has several members from the civil service and business community. It was started in the late 1980s to promote an anti-litter campaign called "Keep Barbados Beautiful," funded by the Canadian International Development Agency. The National Trust has successfully promoted the preservation of historical buildings and landmarks. Both of these groups are hesitant to become involved in a public dialogue about larger environmental issues facing Barbados because of the risk that they would be branded as anti-government.

The potential does exist for a public debate on environmental issues to take place in Barbados because of the openness of the media. Barbadians have an adult literacy rate of over 90 percent and support three privately owned daily newspapers. Indirect public participation in the policy-making process occurs through several national radio call-in shows.[43] At most times of the day at least one call-in show is on the radio. These shows are reportedly listened to by cabinet ministers, and have resulted in the government taking action on issues of concern to the public, such as an investigation of health concerns at a major chicken plant in 1989.

Radio call-in shows could serve as a surrogate for public hearings, which are not part of the national planning process. However,

the fear does exist among civil servants, who are among the best educated and environmentally aware citizens, that their voices will be
recognized on the radio by politicians who will exact retribution for
any criticism leveled at the government.

Two key events occurred in Barbados during the late 1980s
that raised the public consciousness about environmental issues.
The Trading Post fire destroyed an industrial warehouse storing large
amounts of toxic chemicals. For the first time, officials had to find a
way safely to dispose of large amounts of contaminated material that
posed a public health hazard. The waste was finally burned in the
defense department incinerator which raised additional questions
about resulting air pollution problems. The controversy about how
safely to dispose of the toxic material from the warehouse became a
major public issue, and was in newspapers and on call-in shows for
several days.

The second event was a fire that destroyed the White Park Road
farm and garden shop housing pesticides, herbicides, and fertilizers.
The resulting air and water pollution and subsequent clean-up problems also heightened public awareness of the dangers of toxic waste
disposal. As a result of these key events, workers who are exposed to
toxic materials in their jobs are demanding that they be provided
with safety clothes, and the fire department has started to train personnel in how to deal with fires involving toxic materials. Public
consciousness about environmental issues in general has risen in the
past few years since cable television has been available on the island.
News accounts of international environmental problems such the
Greenhouse effect, depletion of the ozone, deforestation in the Amazon, and oil spills now reach many Barbadian households, and has
marginally increased their level of awareness of similar issues in
their own country (B 1, 3, 12). This combination of local and international key events and conditions could lead to an opening of the
policy dialogue concerning environmental issues in general, and the
effects of large development projects on limited natural resources on
this tropical island in particular.

SUMMARY

How interest groups exert influence on the public policy
process can be determined by studying their content and behavior.
Interest groups are an important element of the political system
in the Eastern Caribbean, and their behavior can explain the gap

between the purpose and the result of national environmental policies that are supposed to protect the fragile natural resources of the region.

In all three countries political leaders used similar strategies of influence to promote the interests of pro-development interest groups. These strategies included accepting money from developers, refusing to allow public participation in decision making, holding private meetings to approve projects informally, using public funds to give economic incentives to developers, and excluding key environmental stakeholders from the policy-making process.

The political leadership in all three countries exerted their formal and informal authority to discourage civil servants from implementing environmental policies. Ministers regularly overruled civil servants and disregarded their recommendations to protect natural resources. Governments have dropped their ministerial portfolios for the environment, limited access to information that supports environmental interests—including the restriction of the free press on St. Kitts—and focused on short-term planning that favors quick solutions to current economic problems.

Political leaders also used their informal authority to discourage the implementation of environmental policies. They have created a pro-development atmosphere by continually disregarding existing environmental laws while maintaining strict control over civil servants through patronage appointments and party loyalty. Political leaders have also rebuffed the efforts of civil servants to create new national policies for environmental protection, such as the Environmental Commission in St. Lucia, by withholding the official backing of the government.

Local environmental groups are forming in the region, but they lack the access to political leaders that is needed to influence public policies. Regional environmental organizations have had little influence on local development decisions. Resource users remain unorganized and have no voice in the public policy process, even though they stand to lose the most when decisions are made that lead to the destruction of natural resources. Given the pro-development bias of political leaders, the access to the government that pro-development interest groups have, and the exclusion of environmental stakeholders in national policy making, the future for the limited natural resources of the islands looks bleak.

It is clear that an approach to development decisions that includes the interests of all stakeholders needs to be created if natural resources are to be protected. But other crucial elements reflective of the public policy process in developing countries also need to be taken into account. Culture plays an important role in decision making, especially as it affects the interactions between donor agencies and national governments. The interplay between culture and politics, what I call the culture of decision making, also needs to be accounted for in development decision

Chapter Four

THE IMPACT OF CULTURAL DIFFERENCES

According to Edward T. Hall, "Culture directs the organization of the psyche, which in turn has a profound effect upon the ways people look at things, behave politically, make decisions, order priorities, organize their lives, and last but not least, how they think."[1] There are several ways that cultural differences can create obstacles that undermine environmental initiatives undertaken in developing countries. One reason for this is that programs to promote environmental protection in developing countries are often initiated in the United States, Europe, Canada, and Japan, which have very different cultural conditions and traditions. In turn, the cultural conditions and traditions in these countries are different from those that exist in the developing countries they are attempting to influence. As a result, miscommunication often occurs between well-meaning environmental advocates from developed countries and their counterparts in developing countries. Misunderstandings of local and national cultural norms, added to the complexities of the political, economic, and institutional aspects of environmental policy making, can defeat the most well-intentioned efforts.

Culture affects public policy implementation in two ways. First, the patterns of behavior, customs, and beliefs that people acquire as members of a society shape the way they perceive the settings in which they operate. Second, decision making and particularly, the way power is concentrated in the hands of a few individuals, the ways that political leaders relate to the governed, and the norms of responsibility for civil servants constrain the way policy options are evaluated.

These two effects of culture on the public policy process are inseparable yet rarely understood. The link between culture and decision making has to be understood to see why it is difficult to implement any new public policy, including environmental policies. Often, when new environmental policies are adopted by developing countries, they are based on models borrowed from the United States or Europe. For instance, this happens when international foreign assistance agencies require that new national environmental legislation be adopted as a condition of development assistance. In almost all instances, these imported policies do not take adequate account of cultural conditions. Because cultural conditions are not accounted for in the policy making process, efforts to implement new environmental policies often fail.

SOME GENERAL CHARACTERISTICS OF CULTURE

In addition to examining the importance of the other culture, it is important for a person to contemplate his or her own beliefs and customs. This is especially true when a person is working in an unfamiliar culture attempting to find ways to implement new public policies. How a person is perceived and the biases, beliefs, and customs he or she brings to a foreign country can lead to personal misunderstandings that undermine such work.

Weiss identifies several "ghosts" that can make it difficult to understand the effect of culture on policy implementation.[2] Ghosts are factors that can obscure the identifiable elements of a national, regional, or local culture and make it difficult to determine exactly what mix of personal, societal, or institutional factors affect how people behave. The ghosts Weiss sees include (1) how people are affected by different political, economic, and legal systems and organizations within a national culture; (2) the wide variation in individual behavioral styles people use to negotiate and communicate; (3) the changes that take place over time in a culture; and (4) individual versus group behavior in a culture.

Most cultures, whether they are national, sub-national, or local, exist on a continuum ranging from totally homogeneous to widely varying heterogeneous. In heterogeneous cultures, or those lacking long historical traditions, it is harder to separate the ghosts and focus on the underlying elements of the cultural milieu. In smaller more homogeneous cultures, such as those of countries in the Eastern Caribbean, the elements of culture are easier to identify. Once identified, important cultural factors can be integrated into efforts to implement new public policies, to increase the likelihood they will succeed. The context of a culture, and the beliefs, language, and behavior of its members must be taken into account when designing and seeking to implement new policies.

CULTURAL CONTEXT

Hall and Hall describe *context* as "the information that surrounds an event and is inextricably bound up with the meaning of that event."[3] Events combine with the cultural context to produce different outcomes. Certain indicators can be used to evaluate, and to some extent predict, how different cultural contexts will affect the implementation of new public policies.

Different cultures have different cultural contexts. Countries in northern Europe tend to be low context, a characteristic shared with many Americans of European descent. Countries in Latin America, southern Europe, and the Caribbean have high-context cultures. People from low-context cultures, where the models for new public policies often originate, are described by Hall and Hall as being monochronic. People from high-context cultures, typical of societies in developing countries that adopt imported public policies, are described as polychronic.

Monochronic individuals are generally seen as those who operate on strict time deadlines, show little flexibility, and require great amounts of information to make a decision. Polychronic people are more committed to people and human relationships, are more willing to be flexible and deviate from a fixed plan or strategy, and consider social relationships to be more important than strict objectives. These differences have significant implications for the effectiveness of public policies that are transferred without variation from low-context to high-context cultures.

BELIEF SYSTEMS

Belief systems are at the foundation of culture. A belief system is made up of the values and attitudes expressed by individuals, family groups, and communities who draw upon past events, experiences and traditions to form beliefs about issues of importance to their society. Elements of a belief system that relate to the public policy process include perceptions about the validity of the government and its leaders, and the acceptance of laws and regulations that control personal behavior. This includes how people accept or reject the role of government in implementing environmental laws that alter personal habits.

Belief systems may be represented by a variety of people, including male religious leaders, village elders, clan heads, or women, none of whom usually hold formal leadership positions in the government. The values and attitudes of a belief system may be expressed in ways that are difficult for outsiders to understand, such as localized spoken languages, and non-verbal behavior. It is generally very difficult to understand a belief system, and know how to operate within its norms, without living in a culture for many years. If an outsider does not understand a culture and its belief system, he or she will have a hard time getting any message across.[4]

In some ways it is even harder to become familiar with the culture and belief system of small communities, such as an island or rural village. The tradition of social interdependence among residents of smaller, insular communities may prevent an outside party from gaining the legitimacy needed to influence public policy.[5] This can happen even when an outsider and local people speak the same language.

Written and Spoken Language

The languages of a society, both written and spoken, reflect the underlying culture. If language differences exist it will invariably lead to misunderstandings. To understand a culture, to be able to get inside it and perceive the world as its members do, a person has to understand its languages. There are often two types of language differences that hamper cross-cultural communication. The first type of difference relates to written language, and the second relates to spoken language. It is important to consider how both types of language impact the effectiveness of new policy initiatives.[6]

When public policies originate in a developed country, they typically include legislation, administrative guidelines, and regulations, in the form of long written documents filled with complex legal and technical terminology. For example, environmental legislation may include words like *wildlands, zoning,* or *parks and protected areas.* These words have a clear meaning in the United States or Europe, but are often not understood by officials in countries that lack a tradition of carefully controlled land use and conservation.

Similarly, differences in the use of spoken words are also rooted in culture. In many developing countries, oral traditions are the main way of communication, including political leaders who are responsible for implementing public policies. Even if both countries involved in the transference of policies use the same language, such as the United States and an island in the English-speaking Caribbean, residents of the developing country will often use a localized version of the language, such as creolized English.

Mervyn C. Alleyne describes the Caribbean as having extremely complex languages and almost every type of linguistic phenomenon, including trade and contact jargons, creole languages and dialects, ethnic vernaculars, and non-standard dialects.[7] In St. Lucia, the official language is English, but everyday conversations are spoken in a French-based patois. When people do speak English it is often not the standard form. On several occasions while in St. Kitts I have heard visitors ask local residents "What language are you speaking?" The inevitable reply was "English." Kittians speak English, but it is spoken very quickly with a heavy accent, and can be hard for foreigners to understand.

Public policies that originate in developed countries are based on their written tradition and do not account for either subtle differences in written language or larger differences between written and spoken languages that can exist between people from industrialized and developing countries. Under the best of circumstances, these differences lead to misunderstandings that hinder policy implementation, because the parties simply are not communicating. Under the worst of circumstances, open conflict can result. An example of how this happens is in the history of the Treaty of Waitangi in New Zealand.

The signatories to the treaty in 1840 were representatives of the sovereign of England and chiefs representing several Maori tribes. The English signed versions of the treaty written in English, while the Maori chiefs signed multiple versions written in Maori. The controversy over the treaty has centered on the Maori right to *"tino rangatiratanga"* (loosely translated as "unqualified exercise of their chieftainship") over their *"taonga"* (loosely translated as the land, villages, treasures, and sacred things handed down over several generations). There was, and remains, no literal translation into English of these words. This has led to continuous conflicts over natural resource management in many parts of the country.[8]

BEHAVIORAL CHARACTERISTICS

It is important to consider behavior as an element of culture because the successful implementation of new public policies depends on effective interaction with people from different cultures who will interpret behavior and exhibit behavior quite differently. The emotional, verbal, and behavioral cues that people use to transmit information vary among different cultures. To build the personal relationships seen as normal by high-context people in developing countries, one must understand the meaning of behavioral cues that may not be obvious, even to people that have spent considerable time observing them.

Behavioral cues range from subtleties such as dress, posture, and composure to more obvious behavior like patterns of speech, where people sit at a table, and who speaks first during a meeting. These cues are often related to a standard of etiquette that if breached can lead to a lack of trust and deterioration of the relationship. It can be difficult to grasp the specific characteristics of non-verbal communication in a given culture.[9] Non-verbal language is harder to understand than the spoken word. Non-verbal cues such as the use of silence and eye contact can vary widely among cultures. Direct eye contact, long silences between spoken words, and the time between interventions possess different meanings for different cultures.

Scollen and Scollen describe a communication system that varies among different ethnic groups.[10] Ethnicity is important to consider because policy dialogues between developed and developing countries often involve interethnic communication. The way in which the components of this system are used and perceived affects the quality and outcome of interethnic communication. Some of the components of the system include the traditions, skills, knowledge, group membership, linguistic resources, and politeness phenomena that people bring to a conversation.

Understanding the importance of politeness phenomena in different cultures can be crucial to successful communication in a cross-cultural or interethnic dialogue. For example, if a person from a high-context or indigenous culture uses long pauses while talking, and the other person from a low-context or mainstream culture is used to short spaces between words, a basic misunderstanding usually occurs. The indigenous person, using long pauses out of politeness, will think that the mainstream person does not know how to listen, and the mainstream person will think that the indigenous person is not adept at expressing complete thoughts. Both are wrong. By deferring to politeness this kind of miscommunication can be lessened.

THINGS GO WRONG WHEN CULTURE IS IGNORED

Bad Communication

When people from different cultures enter into a policy dialogue, they use different kinds of communication systems. When one party to the dialogue, typically from a developed country, employs a formal system based on laws and administrative structure, and the other party, typically from a developing country, prefers more personalized, informal methods of communication, it is very difficult to reach a common objective, such as implementing a new public policy. If a person using the formal approach is an alien to the society, it can prevent an informal, personal relationship from developing. This in turn can hinder the establishment of personal trust and reinforce the perception of the formal party as an outsider who does not accept the social norms that exists within the local culture.

As Nader and Todd have noted, "In particular, it is important to see how things work in societies where the boundaries between formal and informal systems are often blurred, and can be crossed when convenient by participants who understand and use the total system for specific ends, and where law often plays a secondary role."[11]

In many instances, conflicts arise when new public policies are introduced, because they infringe on a society's informal system. These conflicts occur because the status quo, the equilibrium of society, is being disturbed. They may be marked by internal competition, strife, disturbances, disputes, quarrels, and struggles, which relate to the cohesion of the underlying social process. In developing countries, especially when an indigenous population is involved, the underlying social process is often more important than the formal legal process. The personal ties, bonds, and cooperation that define formal surface relationships constitute this social process.[12] Yet outsiders rarely understand how the social process works in a community that is unfamiliar to them. The result is bad communication, and the start of a ruined relationship that will almost certainly prevent the attainment of a mutual objective.

Ruined Relationships

Culture is intertwined with political and economic conditions, especially in societies where dependency has marked the relationship. It is difficult to separate the cultural elements that affect a relationship from political and economic factors. Societies that are historically dependent on more powerful countries, for whatever reason, possess a form of cultural dualism based on the convergence of their traditional lifestyles and dependency on the outside group.

Relying on outsiders for new policy initiatives may be frowned upon, as members of the society would rather control their own affairs. At the same time, societies that are dependent on outside parties to meet their basic human needs, such as food, education, and public infrastructure, can experience a weakening of their self-determination. As self-determination weakens, so does the ability to control internal affairs. This is often complicated by other costs of dependency, such as massive emigration that drains the community of educated professionals and skilled laborers and financial concessions to outside investors to promote economic growth factors, in turn, accelerate changes in traditional lifestyles and culture.

Within dependent societies there is often a feeling of exile, as people feel they have no control over their own destiny. Communities can feel so disenfranchised that outside parties are allowed to maintain control over the policy-making apparatus. This allows outsiders to exert control over the political system, reducing sovereignty and reinforcing feelings of dependency and exile.

Elements of Culture in the Eastern Caribbean

The indigenous Amerindian culture of the Eastern Caribbean region included the Arawaks and the Caribs, who were undisturbed for centuries until Europeans started to colonize the islands in the fifteenth century. Although the Caribs, who were more warlike than the Arawaks, successfully defended some islands for many years, by 1630 there was a steady flow of Spanish, British, Dutch, and French immigrants. With the advent of plantation agriculture in the sixteenth century, nearly five million Africans were forcibly brought to the Caribbean to provide slave labor. Abolished in the 1830s, slavery formed the basis for the current Afro-Caribbean culture that dominates life in the region.[13]

The cultures of the islands have much in common due to a shared plantation history, but they each possess unique characteris-

tics based on the relationship with their particular European colo-
nizer. This has created tremendous cultural diversity among the
small societies in the region. The massive scale of social and economic change in the region makes it difficult to trace how the residents of any particular island formed their cultural identity, but
some general statements can be made.[14]

The indigenous Indian people who first populated the islands
were exterminated and replaced by bipolar societies whose resources
were controlled entirely by forces outside of the region. This resulted
in a strong dependency on outside governments and institutions for
political and economic control, and created distinct social classes
based on skin color. These social classes originated with the master-
slave relationship. People were, and still are in many areas, classified
by skin color, with white the upper class, colored (light-skinned
black, brown, yellow, and red) the middle class, and black the lower
class. The white upper class are typically creole-elites, white de-
scendants of European heritage. The smallest islands in the region
such as St. Kitts are more ethnically homogeneous, but still have a
creole-white upper class that retains significant economic power, although opportunities for non-whites are increasing. Other islands,
such as St. Lucia, tend to be controlled by a light-skinned upper class,
who distinguish themselves from all others of all shades.[15]

The importance of color-based class lines is explained here to
underscore the complexity of Caribbean societies. However, there
are many exceptions to rules based on skin color. The importance of
skin color is decreasing as the region modernizes and people of all
classes benefit from better economic opportunities.[16] But the societies of the islands still place significant emphasis on the role of the
individual.

The plantation system diminished the strength of African traditions as African blacks were assimilated into a European-based creole culture. This prevented the creation of a unified culture. In the
vacuum of no overarching culture, individualism started to dominate the island societies, a type of behavior modeled on the old
master-slave relationship.[17] Individualism has had a strong impact
on the political development of the islands. Several countries in the
Commonwealth Caribbean have been ruled by charismatic and personalistic men who serve as top political leaders for several years at
a time.[18]

While some members of the island communities have bene-
fited from the opportunities of individualism, the bulk of the population has not. The people in the islands continue to delegate

responsibility for social control to a few strong individuals, a pattern that started in the plantation era when they had no choice. This has helped create a modern culture where people seem to distrust innovation, are unwilling to take risks to change the status quo, do not engage in long-term planning, and have a perception of helplessness in controlling their lives.[19] I heard these sentiments expressed during personal interviews with civil servants who repeatedly said that their governments lack the capacity for long-term planning (B 10, SK 4, SL 6).

In addition to individualism, feelings of alienation and exile among West Indians affect their cultures and political systems, preventing the region from developing.[20] These characteristics are embedded in the culture and influence how people think about their governments and political systems. A feeling of exile is the result of forced migration during slavery, when millions of Africans were taken from the Ivory Coast. Having arrived in the West Indies, they lived in exile from their African homeland. Their feelings of dispossession were magnified because they were given no control over their new lives in the Caribbean. They were torn from their African culture and were prevented by the plantation system from choosing a new culture to replace it—a double exile.

In the words of the West Indian poet Derek Walcott,

> Where shall I turn, divided to the vein?
> I who have cursed
> The drunken officer of British rule, how choose
> Between this Africa and the English tongue I love?
> Betray them both, or give back what they give?
> How can I face such slaughter and be cool?
> How can I turn from Africa and live?[21]

Mintz notes that many Caribbean researchers have been struck by the relative absence of community-based activity in the region. There is a general weakness in community organizations, including those focusing on church, school, and political and social activities. This may result from the lack of control that West Indians experienced for several generations.[22]

DEPENDENCY, INSULARITY, AND DISTRUST OF OUTSIDERS

There are several aspects of island culture that contribute to insularity in the Eastern Caribbean. The process of colonialization

initially produced a culture of silence. Africans brought to the islands as slaves were prevented by their masters from keeping their
native culture alive. They were forbidden to practice ceremonies and
rituals that portrayed their mythology of life and death.[23]

In turn, the generations of slavery helped the former Africans
to form a strong collective identity, based on their economic op-
pression and desire to be free people. This group identity, born
from a common experience as victims of a racist slavery mentality,
has not been allowed to develop fully because of the islands' geographical isolation and continued economic and political dependency on larger nations outside of the region. These factors have also
created a mentality, common among islands around the world, of insiders and outsiders.

In the words of a Kittian, "an outsider is an outsider, [but] if you
are from here, everyone assumes you know everyone else" (SK 8).
There is an established interdependency among islanders who are
tied together by the need to survive with limited resources and capital. There is always the expectation that "outsiders come with a hidden agenda," an expectation that "grows out of our past misuse" (SK
4). This has led to a grudging acceptance of outsiders who are basically not trusted.

Many West Indians believe that white outsiders are often racist,
or at least carry an air of superiority, looking down on their small societies. This has been attributed to an ignorance of West Indian culture and the needs of people who live in small island communities
(SK 4). This has amplified the insularity of the region that already exists because of its geographical isolation and plantation history.

Growing Influence of the United States

While European colonialization of the region has left a strong
legacy, the cultural milieu is constantly evolving in response to internal and external conditions. The uniqueness of the Caribbean, always recognized in the region because of its religious expressions,
linguistic diversity, native music, and annual Carnivals, is now
known throughout the world. Bob Marley brought reggae to a worldwide audience, along with an awareness of its Rastafarian roots. An
amazing number of writers have emerged on the literary scene, including Walcott, Lamming, Naipaul, Aime Cesaire, and Braithwaite.
But the most influential factor affecting the modern culture of the
West Indies may be its growing relationship with the United States.

The United States has largely replaced Europe as the metropolitan power in the region. Immigration to the United States from the West Indies more than tripled from 1951 to 1980.[24] Large-scale immigration started when islanders had moved outside of the region to find work when the plantation economy severely eroded in the mid-1800s. This trend is accelerating because the regional and local economies cannot support the rapidly growing population.

The Caribbean has grown increasingly dependent on the United States to buy export crops and to finance development. The growth of tourism and industrialization has caused building booms on several islands. The influx of development has changed traditional land-use patterns, displaced communities, and degraded natural resources. Resorts are being developed on beaches that displace local fishers, and new highways are dividing old villages.[25] Satellite dishes have brought American cable television to the most remote communities. Political leaders choose United States-style development to bolster island economies. The result is a dilution of the cultural diversity in the region, another obstacle for West Indians trying to find their own cultural identity.

THE CULTURE OF DECISION MAKING

There is a close relationship between culture and politics among the islands of the Eastern Caribbean. The interaction of culture and politics has a major effect on how new public policies are carried out, including policies intended to protect the environment.

The relationship between culture and politics is evident in statements by West Indians and expatriates who work in the region. "Outsiders don't understand the tremendous intensity of politics here, everything is political. A large part of the culture is political; intense personal communication is part of the culture, and most of the conversations are political" (SK 19). "Party politics is usually all of an issue. Most organizations are split by party loyalties; opposition members will oppose just to oppose, not due to any factual position. Common people are not included in this, just party leaders, so people develop apathy due to being left out; (the) realities of politics go far beyond parties; it tells where the power lies" (SL 7).

These observations by West Indians show how deeply politics are imbedded in their culture. The power of politicians grows from the dependency on individualism that grew out of the plantation system. In many ways, the plantocracy of the colonial era has been replaced by a modern political plantocracy. This is especially true of small islands that have a low level of political and economic development. Strong personalistic leaders are chosen to run the government. These leaders are often paternalistic and have been repeatedly re-elected despite obvious corruption.[26]

The politics practiced in the Eastern Caribbean can be termed "man-to-man politics" as virtually all decisions are made verbally among a small group of male political leaders and their supporters. This concentration of power is magnified by two factors. First, no public record exists of most policy negotiations, including cabinet meetings. This lack of accountability reduces the chances that policies that are adopted will be implemented. Second, politicians use civil servants to carry out their political agendas, causing public institutions to become heavily politicized.

Another reason that political power is so concentrated is a phenomenon that can be called "one person–many hats." This describes how people, usually men, develop several skills on an island. Typically a person will gain acceptance by becoming proficient in many roles, usually combining politics and business, allowing them to wield both political and economic influence. It is common to have politicians and business leaders exert strong influence over public policy because they wear many hats. This is part of the island culture.[27]

There are other cultural norms that shape how political decisions are made in the Eastern Caribbean. One such norm is the lack of public involvement in the political process. This results from a sense of alienation among the citizenry, a lack of community organizations, and a fear among political leaders that members of the opposition will use public forums to attack government policies.[28] The collection of all of these ingredients that constitute the decision-making process can be called the culture of decision making.

THE INTENSELY PERSONAL NATURE OF THE CULTURE OF DECISION MAKING

A handful of individuals control the national policy-making process. The societies in the region are small. It is virtually impossible for anyone to disagree with the political leadership without it becoming public knowledge. This includes civil servants who are responsible for implementing public policies. For example, St. Kitts, St. Lucia, and Barbados have radio call-in shows that allow citizens to express their opinions on political issues. Civil servants fear that their voices will be recognized, so they do not call to express an opinion, although they may know the most about an issue.

In these tightly controlled political systems, everyone knows everyone else. Rumors spread like wildfire. If a person disagrees with the government, they are seen as directly challenging the authority of an individual in the government, such as the prime minister. With the exception of conflicts between the majority and opposition parties, public disagreements are deemed unacceptable behavior. Even when civil servants break from the political leadership because of private disagreements, they generally remain silent because they do not want to make enemies. One former civil servant described this informal code of silence as "not airing your dirty laundry in public" and an official involved in the Pitons controversy alluded to it when he said that civil servants cannot get involved as they fear for their families (SK 4). This informal code of silence quiets potential adversaries, because of a desire to maintain personal relationships and long-term social stability in the community.

The countries of the Eastern Caribbean, in the tradition of the English Commonwealth to which they belong, use the British system of regulation. Under this system, civil servants use their discretion to enforce government regulations, such as pollution laws. But this approach does not work for two reasons. First, the islands lack the tradition of a highly trained and professional civil service that is needed to effectively use the British system. Second, government ministers oversee all actions of individual civil servants, maintaining control over the smallest policy decisions. Civil servants are not allowed to use their discretion. For example, they know that they will be overruled by a minister or permanent secretary if they try to force industry to comply with environmental laws, as the violator will appeal directly to an ally in the political leadership for relief. The civil servant is then rebuked and his or her decision overturned. Once this happens there is a reluctance to repeat the experience, so subsequent attempts to enforce the law are not as enthusiastic. The result is that many laws remain unenforced (SK 2).

POLICY IMPLEMENTATION AND THE COURTS

An important cultural norm that affects how policies are implemented relates to the judicial system in the Eastern Caribbean.[29] In developed countries when a public policy, such as a regulation to control water pollution, is not enforced, an individual or civic organization can usually sue to force the government to obey the law. The situation in the Eastern Caribbean is very different, and is related to the West Indian culture.

The societies in the Eastern Caribbean are not traditionally legalistic (B 19). Personal relations are very important, so disputes are settled informally rather than using an adversarial legal approach that would damage personal relationships. The chances are that a disputant has a relative or friend in the majority party, or in the leadership of the opposition. It is less expensive, takes less time, and is probably more effective to use personal influence to settle disputes, rather than using the courts. This informal approach is used although it would seem to lessen the formal, legal accountability of political leaders and the government. The public also lacks confidence in the courts because of past incidents of corruption, and most people do not have the money to hire an attorney. There is no tradition of legal assistance to provide poor people with legal representation (B 14).

Informal dispute resolution is not used to enforce environmental laws because these laws "are not catching politically" (B 10). Few people are concerned about environmental problems, certainly not enough to form a national constituency. One reason there is so little public support for more effective environmental laws lies in the cultural norms that relate to how people in the region feel about the natural world.

PERCEPTIONS OF THE ENVIRONMENT

A few important themes describe how the people of the Eastern Caribbean perceive the natural environment. These themes include a plantation heritage, subsistence agriculture, and natural disasters. All three themes collectively form what can be termed a cultural attitude towards the environment.[30]

The hallmark of the plantation era was the master-slave relationship. The master used every means at his disposal to force the maximum possible effort from the slave, amid intense hot and humid conditions. As a consequence, many people now have an aversion to manual labor. People who perform manual labor, including major resource users such as fishers and farmers, are looked down upon (B 3, SK 11, SL 14).[31] As a result, many people have a negative perception of the natural landscape, associating it with the plantation era. On St. Kitts, if a student does poorly on high school placement tests, it is said that he or she is headed for "the green college," a derisive name for the sugar cane fields (SK 19). The idea of conserving the natural landscape in its native state free of human impact is not a part of the culture. There is no conservation tradition in the region. Environmental issues have only garnered limited public attention in the last few years.

Natural disasters also have influenced how the environment is perceived. The islands are subjected to frequent large-scale natural disasters including incredibly intense rain storms, hurricanes, floods, droughts, heat waves, and earthquakes that damage crops, buildings, and wipe out entire communities.[32] There are two consequences for the environment. First, it is perceived as hostile. Second, limited human and financial resources must be allocated to repair the damage that results. This dilution of limited institutional resources, combined with the cultural bias against long-term planning, prevents environmental management programs from being implemented.[33]

Of course there are other factors that determine how people perceive and value the environment, including economics, social class, and educational background. But culture is a dominant factor, and if culture is not accounted for in the public policy process, attempts to design and enforce environmental policies will in all likelihood continue to fail, as shown by the following case studies.

UNDERSTANDING HOW THE CULTURE OF DECISION MAKING CAN BE AN OBSTACLE TO ENVIRONMENTAL PROTECTION: THE CASE STUDIES

St. Lucia

In St. Lucia, the culture of decision making played an important role in the Pitons controversy. St. Lucia's political leaders supported the development of a private resort on the Jalousie Estate in 1981 by granting Sir Colin Tennant an Alien Landholding license for the property. This reversed an earlier cabinet decision to purchase the estate as part of the proposed Pitons National Park.

Officials close to the project feel that Tennant's reputation as the successful developer of the island of Mustique in the Grenadines helped him garner support from St. Lucia's politicians. The prime ministers of St. Lucia and St. Vincent and the Grenadines are cousins. This family tie is thought to be a major reason why the license was granted (SL 16). The support of the prime minister was essential, as he has ruled the country for most of the post-independence period, which is reflective of the regional tradition for charismatic politicians to stay in power for long periods of time. There are other ways that the importance of family ties, combined with party loyalty, have affected the Pitons controversy.

The St. Lucia National Trust, established in 1975, is the main government agency responsible for natural resource management, including the maintenance of several important wildlife areas. The Trust was the first agency to document the ecological importance of the Pitons, and recommended as early as 1975 that the Jalousie Estate be preserved as open space.[34] But the official voice of the Trust has been silenced during the Pitons controversy because the chairman of the Trust is also the leader of the opposition. If the Trust were to publicly oppose the resort project, it would be branded as anti-government and a tool of the opposition (SL 13, 16). This would destroy the credibility of the Trust within the government and hamper its other conservation activities that require the support of the political leadership. So, the Trust has remained silent. Another potential supporter of the proposed park is the St. Lucia Archaeological and Historical Society. The prime minister's wife is vice-president of the society. But if she were to support the park proposal, opposing the resort, she would be publicly opposing her husband. She has remained silent. Thus family ties have also nullified the society as a source of support for the park. In both instances, the opposition's silence has supported the government's position of promoting pro-development policies that lead to environmental damage. And there is another way the government silenced its opponents.

The government used the threat of alienation to attack opponents of the resort. The Soufriere Development Committee (SDC), made up of community leaders from Soufriere, supported the proposed park and opposed the resort. They ostensibly supported the park because of the economic opportunities it would provide, although some observers felt that their primary motive was to promote their own financial interests. Nonetheless, the committee supported conservation of the Jalousie Estate (SL 6).

Members of the SDC were active in lobbying the government to drop its support of the resort and support the national park, individually and as members of the ad hoc environmental group called the Concerned Persons on the Environment. However, when one particularly influential member of the SDC started publicly supporting the park, word swept the island that he was "a rumored

member of the opposition" (SL 4). This label was intended to alienate him from the community and the government, damaging his
personal reputation as well as his extensive private business interests. In all probability this tactic discouraged him from further public opposition to the resort (SL 12).

The citizens of Soufriere adhered to another norm of the cultural of decision making by accepting how the developer of the resort influenced the government to support his project. When the
owners and developers of the Jalousie Estate gave a EC$100,000
donation to the Soufriere Hospital Committee in February 1989, residents of Soufriere saw the eventual construction of the resort as "a
done deal" (SL 20). At the time, the developer had not received permission from the national planning authorities to build the project.
Nonetheless, once the people of Soufriere saw the money change
hands between the developer and the political leadership, they saw
the park as a lost cause.[35]

The Pitons are an important part of St. Lucia's culture. As one
St. Lucian said, "They are seen as the guardians of the island. They
have entered the psychological consciousness of the people, as
shown by stories told about them in wedding ceremonies that relate
the importance of a strong, durable bond in marriage. The Pitons are
seen as symbols of the country. If they are given away, anything in
the country can be given away. They are a focal point for all of our
national concerns" (SL 7). Another said, "The Jalousie Estate is the
bosom of St. Lucia. The people know this and have to be involved.
The resource users, like charcoal cutters, have to be trained as resource managers" (SL 2).

If the planning team from the OAS, who prepared the proposal
for the Pitons National Park, could have tapped this popular senti-
ment to protect the Pitons, it may have gained the national support
needed to be successful. There was a lack of grassroots participation
when the park was being planned. This occurred in part because the
government disapproves of public meetings, but park proponents
also seemed to underestimate the importance of culture in the public policy process (SL 8). As one official said, "The OAS park proposal
was prepared with the input of a small group of technicians, not reflecting the people of Soufriere, but their own views of the area"
(SL 2). This had several repercussions.

First, it prevented local people from becoming politically organized to challenge the culture of decision making that has kept this
isolated part of the island relatively powerless in national political
affairs. Second, it prevented local people from becoming involved in

promoting the park as a way to provide development opportunities consistent with the scale of the local community, minimizing disruption to the culture, compared to the large resort at the Jalousie Estate. Third, it prevented people from being educated about what a conservation-oriented national park is. As one observer said, "To the average St. Lucian, a park is a soccer field; the concept of setting aside a large area as a wildland, without any obvious productive human use, is foreign" (SL 6). The park planning process could have been used as a vehicle to increase local understanding of environmental conservation, and to help make it an element of the national culture. Finally, it would have allowed planning technicians to create a park to meet the specific needs of local people. This could have included enlisting the many resource users in the area (small farmers, herders, charcoal producers, fishers) to become resource managers to protect the local environment, which would also have helped to create an environmental tradition for the island.

St. Kitts

The culture of decision making that exists on St. Kitts leads to a type of government similar to the plantocracy that existed in the plantation era, with politicians replacing foreign elites. This results from the relatively low level of political and economic development on the island, and the importance that Kittians place on electing strong leaders.[36] A very small group of politicians and party loyalists control the public policy apparatus, supporting a pro-development policy agenda that prevents environmental policies from being implemented.

The planning process for the Southeast Peninsula Development Project is controlled by a two key political leaders, illustrating the premium given to individualistic behavior by the island's culture. The minister of development and the attorney general were the chief negotiators for the government with USAID. The minister had a broad portfolio with jurisdiction over the peninsula advisory board, the Central Planning Unit, and agencies related to housing and agriculture. He exercised total control over the peninsula's development, and failed to enforce environmental policies in the rest of the country. He epitomized the culture of decision making that exists in the country.

The Southeast Peninsula Development Project is simply huge by island standards. Its 6.4-mile–long road, costing $17 million, runs over steep coastal hillsides while skirting numerous beaches and bays. The road was built to provide access to 4,000 acres of undeveloped land, and in this it has succeeded. But the project was designed and carried out with little thought given to its cultural impact. The constraints that the Kittian culture impose on the political system were ignored by USAID when it designed a program to implement policies to protect the abundant natural resources on the peninsula, and this has led to severe problems.

USAID took several steps intended to protect the natural resources of the southeast peninsula. It required that politicians pass national conservation legislation, hired consultants who cataloged natural resources and recommended how to manage them, and prompted the government to establish an advisory board to oversee the development of the peninsula. USAID envisioned that these and other policy-oriented elements of the project would be operational by the time the road was completed. But this has not happened.

In St. Kitts, as in other Eastern Caribbean countries, policy implementation is a long, slow process. It is based on "man-to-man" communication and trust between individuals that takes years to develop. It takes most outsiders several years to be accepted by local people, including local political leaders. It also can take several years to learn how to recognize and respond to numerous subtleties of the culture that are simply very difficult for outsiders to understand, such as classism, power relationships, and the way that the culture of decision making works. Outsiders who try to promote policy reform, including USAID, operate on a fixed, fast-paced schedule, reflective of continental lifestyles and American institutional protocols. But St. Kitts continues to have a pace of life reflective of the tropical heat, humidity, and one-on-one relationships that mirror the insularity and interdependence of island living. As a result, many of the environmental policies designed by USAID are taking years, rather than months, to be adopted. When discussing how slow the public policy process works in St. Kitts, one official paraphrased a top politician who was protesting a policy change: "Man, you are laying too much on the people" (SK 4). This response has been given to efforts to preserve the natural resources on the peninsula, which have been proceeding slowly. In the words of an official close to the project, the country is learning very slowly how to deal with the planning process for the peninsula (SK 25).

As described by a former government official, the slow process of policy implementation has several distinct steps. Unlike the United States, there is a huge gap between a law and the regulation to implement the law. Once a law is adopted, discretionary guidelines are informally developed by civil servants to carry out the law. As the voluntary guidelines are used more and more, the government starts to think about creating formal regulations. Politicians test the waters with the guidelines to find out what kind of regulation is politically feasible. Then a way has to be found to present the proposed regulation in a simple and concise manner. This process requires that civil servants responsible for implementing new policies possess a lot of political skill, are patient, can work effectively in an informal manner behind the scenes, and do all this without much in the way of financial and technical resources.

Another factor leading to the slow acceptance of new policies is the desire to preserve harmony in the society. When a new policy is introduced, it often causes conflict with traditional values. For example, the National Conservation and Environment Protection Act contained a definition of beach and foreshore that was disliked by land owners on the peninsula as it could adversely affect property values. Sensitive issues such as this are generally discussed bit by bit over a long period of time. After the new idea has had a chance to sink in, which may take a year or two, it may be acted on. This pattern of gradual disclosure of new information is done out of a need to preserve harmony in the society, and will not change due to pressure from outsiders. A continental bias has underlain the entire environmental planning process for the peninsula, designed by outsiders who do not understand the scale of St. Kitts and how its culture influences the political process (SK 4).

Barbados

Although it is more developed politically and economically than St. Lucia or St. Kitts, Barbados possesses some of the same cultural characteristics common to countries in the Eastern Caribbean. It has a political culture that favors strong individuals, a plantation heritage that has alienated many people from direct involvement in the public policy process, including the advocacy of environmental issues, and a closed decision-making system that favors development over environmental protection. Because the Bridgetown Fishing Harbor originated in the political directorate of the national government, the cross-cultural problems affecting policy implementation in the Pitons controversy and the Southeast Peninsula project did not exist. But problems did arise when the government chose a foreigner to design the harbor, a Canadian consultant who was unfamiliar with conditions in the tropics. This in turn raises a concern about the suitability of sophisticated technologies used for development projects such as the harbor, and this concern is related to the culture of decision making in Barbados.

Several Barbadians familiar with the fishing harbor were alarmed when the consultants designing it seemed to be unfamiliar with the tropical conditions in which they were working. Specific mistakes in the design included the fact that the original design of the ice processing plant was based on the ambient temperature of sea water in the Atlantic Ocean, where the consultants were from, rather than that of water in the warmer Caribbean Sea. Another mistake was the improper placement of input pipes, which caused the pumping system for the ice plant to be destroyed, delaying the opening of the harbor for several months. Civil servants who were knowledgeable about the day-to-day operation of the Barbados fishing fleet, and how the operation of the plant would be constrained by the less sophisticated technological knowledge available in the country, felt that the foreign consultants designed a project that is too dependent on complex technologies. Yet, they found it very difficult to gain a voice in the design of the facility so that it would use less complicated technologies. Finally, after much conflict between the consultants, the Ministry of Agriculture who employed them, and the Fisheries Division, the government designated a liaison between the consultants and the government to address these concerns (B 13). Still, many government officials close to the project, after seeing the smaller fishing harbor at Ostins fail, feel that the Bridgetown project will be a white elephant because it depends heavily on sophisticated technology (B 22).

Cultural conditions could influence the technical feasibility of the Bridgetown project in two ways. First, political leaders operating within the culture of decision making are likely to reward their political patrons with jobs in the new facility. This will place an emphasis on filling jobs with local people who lack the management skills to operate the harbor. Second, when any one of the many pieces of machinery in the facility (pumps, motors, scales, water and electrical lines, cranes, the ice plant, etc.) breaks, as will inevitably happen in the harsh tropical environment, it is doubtful if replacement parts will be available on the island or in the region. The large scale of the project, with its many complex interconnected components, appears to exceed the technological constraints of the island. Although the project included some technical training, Barbados does not have enough trained personnel to operate the project or the replacement parts to fix the equipment when it breaks. The project was not adapted to the technological and cultural limitations of the island.

Summary

Culture and political decision making in the Eastern Caribbean are inseparable, and the link between them has to be understood in order to find new ways to implement policies intended to protect natural resources. When environmental policies are adopted by developing countries in the region, often as a requirement of development assistance, they are based on models from the United States and Europe. In almost every instance, these imported laws do not take adequate account of local and national culture, and as a result, fail.

The elements of a culture that must be taken into account include language, kinship, attitudes towards formal authorities, attitudes towards outsiders, the differences between informal and formal systems used to resolve conflicts, and the role of non-verbal behavior cues in communication. The different cultural perspectives of people who are either polychronic or monochronic have to be examined so that misunderstandings do not occur when public policies are transferred from developed to developing societies. It is crucial to understand the use of written versus spoken language, especially in countries whose residents have a strong oral tradition, and to design a specific strategy for policy implementation that respects how people within a cultural group use language in their everyday life. Culture is interconnected with the political and economic conditions in countries, especially in societies that have been dependent on outsiders to meet their basic human needs. Understanding how dependency has shaped a society, and possibly undermined its self-determination, is essential to designing public policies that work.

To implement environmental policies it is critical to know how to account for the special characteristics that make up a country's unique culture. In the eastern Caribbean, the plantation system that dominated the region from the early sixteenth century until the mid-1800s formed the basis for the Afro-Caribbean culture that is dominant today. The premium on individualism, a distrust of outsiders, and pervasive feelings of alienation and exile are the legacy of the plantation era. These elements of culture, combined with the small size of the societies, have had a pronounced effect on the public policy process.

Outsiders often simply do not understand the intensity of politics in the Eastern Caribbean. Intense personal communication is part of the culture. Public policy decisions are controlled by loyalty to people and political parties among top political leaders. "Man-to-man" politics is dominant, reflecting the vitality of personal relationships and the need for trust. The distrust of outsiders, a strong desire for self-governance, the small size of public agencies, and the politicalization of civil servants make innovation and creativity in policy making very difficult. People prefer to settle disputes informally rather than to risk damaging personal relationship by resorting to the courts. This lack of legal leverage weakens pro-environmental interest groups trying to strengthen environmental policies.

The way that people in the region perceive the natural environment affects the way that natural resources are managed. The plantation system's abuse of people through manual slave labor has created a negative perception of the landscape. There is no widespread conservation tradition in the region. The concept of setting aside large areas for wildlife and public use is not widely understood. Natural disasters are a regular occurrence, and recovering from them diverts limited technical and financial resources away from long-term efforts to improve natural resource management.

An overarching cultural theme that relates to the efforts of outsiders trying to intervene in the region's political systems is the vast difference between island and continental cultures. It is simply very difficult for people from large continental countries to fully appreciate the huge differences between their cultures and those that exist on small and geographically isolated islands. The linkages between culture and policy making in an island environment, including the use of oral traditions to convey information, social interdependencies, and the effect of a tropical climate on the pace of business and life, largely define how these societies operate and are often not understood by people from continental cultures in the United States and Europe.

In the three countries studied, St. Kitts, St. Lucia, and Barbados, among the elements of culture that cause environmental concerns to be ignored are concentrated political power through individualism, family ties, and party loyalty; the risk of alienation to environmentalists; and the citizens' acceptance of a closed political system. The elements of culture that cause international foreign assistance agencies to fail in their attempts to implement environmental policies are use of massive projects that are out of scale with the islands; not understanding how long it takes for new policies to be accepted; the pervasive distrust of outsiders in the region; and the use of sophisticated technologies to convey information and operate projects that are in conflict with the cultural norms in the islands.

Chapter Five

THE IMPORTANCE OF ECONOMIC CONDITIONS

In the Eastern Caribbean and developing countries in general, the basic imperative for economic growth drives most development decisions. In the face of severe economic pressures, governments generally favor large development projects that are designed to provide major financial benefits. It is these large projects that often cause the most environmental damage. Environmental policies intended to protect the environment are seen as obstacles to economic growth and are often ignored.

Attempts to improve environmental policy implementation cannot be separated from the economic realities that political leaders face on a daily basis. In the Caribbean, these realities include the history of dependency on the North Atlantic states, problems encountered when trying to diversify national economies, a shortage of foreign exchange to finance imports, persistent high unemployment, and the difficulty in achieving regional integration. To help understand how these elements of the regional economic system have evolved, and in turn how they relate to environmental policy implementation, it is necessary to describe briefly the economic history of the Eastern Caribbean.

ECONOMIC HISTORY OF THE REGION

The history of how the economies of the islands in the Eastern Caribbean developed is tied to what happened in the Wider Caribbean region. When Christopher Columbus made the first of three voyages to the region in the late fifteenth century it marked the beginning of the colonial era which did not end until the independence movement in the latter half of the twentieth century. The hallmark of the colonial era, which lasted more than 300 years, was the mercantile system that controlled the economies of the island states.

The mercantile system was based on a triangular trading pattern between Africa, the Caribbean, and Europe. The entire system was managed and capitalized by various European powers in the metropolitan capitals, and exploited the people and resources of their colonies in the Caribbean. Slaves were brought from Africa to the islands, where sugar and rum were picked up and brought to Europe. Finished products were then taken back to the Caribbean to feed and cloth the expanding population, completing the cycle. The financial rewards to European merchants, absentee landowners, and heads of state were great. By the end of the eighteenth century one third of England's trade was taken up by the sugar industry. Profits from the slave trade were also immense. The sovereigns of Spain, the Netherlands, and England granted licenses to allow traders to buy and sell slaves, and received large fees in return.[1]

Several economic patterns that were established in the plantation era persist today. Because virtually all fertile soil was planted in sugar, no land was left to grow crops. As a result, food had to be imported, which created a dependency that has grown in recent years as the population of the islands has increased.[2] Food and consumer durables that must be imported continue to drain national treasuries of highly prized foreign exchange. A common expression in the region is that "the islands consume what they don't produce, and produce what they don't consume."

The geographical isolation of the islands and their small size made them ideal candidates for colonialism and external dependency. Although the plantation economy has changed to some extent, most island economies in the Eastern Caribbean, especially the smaller islands such as St. Kitts, are still struggling to escape from their multiple burdens. Most of these economies are still underdeveloped and dependent on external decisions.[3] This is due in large part to the general neglect given the West Indies by its colonizers after the sugar economy declined in the nineteenth century. The reasons for this neglect are important elements of the modern economic problems in the region: the economies are small, the expense of communicating and transporting supplies over the long distances between islands and the continents is great, and the relatively small population base means a small political constituency to voice its demands to the international community.[4]

CURRENT ECONOMIC REALITIES

A common characteristic of all island economies in the region is their vulnerability to external circumstances. In part this reflects the cycle of low domestic savings and low investment that existed for many years. In the 1960s foreign investors became interested in the region, spending foreign exchange to build hotels and resorts, refurbish sugar plantations, and develop mines. As a result, the region has experienced positive economic growth over the last several years, but at a slower rate than was anticipated in the 1970s.

The flow of foreign capital, a necessary component for development because of the lack of domestic savings in the region, slowed when initial investment opportunities were exhausted.[5] The decline of the global economy in the 1980s brought disruptions to the island economies because of declining commodity prices, unstable currencies (especially the fall of the United States dollar), and wide variations in export prices. Nonetheless, a moderate rate of overall growth has lifted most Eastern Caribbean countries to an intermediate position between industrialized nations and the rest of the developing world.[6] This has been due in part to large grants and low-interest loans made to countries by development assistance agencies that have funded a wide variety of projects. This new source of capital has made up for the decline in private foreign investment and contributed to the positive growth rate of the last few years.[7]

In general, economic growth has been based on the diversification of exports, but has been unsteady and highly reactive to fluctuations in the world economy. The region is oriented heavily toward international trade, and there is no reason to believe this will change.[8] The economies of the islands are unstable because they are typically dominated by one sector, and if adverse conditions affect that sector, the whole economy suffers. One obvious example was the effect of hurricanes in 1979 and 1980 that destroyed most of St. Lucia's banana crop, which accounts for about 50 percent of its total exports. Another example is illustrated by recent economic conditions in Barbados. In late 1991 Barbados entered an 18-month Standby Arrangement with the International Monetary Fund (IMF). Economic austerity measures were instituted to limit government borrowing, stop large publicly funded construction projects, reduce government spending, and cut civil service jobs. These measures were taken to attempt to counteract the effects of a national recession.[9]

Because the countries in the region must import large amounts of food and consumer products, their external debt is increasing, requiring large payments to service it. Growth in the economy depends on an increase in the value of exports that earn foreign exchange. As debt payments increase, so must export earnings if the economy is to grow. All of the islands have large trade deficits, but these deficits are partly or wholly offset by increased earnings from tourism, remittances from citizens working abroad, and grants. Although their debt-to-service ratios have steadily increased, reflecting the rise in debt and decline in export earnings, compared to other developing countries the overall performance of the island economies has been good.[10]

The region's overall terms of trade improved in the late 1980s due to an expansion of tourism and a decline in international interest rates.[11] As a comparison, the debt to service ratio for larger countries in Latin America has grown much faster, requiring massive structural adjustments to enable external debt obligations to be met, reversing much of the economic progress made since the 1960s.[12]

Although it is difficult to document precisely because of poor record keeping, language differences, and the existence of a vibrant informal economy, high rates of unemployment have been a persistent problem in the Caribbean. Every country has seen a mass migration of its workers that have moved to another country to find work and send remittances back home. Remittances are a major source of foreign exchange for all of the islands and without them the expanding foreign debt could not be paid off.

Unemployment has several root causes. The most obvious is the underdevelopment that plagues the region and the inability to provide investment capital, through domestic savings or foreign investment, to diversify national economies fast enough to provide jobs for the expanding population. Unemployment rates of 20 to 30 percent in the agricultural, industrial, and service sectors are not uncommon. Industrialization has not occurred fast enough to employ workers who have left the agricultural jobs, which has created a major labor surplus.[13] The persistence of both unemployment and underemployment means a loss of productivity for the island economies of the region, and perpetuates a cycle of poverty, poor health, and frustration that prevents people from enjoying productive lives.[14]

THE MULTI-SECTORAL ECONOMY

The economy of the Caribbean, including the islands of the Eastern Caribbean, is still dependent on the interest and activity of major investment centers outside of the region, mainly in the United States, Canada, and Europe. The island economies are based on a narrow range of domestic products that are increasingly subject to competitive pressure from the global marketplace and instability due to scarcities of foreign exchange, technical expertise, and raw materials.[15] Economic conditions in the region can best be described by briefly reviewing the status of agriculture, tourism, and manufacturing.

Agricultural Exports: Boom or Bust

The agricultural sector has historically been based on the production of single-commodity export crops that garner large amounts of foreign exchange, such as sugar on St. Kitts and bananas on St. Lucia. Problems are caused by depending too heavily on export crops, including the ill effects of regular natural disasters, labor unrest, and oscillation in world prices for agricultural commodities. The response has been an increased emphasis on diversifying national economies to prevent them from being subject to these uncertainties.

The problems of depending too heavily on export crops are illustrated by the situations in St. Kitts, St. Lucia, and Barbados. In St. Kitts, the sugar industry, which was nationalized in 1975 so the government could centralize its management and production, accounts for about 60 percent of domestic exports and employs 25 percent of the working population. The industry has been in decline since the 1960s.[16] In 1986 the United States imported 12,500 tons of sugar from St. Kitts, but this declined to 8,000 tons in both 1988 and 1989 due to a United States sugar import quota. The amount of sugar harvested in 1989 was substantially less than in 1988, a drop from about 25,000 tons compared to 18,000, due to Hurricane Hugo and a shortage of cane cutters on the island.[17]

In St. Lucia the banana crop has been the mainstay of the economy. The government initiated a costly program in the early 1980s to reorganize the industry andincrease its efficiency. Foreign earnings from this single crop have increased more than fivefold since 1983. Despite a slow recovery from damage incurred during hurricanes in 1979 and 1980, the largest earner of foreign currency brought in a record $65 million in 1989.[18]But by world standards St. Lucia's bananas are expensive. Most of the annual crop is purchased by the United Kingdom, which pays more than the world price to be helpful to its former colony. St. Lucia benefits from the Lome Convention under which its bananas have first preference in the United Kingdom market, but this may not continue after the European Union consolidates. The new unified European market could produce bananas cheaper than St. Lucia can, substantially reducing the value of the island's crop and the foreign exchange it earns.[19]

In Barbados the importance of sugar has declined steadily since the early 1960s but still accounts for about 5 percent of the gross domestic product. Stagnating production in the mid-1980s contributed to a general slowdown in the economy, and efforts are under way to diversify into non-sugar agriculture and related agroindustries. Production has continued to be hampered by poor operating efficiencies and low crop yields. The government initiated a program of price supports in 1983 to support the industry, but the low price of sugar on the world market, in part due to the weakness of the United States dollar, has contributed to the general sluggishness of the economy.[20]

Efforts are under way throughout the Eastern Caribbean to diversify agricultural production by shifting emphasis from sugar and bananas to small-plot-row and fruit crops, to provide local foodstuffs and decrease the amount of foreign exchange spent on food imports. The failure to expand local food supplies impedes economic development in general because it uses limited resources that cannot be utilized by other sectors of the economy as it expands. Problems with securing title to arable land and being able to pay for expensive agricultural inputs such as fertilizer and irrigation systems are barriers to diversification.

Agriculture, Land Use, and Distribution of Wealth

There is an economic pattern among the countries of the Eastern Caribbean tied to historical export-oriented agricultural production and subsequent effects on land use, land ownership, and the distribution of wealth. This economic pattern in turn has both social and political implications.

Because plantation-based sugar and banana production has dominated the use of land and the generation of capital for the entire history of St. Kitts and St. Lucia, and to a lesser extent Barbados, large parcels of land have tended to be held by a small group of people. Because the majority of jobs generated by large-scale agricultural production are generally menial labor, the wages paid to workers are historically low, while the profits from selling export crops are kept in the hands of the land owners. This is not always true. In some instances agricultural lands have been nationalized, as was the case with several plantations in St. Kitts, in order to consolidate government control over national economic development. Most of the time, however, land has been kept in private hands.

In St. Kitts, for example, the 4,000-acre southeast peninsula, which was not nationalized, was owned by only thirty landowners in 1989. Parcel sizes generally ranged from 200 to 900 acres. When the road and utility improvements part of the Southeast Peninsula Development Project were installed, land values rose from $2,500 per acre up to $50,000 per acre. At the same time, hourly wages in St. Kitts were $.90 in 1988 for the average worker.[21] One apparent reason for such a low hourly wage is that an estimated 35-40 percent of the jobs in St. Kitts are in sectors related to agricultural.[22]

What can be inferred from this situation? While the hard data on distribution of wealth in these countries are hard to come by, the juxtaposition of land ownership patterns and low wages suggests that economic resources, and related political power, are concentrated in the hands of a relatively few individuals. This may explain why certain entrenched interest groups that possess political power favor national policies that encourage economic development at the expense of protecting limited or scarce natural resources.[23] This also explains why short term economic goals are pursued in lieu of long-term environmental protection.

The pattern of allocating limited land, human, and financial resources to continue producing large-scale export crops has been hard to change. To deal with these problems, governments are being urged by the World Bank and other donor agencies to review existing economic incentives, support services, and public policies that are hindering diversification.[24] However, given the politically sensitive nature of making changes to the economic and political status quo, such as large-scale land reform, it is doubtful that the changes needed to alter the pattern of agricultural production will occur as long as tourism and foreign remittances continue to compensate for expenditures spent on importing food. The problems that derive from depending on agricultural export crops are shared by these Eastern Caribbean countries, which has motivated them all to increase their reliance on international tourism to contribute to their economic stability.

The Emergence of Tourism

The rapid growth of tourism in the 1980s catalyzed the economic growth among the islands of the Eastern Caribbean, with few exceptions. Countries have pursued aggressive strategies for promoting tourism because of its multiplier effect in the economy. Tourism increases local incomes, stimulates investment and employment, and raises foreign exchange earnings.[25] It also benefits other sectors of the economy, especially agriculture, which in many islands is capable of providing increased quantities of fruits, vegetables, and meat to meet the needs of tourists. The manufacturing sector also benefits as the demand increases for tourist-related products.[26]

In the mid-1980s countries in the region initiated efforts to formally integrate tourism into national economic planning. The relatively young industry started to aggressively promote its benefits. The result has been an emphasis on improving the public infrastructure, such as airports, roads, public utilities, waterfront areas, and duty-free concessions, to serve new resorts and cruise ships. This trend can be seen by reviewing the experience with tourism in Barbados, St. Lucia, and St. Kitts.

Barbados aggressively promoted tourism in the 1970s. Several major resorts were built on the south and west coasts and daily chartered air flights were started to bring Americans, British, and Canadians to the island. A new airport was built with the financial assistance of the Canadian government in the early 1980s and several other government sponsored programs started to improve the quality of the tourism experience. By the mid-1980s the revenue from tourists started to drop as other destinations in the Caribbean and South America provided better facilities and benefitted from more favorable exchange rates. This trend changed in 1990, which was a boom year for tourism in the Eastern Caribbean, except for hurricane-damaged Montserrat.[27] These up and down trends in tourism show how fickle this source of revenue can be. It should also be noted that real wages have fallen in the industry in recent years.[28]

St. Lucia promoted tourism later than Barbados but is emerging as a major visitor destination. The St. Lucia National Development Plan promotes development of the tourist industry as a major part of the island economy. The number of hotel rooms on the island has grown from 700 in 1973 to 2,500 in 1989 and several projects have been recently completed or are under way. The Caribbean Development Bank estimates that 2,000 new rooms are needed to accommodate an expected increase in visitors from Europe. The government's commitment to the industry is reflected by its plans to rebuild the west coast road and construct a dam to supply additional water. A major new power station has recently been completed and a duty-free shopping area added to the harbor in Castries to accommodate cruise-ship passengers.[29] These projects are consistent with the recommendation of the World Bank that hotel capacity should be expanded by strengthening the national Tourist Board, increasing promotional efforts, and improving infrastructure.[30]

As the least developed of the three islands, St. Kitts has only recently started to develop its tourist industry, but it has adopted a very aggressive posture to promote it. The government has a program to grant incentives to develop the Frigate Bay area and the USAID-funded Southeast Peninsula Development project recently provided access to 4,000 acres of land for resorts, condominiums, a marina, cruise-ship facilities, duty-free shops, and houses. Cruise-ship stopovers increased in the mid-1980s but decreased in 1989, apparently because of a lack of tourist facilities on the island. With the decline in the sugar industry and its uncertain future, St. Kitts is banking heavily on tourism to provide the impetus for economic growth well into the twenty-first century.

Tourism is viewed by the island governments as the savior of their unstable and marginal economies. Although tourism provides many economic benefits, it does have drawbacks. The demand for tropical tourism varies with the health of the international economy. As a luxury product, tourism responds to the ebb and flow of the national economies in the countries where tourists originate. For example, tourist arrivals in the region declined in the periods 1973–75 and 1981–83, corresponding with a drop in income in the United States.[31] In addition, a large portion of the earnings from tourism goes towards financing imported goods to supply the industry and does not enter the local economy.[32] In the region there has been a trend of building all-inclusive resorts, such as Club Med and Couples, where visitors do not ever have to leave the confines of the hotel complex during their stay. Many of the hotel rooms in St. Lucia are of this type. This prevents lower income people, who tend to be self-employed vendors and craftspeople located in urban areas far from the resorts, from sharing in the economic benefits of tourism.

In some communities in the region, such as Bridgetown, Barbados, public officials are expressing concern that the demands of increased tourism will exceed the carrying capacity of the island. The tourist-related building boom in Barbados has caused widespread coastal erosion; increased the runoff of raw sewage into the ocean, killing large portions of the reef system; placed stress on freshwater supplies during the December–April dry season; and contributed to increased overcrowding in the downtown (B 30, 33).

Manufacturing: Mixed Results

The islands have had mixed results from attempts to expand their manufacturing sectors, despite substantial financial incentives offered to entice international companies to locate in the region. A shortage of raw materials and spare parts are a major limiting factor to the growth of this sector. The electronics industry, which assembles completed components from parts made abroad, showed an increase of 26 percent in 1984, but declined in 1986 because of a deterioration in the United States market and competition from Asia. There are several businesses specializing in the production of food, beverages, tobacco, clothing and chemicals. The sizable garment industry has been hurt by trade barriers in Trinidad and Tobago. In the last five years several international companies have registered in Barbados to benefit from a tax agreement with the United States, but in general Barbados is not competitive due to its limited marketing capabilities and high cost of living.[33]

The small size of St. Kitts and St. Lucia has made it difficult for them to develop sizable manufacturing sectors. In St. Kitts the government has tried to encourage manufacturing by promoting electronics, clothing, and shoes. Several garment operations have closed because of trade restrictions imposed by the Caribbean Community (CARICOM) market.[34] These restrictions require St. Kitts, as a CARICOM member, to impose tariffs on goods imported from outside the CARICOM area.[35] This has served to protect some infant industries in the region, while causing others to close or curtail operations. The recent increase in local wages has also made this sector less competitive.

In St. Lucia the manufacturing sector accounts for only about 10 percent of the gross domestic product. The island supports a wide variety of small-scale industries producing for local and international consumers, including beverages, food, wood and paper products, and textiles. St. Lucia is one of the most industrialized of the small islands in the Eastern Caribbean because of the quality of its infrastructure. The Hess Oil Corporation built a major oil storage area at Cul de Sac Bay in 1983 but it has not had the anticipated spin-off effects for the local industrial economy.[36] A refinery to accompany the oil terminal was never built because of the worldwide decline of the oil industry in the 1980s. The government has provided a customs-free zone to attract international firms but this has had mixed success.

The same themes appear repeatedly when experts discuss the problems that impede improvements in the economic climate of the region. These themes include the lack of political will among governments to aggressively pursue regional integration, the desperate need to diversify island economies, the instability of depending on mono-crop exports for foreign exchange, growing trade deficits, uneven production in the agricultural sector, and continued dependence on the North Atlantic states, especially the United States, for outside capital and technology needed to fuel growth. To understand the economic ramifications of the relationship between the Eastern Caribbean and the North Atlantic states, the next section will describe how this situation has developed.

THE EASTERN CARIBBEAN AND THE NORTH ATLANTIC STATES

Orlando Patterson, the noted sociologist from Jamaica who is now a member of the Harvard faculty, describes how the increasingly close relationship between the United States and the Caribbean is causing more direct and immediate economic influence by the former over the latter. This is characterized by the flow of investments, loans, and remittances from the United States and profits, flight capital, and illegal capital (i.e. drug money) to the United States.[37]

The islands were colonies dependent on the United Kingdom until the independence movement started in the 1960s. St. Kitts was the last country to gain full independence, in late 1983. The economic dominance of Britain ended with the independence movement and was quickly replaced by that of the United States, but this did not immediately translate into closer political ties between the United States and the Caribbean.[38]

After the independence movement created several new sovereign states in the Eastern Caribbean, the United States did not step in to fill the vacuum left by the British. The attention of the United

States government in the region was on Latin America, and the people of the West Indies continued to look to the British for support and guidance. However, the British did not offer much in the way of support in the post-independence era, which probably reflected a desire to rid themselves of their island dependencies.[39]

After it became clear that Castro was going to remain in power in Cuba, foreign policy analysts in the United States government realized that persistent underdevelopment in the region could lead to political instability, and this in turn could impinge upon the security of the United States.[40] The involvement of Cuban technicians in Grenada, and the bloody revolution there in 1983, solidified the belief of the United States government that it should take a greater interest in the region.

The Caribbean Basin Initiative (CBI) took effect in 1984. It is an attempt by the United States to promote economic progress in the region, and to strengthen United States financial ties to the islands. The initiative has three central components. It allows duty-free access to the United States market for most goods, provides emergency economic and military funding, and creates tax incentives for United States investors in the island economies.[41] The CBI also established the CBI Center which in cooperation with USAID provides information about opportunities for investment and export in the region, and promotes joint United States–Caribbean ownership of industry, which could reduce the region's economic dependency.[42]

While the CBI has promoted some direct investment in the region, including the islands of the Eastern Caribbean, it has not been as effective as it could be in providing economic security. Key exports such as textiles and leather goods are excluded, and many goods that were entering the United States were already benefiting from lower tariff levels through the Generalized System of Preferences.[43] Despite the existence of the CBI, exports from the region have grown at a slower rate than those from other developing countries as a whole.[44] This indicates that the economic problems of the region result from structural problems that are difficult to resolve. In addition, it has been suggested that the North American Free Trade Agreement (NAFTA) may harm export businesses in the Caribbean in the short term, as they will be pressured by a strengthened manufacturing sector in Mexico, but that the increased economic activity in the Western hemisphere over the long run will benefit the region.[45]

Another standard used to measure the success of the CBI is the extent to which it encourages indigenous growth in the region. The quest for economic self-reliance has spawned several attempts at regional cooperation within the Caribbean community.

REGIONAL COOPERATION AND INTEGRATION

The crucial need for increased cooperation among the newly independent and widely scattered islands of the Eastern Caribbean has been a clarion call in the region for decades. This is because there is a direct relationship between the size of a country and its economic efficiency. A cooperative institutional arrangement among countries could compensate for the small size of the island economies. Such an arrangement could standardize taxes, tariffs, currency, and the flow of workers. Trade and monetary agreements are the basic reason for integration. These could provide economies of scale for production, marketing, and investing, benefiting each individual country and the region as a whole.[46] While virtually all of the political leaders in the region agree that regional integration is essential for the modern development of the islands, it has not been achieved, and political and economic fragmentation continues to haunt them.

For a variety of reasons repeated attempts to formalize an institutional arrangement to foster regional cooperation, or regional integration as it is sometimes called, have failed to achieve expectations. The history of the short-lived West Indies Federation illustrates some of the most obvious problems that are obstacles to achieving regional integration.

The West Indies Federation came into being in 1958 after many years of negotiation. Its purpose was to create a single economic and political entity from the many English-speaking islands, including the entire Eastern Caribbean. This was before any of the islands became independent; they were still British colonies. If the federation had lasted until 1962 it would have achieved independence as a "super colony."[47]

This attempt to create a central federal government was short lived, and some historians believe was destined to fail. Jamaica was the most economically powerful country in the federation and despite its early leadership to form a cooperative union, it pulled out after a voter referendum supported this move in 1961. The people of Jamaica apparently believed, with justification, that it would more advantageous to pursue independence on their own, rather than diverting resources to support the smaller, poorer islands in the Eastern Caribbean. Shortly after Jamaica withdrew from the federation, Trinidad did the same, causing the union to fall apart.

The most obvious reason for the failure of the federation was the uneven economic power of the islands. Jamaica and Trinidad had the most to lose and least to gain so they opted for independence as separate entities. The smaller islands were left to fend for themselves. This disparity in economic power still exists today, but it is only one reason why the attempt to form a central, federal union failed.

The federation was designed by the British, and reflected their perspective of the region. Its political arm would been made up of what Lewis termed "an indigestible plethora of politicians" including a governor-general, five governors, a minimum of five commissioners and about fifty-five ministers without portfolio.[48] The size and complexity of this political body, and the constant calculation its members would have to make of the local and regional payoffs of their actions, make it doubtful that it would have been able to operate effectively.

Every potential member of a cooperative movement calculates whether they will be better or worse off if they join. In each country political leaders have to convince their constituencies that they will be better off economically if they cooperate, while at the same time at the regional level they must argue that they are worse off than other islands, so they can claim more gains from the cooperative venture to justify their participation at home. Since the governments have to pay attention to the demands of each island's leaders to justify integration, democratic political systems probably pose an obstacle to the integration process.[49] In addition, the insularity, geographical isolation, and independent path that each island pursued in its political and economic development also contributed to the collapse of the federation.[50]

In the region, each island has developed independently, based on its own set of cultural, political, and economic conditions. Any institutional program intended to foster cooperation between the islands has to account for these factors. This is very difficult to accomplish given the diversity in the region and the desire of national political leaders to maintain the sovereignty of countries they govern. There are several efforts currently under way to promote regional integration. They are less ambitious than the West Indies Federation, and are forming the basis for the cooperation needed to jointly address the economic problems of the region.[51]

Regional Economic Programs

There are several programs and institutional arrangements to improve regional economic integration. CARICOM, the Caribbean Development Bank (CDB), and the East Caribbean Common Market (ECCM) illustrate the dominant strategies being used to promote economic integration.

CARICOM was founded in 1973 by the Treaty of Chaguaramas whose goals were the coordination of economic policies, regional institutions to improve credit and finance, regional trade, and investment capital. The one area in which CARICOM has been successful is its initiation of free trade between member nations, but problems even in this area reflect the difficulty facing any attempts at improving regional cooperation.

In 1977 Guyana and Jamaica, both members of CARICOM, were forced by their own desperate economic conditions to violate the community's free-trade agreement by restricting imports from fellow member states. Both countries later reinstated CARICOM imports, but their temporary cessation showed the fragility of the community.[52] The economic integration sought by the CARICOM initiative has also been hampered by different exchange-rate policies among its members. Because countries receive no compensation for sudden changes in exchange rates, several responded in the mid-1980s by placing restrictions on regional trade, nullifying the community's trade agreement.[53] The invasion of Grenada deepened the divisions already caused by the many devaluations and trade restrictions implemented by individual countries. Regional trade restarted in the late 1980s, and in 1989 the community initiated work on harmonizing structural adjustment, credit, and exchange-rate policies.[54]

The CDB was established in 1969 as the first regional lending agency in the Eastern Caribbean. All seventeen English-speaking countries are members. The chief purpose of the CDB is to raise funds from several sources: the main trading partners of the region (the United States, United Kingdom, and Canada), the European Community, Latin American nations, and other international lending agencies (World Bank and IDB). The main benefit of the CDB is its ability to raise capital from outside the region, and to provide these funds to member countries with concessions such as low interest rates.

The CDB has initiated several projects aimed at improving regional economic integration, focusing on agriculture, fisheries, and the food supply, in addition to regional transportation facilities. It also coordinates national and regional economic development programs with CARICOM, and has improved the institutional capacity in the region by assisting several institutions, such as the Caribbean Agricultural Research and Development Institute, the Caribbean Tourism Organization, and the Caribbean Association of Industry and Commerce.

The ECCM is made up of the island countries of the Eastern Caribbean, who are also members of CARICOM. Its purpose is to coordinate the positions of members on CARICOM-related issues, and to aggregate their efforts to compensate for the differences in size and level of development between the ministates and larger CARICOM members such as Jamaica and Trinidad-Tobago. The ECCM also serves as a clearinghouse that its members can use to gain access to technical expertise from a variety of economic sectors, such as agriculture, tourism, and manufacturing.[55]

The existence of the ECCM reflects the separate identity and economic problems of the ministates in the Eastern Caribbean, because of their limited economic, technical, and human resources. Integration in the context of the Eastern Caribbean means cooperation on three levels: among the island ministates on an area basis; between the ministates and larger countries in the Caribbean, including mainland nations in Latin America on a regional basis; and among all Caribbean countries, both island and mainland nations, and their trading partners in the North Atlantic region, Europe, and the rest of the world.

There are many other organizations working to improve regional cooperation and integration, too many to list here, such as the family of the United Nations. These organizations are working to plan, coordinate, and implement a wide range of economic development activities, ranging from cooperative training in different industries to financing and building new roads, airports, electric plants, and water supply facilities, in addition to providing emergency relief for natural disasters.[56]

INSTITUTIONAL LINKAGES THAT INTEGRATE ECONOMIC AND ENVIRONMENTAL CONCERNS

In recent years, several organizations whose primary responsibility has been economic development have initiated programs in environmental resource management, in response to the growing deterioration of natural resources in the Eastern and Wider Caribbean. This reflects a growing realization by economic planners that sustainable economic growth is dependent on prudent management of limited and often fragile natural resources.

The CDB issued a directive in early 1989 requiring that the environmental impact of all of its projects be evaluated prior to loan commitments. The CDB also sponsored a regional conference in environmental issues to advise members how to improve project design to mitigate environmental damage. However, even though the CDB theoretically has the leverage to enforce environmental protection through loan conditionality, it has not created any mechanism to require that countries implement these new policies. By the time projects are selected for funding, the pressure to complete them makes enforcement of environmental standards very difficult (B 3).

The Economic Commission for Latin America and the Caribbean (ECLAC) is primarily responsible for promoting regional cooperation for economic development, but has recently become interested in a wide variety of environmental policy issues. It has sponsored a project on the effects of tourism in the wider Caribbean with case studies on several islands, and has examined the socioeconomic impact of climate change in the region.[57]

CARICOM held its first conference on environmental issues in mid 1989. It was attended by ministers, top civil servants, educators, and professionals and resulted in the Port-of-Spain Accord on the Management and Conservation on the Environment. The accord prioritizes environmental issues shared by all countries in the region, including local management of toxic and hazardous materials and the dumping of toxic materials that originate outside of the region; coastal protection and marine pollution; solid and liquid waste management; forest and watershed management; housing and human settlements; and several others.

The accord contains several general recommendations for addressing these environmental problems, such as preparation of national environmental plans and policies, but lacks specific measures to enforce them. However, it does strongly recommend that CARICOM countries establish institutional arrangements to enhance the integration of environmental management at the political, technical, and administrative levels. That the accord even mentions the political process is an encouraging sign.

There are several regional environmental programs working to strengthen the linkage between economic and environmental issues to improve natural resource management among the islands.

The Natural Resource Management Project of the Organization of Eastern Caribbean States (OECS-NRMP), headquartered in St. Lucia, has sponsored several country studies examining the adequacy of environmental policies, and the relationship between community development programs and environmental management. The Department of Regional Development of the OAS, with headquarters in Washington, D.C., and field offices throughout the region, has assisted several countries in preparing economic development plans. These have included projects in integrated development, tourism, agriculture, and downtown revitalization. Both the OAS and the OECS-NRMP only provide assistance when a government has requested it.

The United Nations Environment Programme (UNEP) sponsors the Caribbean Action Plan, administering the plan from its office in Kingston, Jamaica. UNEP convened governments from throughout the region for its first meeting in Cartagena de Indias in 1983; this meeting resulted in two agreements: the Convention for the Protection and Development of the Marine Environment of the Wider Caribbean Region, and the Protocol Concerning Cooperation in Combating Oil Spills in the Wider Caribbean Region.[58] Subsequently, in 1987, at its fourth intergovernmental meeting in Guadeloupe, additional protocols were added to support specially protected areas and wildlife. These protocols include provisions for establishing protected areas to preserve marine and terrestrial resources for recreational, educational, and scientific use.[59]

Working with ECLAC, regional environmental organizations, and country governments, UNEP is facilitating the integration of economic development and natural resource management by creating agreements designed to carry out its protocols. However, the procedure for implementing the protocols is limited to language requiring that the parties "take all appropriate measures to protect, preserve and manage" affected resources. The agreements lack legal provisions binding the signatories, so they are not enforced.

There are many smaller NGOs working to integrate economic and environmental linkages in regional and local development strategies. These include the Caribbean Conservation Association (Barbados); the Caribbean Natural Resources Institute (St. Lucia); the Eastern Caribbean Natural Area Management Program (United States Virgin Islands); the Centre for Environmental Studies and Natural Resource Management, University of the West Indies (Barbados); and the Island Resources Foundation (United States Virgin Islands). These organizations are involved in a wide variety of projects throughout the Eastern Caribbean, including training conservation technicians, preparing national conservation strategies, analyzing the specific environmental costs of different agricultural, tourist, and industrial projects, and providing governments with objective criteria to make environmental policy decisions.

THE ST. LUCIA SOUTHEAST COAST PROJECT

A project undertaken by the Caribbean Natural Resource Institute (CANRI) on St. Lucia illustrates how a small organization can effectively use economic incentives to promote environmental protection. The southeast coast of St. Lucia was facing severe environmental problems. Fishers dynamited reefs to collect lobsters, sea urchins were overharvested, nesting bird colonies were destroyed by people taking eggs, charcoal producers stripped hillsides bare, sand mining was rampant on beaches, and raw sewage flowed into prime fishing and beach areas.[60]

To resolve these major environmental problems, CANRI focused on solutions that would raise the personal income of people causing the damage. This created a link between the equity needs of the poor and environmental management. A multiyear public participation program resulted in the establishment of the Maria Islands Nature Center, funded by the World Wildlife Fund and administered by the St. Lucia National Trust. Its purpose is to manage the wildlife on the island and to coordinate an environmental program for local residents.

A key part of the project focused on the problems of the local fishing community, which was marginal due to its lack of organization. After working extensively with many fishers, CANRI received permission from the government to build a facility to store and market fish at Palmis. In addition, fishers were trained in more effective fishing techniques, as they had been resorting to dynamiting reefs and overharvesting local species. This program addressed the problems of the fishing community by creating economic incentives, better marketing, and more efficient fishing practices, all of which also protected limited fisheries resources. The project also created sea moss farms to produce a material used in beverages used to promote good health, a fuelwood plantation to provide charcoal producers with trees, and a solid waste management program. The success of the CANRI project reflects the need to integrate economic and environmental concerns on the community level to protect limited natural resources.

IDENTIFYING CONFLICTS BETWEEN ECONOMIC PRIORITIES AND ENVIRONMENTAL PROTECTION: THE CASE STUDIES

In St. Lucia, St. Kitts, and Barbados there are no economic incentives to promote environmental protection. On the contrary, the short-term economic gains derived from large development projects are a disincentive to protect natural resources. Environmental standards are typically perceived as obstacles to development. The following case studies show how this occurs.

When the St. Lucia cabinet granted permission for the M-Group to purchase the Jalousie Estate it granted several financial incentives to the developer. These incentives promoted the resort at the expense of the national park which would have protected the site's fragile natural resources. Incentives granted to the developer included repatriation of profits, waiver of duties on construction materials and supplies for the resort, and a multi-year tax holiday (SL 15). In addition, the government took the unusual step of granting a direct subvention to the resort, agreeing to construct the major access road to the Jalousie Estate with public funds.

The park project, although supported by previous governments who had voted to purchase the Jalousie Estate as public open space, has not been officially supported by the government. Although it would have required a modest capital outlay estimated at $1.63 million for acquisition of the estate and surrounding lands, the government was not willing to provide the necessary funds. Given the $57 millon that is budgeted for capital improvements in St. Lucia in 1990, it appears that the government could have afforded to fund the initial costs of the park if it so desired.

In St. Kitts the 4,000-acre southeast peninsula was owned by less than thirty parties, most of whom owned large parcels measuring 200-900 acres each. The peninsula is the only area in the country with large parcels in private ownership, as all land in sugar production on the main part of the island was nationalized in 1975. The installation of the road caused land values to increase dramatically in a short period of time, providing a direct incentive to develop the peninsula as rapidly as possible, before environmental policies intended to protect its abundant natural resources were operational.

It was estimated that the owners of the peninsula paid about $8.5 million in 1985 dollars for it, equal to $2,500 per acre. In 1990 large parcels in prime locations were selling for about $50,000 per acre, an increase of 2000 percent.[61] Several purchasers were foreign investors buying large parcels, which reflects the strong demand for resort sites in the region.

As a condition of approval for the USAID-funded project, St. Kitts was supposed to take several steps to protect the environment on the peninsula. A National Conservation Commission was to be operational, and a new Environmental Unit was to be created in the national planning office to help implement laws and regulations to protect the marine and terrestrial resources on the peninsula. These steps were not taken by the time the road was complete and the first development proposals were submitted to the government.

It is apparent that the tremendous increase in the value of the peninsula, coupled with the government's strong desire to strengthen the tourism economy, created major financial incentives to develop the peninsula as rapidly as possible, without the possible delays that environmental policies would cause. In turn, there were no incentives to protect the peninsula's natural resources.

The economic development process in both St. Lucia and St. Kitts is geared to attract private projects that are given financial incentives to attract foreign exchange. This system of incentives is contrary to national policies intended to protect the environment. As long as this conflict exists, public policy decisions will continue to be made that favor economic growth and cause fragile natural resources to be destroyed.

In Barbados, the Bridgetown Fishing Harbor was built without any precautions to mitigate against environmental damage. Even though civil servants in the Coastal Project Planning Unit warned of possible problems with coastal hydrology, sedimentation, water pollution, and the sustainability of the fishery, the Ministry of Agriculture ignored these concerns.

The basic economic incentive for building the harbor was immense, as a large part of Barbados's trade imbalance occurs because the island has to import food. The project was proposed in several National Development Plans as part of the solution to the island's economic problems. The harbor will theoretically improve the efficiency of the fishing industry and reduce the expenditure of scarce foreign exchange for imported protein. Of course, this will only happen if the fish population in the region is sustainable, which is highly suspect after a 40 percent drop in the fish catch during the 1989 fishing season.

The environmental concerns of civil servants were ignored because of the perceived importance of the project to the national economy. Conducting the necessary field research to evaluate the full extent of the project's impact on the environment would have been time consuming, compounding the uncertainty as to whether it would proceed. The project's feasibility was already uncertain due to its razor-thin rate of return, estimated at 12.1 percent, compared to the IDB's minimum requirement of 12 percent (B 42).

As a result, the government now has a harbor which may contribute to the national debt. The harbor already depends on a government subsidy to operate (B 26). If the regional fish catch continues to decline, it will reduce the revenue to the harbor, requiring the government to increase the amount of its subsidy. This will subject the operation of the harbor to the general instability that exists in the island economy. In addition, if the environmental problems that were forecast occur, such as sedimentation of the river mouth, the government will have to pay to fix them, causing a further drain on the treasury. This was allowed to happen because the potential environmental costs of the project were treated as external costs not associated with the project.

LACK OF LONG-TERM ECONOMIC PLANNING

The government of St. Lucia favored the resort at the Jalousie Estate because the national economic planning process favors short-term solutions. The short-term economic benefit of the resort is mainly derived from the creation of a few dozen jobs, mostly for unskilled labor, and income from a 12.5 percent hotel room tax (SL 13). Although the developer publicly said in early 1989 that the resort would create several hundred construction jobs to benefit locally unemployed people, these benefits were reduced when he chose a Brazilian company to build the resort, despite the existence of qualified companies in the region.[62] It does not appear that the resort will result in any substantial economic benefit to the island other than a modest contribution to the treasury from the room tax, and whatever money tourists spend when they leave the confines of the resort. But the trickle-down or spin-off effects are expected to be minimal as the project will be an exclusive destination resort, with its health club and convention facilities designed to keep visitors on the site.

The Pitons National Park would have provided far more economic benefit to the local community. It would have generated about 500 jobs by the third year of operation, growing to nearly 1,200 by the year 2000.[63] The government's push to replace the banana crop, which accounts for over 60 percent of its foreign exchange earnings, is causing it to focus on short-term solutions, although the park could have become operational by 1991–92, the same time as the resort.

The government has made a policy decision that hotels are the answer to its economic problems. It has geared the national budget and capital improvement program to promote the tourist sector, creating a bias against other development alternatives that require a longer planning horizon to implement.

As described in chapter 4, the cultural tradition of the islands creates an aversion to risks, and the small size of public institutions makes it difficult for them to undertake innovations in public policies. These factors, when combined with such long-term economic risks as those the park entails, causes governments to favor solutions that are perceived as being more certain.[64]

The economic development strategy of St. Lucia's government is to aggressively pursue international investors to build new tourist projects. Once it provides the basic infrastructure and permission to build the hotels, the government does not have to incur any additional risk to collect revenue from the projects. It does not have to make the many day-to-day decisions that the hotel owners will be required to make, or risk additional public funds to generate revenue.

The proposed Pitons National Park is a public project. To plan, design, and implement the park's master plan would require the government to continuously allocate limited financial and technical resources in perpetuity. Just to get it off the ground would require a complex series of government actions that are difficult to make given the limited technical resources in the country (SL 6, 12). To keep it operating and generating revenue would require the ongoing commitment of several new civil servants, as existing government employees are stretched to their capacity (SL 5). St. Lucia does not have the institutional capacity to carry out large public projects such as the park, which require substantial inputs for design, construction and operation.[65]

The similar situation exists with the Southeast Peninsula Development Project on St. Kitts. The land-use management plan for the project recommended that large portions of the peninsula with outstanding wildlife and open space values remain undeveloped. The natural resources in these areas are supposed to be protected by implementing a conservation program, but the government has not been willing to make the financial commitment to support such a program.

By using the financial and technical resources of the tourist industry, the governments are avoiding the risk associated with using their own limited resources. This is an important factor that limits the ability of governments in the region to undertake development projects that preserve the environment, such as the Pitons National

Park and the southeast peninsula, which both represented opportunities to create large tourist projects while leaving the natural environment intact. This could have been done by leaving the sites in their natural state, installing minimum improvements, and catering to the growing international clientele for "nature tourism." This approach would have required far less capital, but would be somewhat less certain than the traditional approach to tourism of building resorts on every beach and a cabana under every palm tree.

SUMMARY

In the countries of the Eastern Caribbean economic uncertainties cause governments to choose large development projects that damage fragile natural resources. Among the economic realities these countries face are dependency on the North Atlantic states, a lack of diversification, persistent high unemployment, and a shortage of foreign exchange to pay for imported food and consumer durables. Although their recent economic performance has been better than that of developing countries in general, vulnerability to price shocks for exported agricultural commodities make the regional economies unstable. These difficulties occur in the context of political, social, and economic patterns that concentrate power and wealth in the hands of a relatively few individuals who are resistant to change.

There have been several attempts to integrate the economies of the islands by promoting regional cooperation. Regional economic integration could compensate for the small size of the islands by providing for economies of scale for production, marketing, and investing. But problems rooted in the different cultures and political systems of the islands have prevented integration from taking place. Nonetheless, there are several efforts under way to improve regional cooperation, such as CARICOM and the CDB, efforts that are helping to build the tradition of cooperation needed if integration is to work in the long run.

Because domestic savings are too low to finance development, the islands must look outside the region for investment capital. The best investment opportunities were exhausted in the 1970s, so the island economies are increasingly dependent on international development assistance agencies, such as USAID and the IDB, to provide capital. These agencies have been funding large projects intended to diversify island economies, with a heavy emphasis on tourism and agriculture.

Regional organizations such as CARICOM, the CDB, and UNEP are working to promote more effective linkages between economic development and environmental preservation. The results have been mixed. Regional environmental agreements, such as the UNEP protocols for protection of wildlife areas, lack enforcement mechanisms that bind governments. Several NGOs are integrating economic and environmental planning, with the Southeast Coast Project on St. Lucia managed by the Caribbean Natural Resource Institute being the most notable example.

The government of St. Lucia chose to support a private resort on the Jalousie Estate rather than the Pitons National Park because it is promoting growth of the traditional tourist industry to alleviate its economic problems. The government of St. Kitts chose to develop the 4,000-acre Southeast Peninsula for the same reason, but has instituted only a few of several recommended measures to protect its natural resources, deemed to be among the most abundant in the Eastern Caribbean. In Barbados, the government built the largest and most technically complex fishing harbor in the region, but it failed to evaluate the environmental impact it could cause.

In all three instances, economic incentives favored large development projects and undercut environmental protection policies. There are no economic incentives for preserving natural resources. In addition, the uncertainty of depending on long-range economic planning using public funds prompted both St. Kitts and St. Lucia to pursue traditional, capital-intensive tourist projects rather than developing nature tourism that would both earn foreign exchange and preserve the natural resources of the islands.

Chapter Six

DEVELOPMENT ASSISTANCE AGENCIES

International development assistance agencies, such as the World Bank and the USAID, have been under increasing political pressure to adopt policies and programs that help protect limited natural resources in developing countries. Yet conditions within these agencies have prevented many such initiatives from taking hold and being implemented in the field, in the countries that receive development assistance. To complicate matters, the lack of effective environmental policy initiatives within development assistance agencies reinforces the behavior of political leaders in developing countries who also fail to protect the environment. Even though most countries have national laws and policies aimed at protecting limited natural resources such as forests, fisheries, rivers, and ocean waters, they often remain unenforced (see chapter 2). The combination of weak environmental protection by both development assistance agencies and developing countries creates a political and institutional atmosphere that seems to tolerate, and sometimes encourage, the widespread destruction of natural resources that often accompanies large donor-funded projects.

As the three case studies will show, efforts to improve the environmental accountability of the donor agencies are in conflict with many elements of the development process. The goals of donor agencies involve several competing objectives, including economic growth, good foreign relations, and—in recent years—conservation of natural resources. Many developing countries depend on the foreign investments created by donor-sponsored projects. These factors create a tension between environment and development that makes it difficult for donor agencies to implement their own environmental policies.

THE NECESSITY FOR DEVELOPMENT ASSISTANCE

Theories of what development is, and how it can best be achieved, have undergone constant revision in the last thirty years. Early theories perceived economic growth as consisting of a series of linear stages through which all national economies have to proceed. With adequate domestic savings, foreign-aid, and investment, all developing countries could theoretically create their own independent, industrialized economies. The linear-stages model was succeeded by the neoclassical structural change model and international dependence paradigm, the latter being an attempt to reflect the importance of political relations and equity in development planning.

These traditional theories of development have been somewhat de-emphasized and augmented in the last ten years as the basic assumptions of the development process have been challenged. It had been assumed that if countries can progress through a series of set economic changes, the general quality of life in a society would undergo a definite improvement. This improvement in the quality of life was measured using economic indicators, such as per capita income, gross national product, increased growth, and efficiencies in major economic sectors such as manufacturing, agriculture, and professional services, which result in greater domestic production, savings, and trade exports. But these economic indicators have not proven to be a reliable way to measure the effectiveness of development. They undervalue or ignore non-economic factors such as improved health care, education, and environmental protection.[1]

As a result, more recent theories of development have focused on how countries can improve standards of living and quality of life in a broader sense than just general economic betterment. Development assistance has diversified and shifted to include the needs of rural communities by integrating the agricultural sector into growth strategies that previously focused on industry as the engine of the economy. Residents of new squatter communities springing up on the outskirts of urban megacities, having migrated from poor rural areas, are targeted for small scale development assistance programs as a way to improve the economy by promoting the informal sector, sometimes still called the "black market." New, non-traditional development initiatives such as these are part of comprehensive integrated development strategies that have become quite sophisticated. As a result, development assistance in the Eastern Caribbean includes a wide range of urban and rural projects designed to diversify the traditional plantation economies of the islands. But, as discussed in chapter 5, the island economies have a whole set of problems, including geographical isolation, small size, the high cost of doing business over great distances, and difficulties of achieving regional economic integration that have prevented them from becoming more fully developed.[2]

The islands are heavily dependent on foreign investment because they lack sufficient domestic savings to provide the capital needed to fund development of the manufacturing, agricultural, and tourist projects needed to diversify their economies.[3] To stimulate private investment in what are considered to be marginal economies, they are heavily reliant on donor agencies. The donors provide the money and technical assistance needed to build infrastructure, such as roads, utilities, and major public facilities, creating a financial climate that ideally should promote private investment. Sometimes this strategy works and sometimes it does not. Hoping that this approach will work more often than not, donor agencies use several types of development assistance to funnel aid to the Caribbean, typical of approaches used for other developing countries.

DEVELOPMENT ASSISTANCE PROGRAMS

There are basically two kinds of development assistance agencies, multilateral and bilateral. Aid given from one government to another is considered bilateral assistance, while multilateral assistance is from agencies that give aid on behalf of several governments, such as the multilateral development banks (MDBs). Grants and low-interest loans, known as concessional financing, fund a wide variety of projects. In the Eastern Caribbean, capital from donor agencies has made up for the decline in private foreign investment, and has been largely responsible for the continued rate of positive growth in the 1980s.

There are several bilateral and multilateral organizations that provide financial and technical assistance in the region. The World Bank is the largest multilateral lender in the world, providing aid through its three institutions, the International Bank for Reconstruction, the International Development Association, and the International Finance Committee. As with all MDBs, the World Bank uses capital contributed from its members to raise additional funds in international money markets. It then finances projects by giving loans to recipients at lower interest rates than are available from commercial banks. Funds raised from its members also allow the World Bank, and other MDBs, to provide soft loans to lesser developed countries and projects that have a low rate of return.

The World Bank funds some projects in the Caribbean through its regional division for Latin America and the Caribbean, and provides funding for the IDB and Caribbean Development Bank so they can conduct their own development programs. The Caribbean Development Bank (CDB) is the smallest of the regional MDBs. Founded in 1970, its members include all of the countries of the Commonwealth Caribbean, three Latin American states, and five non-regional members from Europe and Canada. Several countries, including the United States, make substantial contributions to the CDB by contributing to its Special Development Fund. As its charter requires the CDB to promote economic cooperation and integration among its members, it focuses on promoting projects that meet this objective. Most projects funded have been in the agricultural, transportation, and industrial sectors. In 1987 the CDB, in association with the World Bank, made its first loan to assist a structural adjustment program in a member country.[4] The European Development Fund (the development agency of the European Community), the Canadian International Development Agency, and the United Nations Development Program also provide substantial assistance to the region.

The Inter-American Development Bank

The largest regional bank in the world, the IDB, funds several projects in the Eastern Caribbean. The IDB was organized in 1959 and is owned by forty-four countries, including twenty-seven from North and South America, and sixteen from outside of the region that were admitted in 1976. The focus of the IDB's aid programs is the developing countries in South American and the Caribbean.[5] The IDB was set up so its members could have greater participation in adopting lending policies that meet the needs of the region, and pursue regional economic integration as a part of the inter-American system.[6]

The headquarters of the IDB is in Washington, D.C. It also has regional offices in many countries. It is managed by a board of governors, with one governor and an alternate governor appointed by each member. The voting power of each member is linked to its share of the IDB's capital stock. Latin American members have the most votes, followed by members from the United States. Canada and other non-regional members hold small percentages of capital stock.

Projects that are proposed by developing countries in the region are presented to the IDB for funding at an annual Donor's Conference in Washington, D.C. All countries seeking aid and all donors providing it attend this conference, where projects are tentatively selected by agencies, who tend to specialize in certain types of development assistance (i.e. providing infrastructure, agricultural technology, support for manufacturing, tourism, etc.). Over the past several years the IDB has lent between $2.3 and 3.0 billion each year. This includes projects in the Eastern Caribbean such as a new highway system, a sewage project, and a fishing harbor in Barbados.

The IDB uses a system for evaluating and implementing projects that is common to most donors. Once a project is tentatively selected by the IDB, it goes through a standard project cycle that takes 12–24 months to complete. A "Country Programming Paper" puts a project in the pipeline, followed by an orientation mission in the field to help the borrower prepare the loan application. Next, the IDB forms a project committee, and dispatches an analysis mission to prepare a project report. The report includes information on the national economy, the experience of the IDB in the type of project to be funded, how the objectives of the project will be carried out, and the steps needed to execute it. A loan proposal is then prepared and submitted for approval to the IDB's board of directors, which delegates authority for project implementation to a field office.

The Organization of American States

The OAS is a regional body that provides technical assistance to its members, but is similar to a multilateral development agency. The charter for the OAS was created in 1948 and gave a new name to the structure of the inter-American system. Its broad purpose is to promote economic, social, and cultural progress in the Americas. The policy of the OAS is set by its general assembly, which has an elaborate system of special committees, conferences, commissions, institutes, and boards specializing in a wide range of issues.[7] The General Secretariat of the OAS is controlled by the cabinet and secretary general, assisted by an Advisory Group, and in turn by a tier of executive secretariats and secretariats, each specializing in a different topic.[8]

The Department of Regional Development and Environment of the Executive Secretariat for Economic and Social Affairs was created in 1963 as the Natural Resources Unit.[9] It provides technical advice for the design of development projects that are based on the sustainable use of natural resources. In the Eastern Caribbean the department coordinates with many other agencies, such as US-AID, the IDB and the Organization of Eastern Caribbean States, to evaluate the feasibility of development projects and to increase the institutional capacity of island governments to carry out environmental planning.[10]

The department is staffed by specialists in natural resources, economics, regional developing planning, and related areas, and regularly sponsors several technical cooperation projects, policy exercises, and workshops aimed at developing sustainable development practices in Latin America and the Caribbean. It operates in several countries and has been very active at the policy level throughout the Caribbean, attempting to find solutions to a range of environmental problems.

This department of the OAS has been a pioneer in the field of integrated planning, defined for its purpose as the integration of regional development planning and natural resource management. A major focus of its policy-level environmental work has been to recommend to national governments in the region how to integrate economic development and natural resource protection. It has done so, for example, in the workshops it has sponsored for member nations on national natural resource accounting methods. This work has taken several forms. As early as 1983 OAS was concerned about the possible adverse effect of increasing tourism on indigenous cultures in the region. It made several recommendations on how to preserve the cultural heritage in the Caribbean while catering to the burgeoning tourist industry.[11]

In 1984 OAS, in cooperation with the United States National Park Service and USAID, undertook a major effort to evaluate the effectiveness of efforts throughout the Caribbean to integrate regional development planning and environmental protection.[12] This effort involved documenting six detailed case studies of integrated regional planning in Latin American and the Caribbean.[13] In 1987 the department issued a report titled *Minimum Conflicts: Guidelines for Planning the Use of American Humid Tropic Environments.* This piece of work discusses methods that can be used to deal with policy-level and intergovernmental conflicts that arise when opposing parties compete for the use of limited natural resources. The OAS has sponsored examinations of how to control the size of new hotel developments so they are compatible with limited natural resources and has done extensive work to lay the foundation for establishing several major national parks and protected areas throughout the region.[14] A master plan for developing the tourist industry in St. Kitts–Nevis was recently completed.

Although the OAS is increasingly becoming actively involved in environmental initiatives in the region, as evidenced by its Environmental Commission, established to provide policy guidance to the OAS permanent council—and its Inter-American Program for Environmental Protection—which closely overlaps Agenda 21, which was ratified by many countries at the Earth Summit in 1992—it does not intervene in the internal operations of the nations where it works. Its Department of Regional Development and Environment, which has done much to promote the use of natural resource planning and management in the Caribbean, can only go so far. This department acts in a technical advisory role to the nations of the region and is thus prevented from taking a more active role in implementing the approaches it recommends.

The United States Agency for International Development

USAID is the main development assistance agency of the United States government, carrying out bilateral economic assistance through several programs and organizations. The USAID administrator, assisted by a deputy administrator, oversees the actions of the agency, and is responsible to the secretary of state on matters of policy and budget, while retaining authority for administration and operations. USAID is part of the executive branch of the United States government, so the president has the power to fill many senior offices with political appointees.

USAID works closely with the Department of State and the Department of the Treasury to coordinate its programs to be consistent with the direction of the government's foreign policy and budget priorities. Several committees and subcommittees of the Senate and House of Representatives oversee its policies and projects.[15] USAID uses a method of analyzing and designing projects similar to that of other donors. It generally requires that goods and services purchased by recipients be provided by United States suppliers and consultants.[16]

To coordinate its projects in the Eastern Caribbean, USAID has a regional development office in Bridgetown, Barbados, which has a director and deputy director who are responsible for policy decisions. Projects in the region are targeted in three key sectors, agriculture, light manufacturing, and tourism, and stress linkages to the private sector and provide improved public facilities to support economic growth. Between 1982 and 1990 the regional office sponsored a wide variety of aid projects for the islands including several in Grenada after the United States intervention in late 1983, roads and power plants in St. Lucia, St. Vincent, and Dominica; water supply projects in Antigua; and the Southeast Development Project in St. Kitts. Expenditures during this period were about $130 million, not including a region-wide program to improve agricultural production and management known as HIAMP.[17]

In addition to its large presence in the Eastern Caribbean, USAID is sponsoring other programs in the Caribbean–Latin America region to promote unity with the United States. The Central American Initiative is currently providing about $8 billion in economic assistance; in El Salvador USAID projects involve public works, health care, and repair of facilities damaged by that country's war.[18]

USAID and other donors active in the Caribbean have showed an increasing interest in incorporating environmental safeguards in their projects, and undertaking major policy initiatives to include these concerns in their long-range planning. A series of events that started in the 1980s has caused USAID and other donors to take environmental concerns more seriously.

Environmental Reform in the Donor Agencies

Since the early 1980s donors have come under increasing pressure, mainly from United States environmental groups, to consider the effects on the environment when they fund development projects. This concern arose from a basic belief that the health of the natural environment is integrally linked to the social and economic well being of people in a society, especially in countries with marginal natural resources. The political movement to improve the environmental policies of the donors also reflects the difficulty of implementing new policies in these large and complex institutions.

There are several reasons why donors have been slow to adopt more effective environmental policies. Such policies represent a major change in the direction of development assistance. The established interdependencies, decision-making mechanisms, and centers of power make it very difficult to implement new policies in large institutions.[19] Entrenched bureaucrats who are threatened by new policies form coalitions that promote their self-interest, shortsightedness, and resistance to change.[20] The resistance to change that individuals often bring to a policy dialogue is compounded by the inherent difficulty of integrating environmental factors into the complexities of evaluating and designing large development projects.

Hirschman stresses how complex the development process is, especially when projects are enmeshed with natural resources. He proposes that a "long voyage of discovery" is needed to properly integrate the two. His "hiding hand principle" holds that development planners underestimate the effort it takes to implement a project, and overestimate their ability to solve difficulties that arise.[21] Sachs mentions how development is defined very narrowly, often ignoring local conditions, including the natural environment.[22] International donors have difficulty implementing new environmental policies for several reasons, including rapid staff turnover in field offices that are responsible for project implementation, a lack of field personnel trained in natural resource management, miscommunication between field offices and headquarters, the lack of an environmental tradition among development planners, and the technical difficulty of implementing new environmental management practices in the field. In addition, an effective natural resources management program requires the careful integration of several disciplines that typically touch on a wide variety of topics and issues, such as forestry and fisheries management, and watershed, land use, transportation, and energy planning. Add cultural concerns, such as the preservation of indigenous communities and lifeways, in additional to economic requirements such as cost effectiveness and providing an internal rate of return adequate to service the debt incurred by project design and construction, and the level of complexity demanded for a well designed and environmentally safe project becomes apparent.

Sparked by international concern over the severe environmental damage being caused by large donor-funded projects, such as the Polonoroeste Project in Brazil, the Narmada Valley Dam in India, and transmigration in Indonesia, United States environmental groups have worked to reform MDB lending policies.[23] Because the United States Treasury contributes millions of dollars to various donors, including the World Bank, the IDB, and of course, USAID, environmentalists focus on the congressional budget process to voice their concerns. As a result, several donor agencies have instituted procedures to protect natural resources.

The Working Group for Multilateral Assistance is made up of several agencies, including USAID and the United States Treasury, and helps review about 500 MDB projects a year. The USAID Early Warning Project Notification process was initiated in 1982 to identify environmental problems of MDB projects early in the planning process. The 1987 and 1988 Appropriation Acts required the United States Treasury to instruct United States executive directors of MDBs to promote new environmental review processes.[24] Most importantly, in 1987 the Congress passed legislation as part of the Foreign Assistance and Related Programs Act requiring that specific actions be taken to integrate more effective environmental protection policies into the operations of MDBs. In 1988 a second Congressional mandate was passed making the previous year's requirement a permanent part of the authorizing legislation for MDB funding.

The 1987 and 1988 legal reforms were major steps forward in promoting donor accountability for environmental reforms. The Treasury Department must now present detailed progress reports each year to Congress that document how each donor is implementing the act. The progress reports evaluate the environmental programs of the donors in several areas including the adequacy of their environmental staff, whether bank presidents have appointed environmental advisors, the provision of career incentives for environmental staff, the protection of indigenous people, and consultations with NGOs in the field.[25] In addition, the MDBs must prepare environmental impact statements on all projects that may damage natural resources. These reports also examine the potential adverse and cultural effects of large development projects. However, it is unclear how recommendations from these reports will concretely alter large projects that have been in the pipeline for many years.

So, the progress of the MDBs in protecting natural resources, and incorporating environmental protection measures in their own projects, has been mixed. For example, the World Bank, which is the largest MDB, does sponsor some environmental improvement projects, such as a $117 million National Environment Project in Brazil to create a national system of Conservation Units and provide protection for the Pantanal, a huge interior wetlands system, and endangered coastal rainforest areas. The World Bank is also sponsoring several other major environmental initiatives, including a $18 million project in Poland for environmental protection related to solid and hazardous wastes, a $26 million credit to fund the Madagascar National Protection and Management Project in Africa, $450 million in projects in China for pollution control in Beijing and for urban and industrial pollution in Liaonging and Southern Jiangsu provinces, and a $200 million project in Mexico to address air pollution and transportation issues in Mexico City. The World Bank is also sponsoring major projects in Indonesia and Brazil to support the efficient use of non-renewable energy resources while promoting energy efficiency.[26] But at the same time, many large-scale development projects sponsored by the World Bank are still causing severe environmental and social impacts, despite repeated requests expressed by environmental groups before the United States Congress over the last ten years that the World Bank revise its design and construction of projects to minimize damage to natural and social resources.

An example of why it is difficult, some would say nearly impossible, for the World Bank to drop projects that cause large-scale environmental damage lies in the findings of the Morse Commission. This commission was convened by then–World Bank President Barber Conable in 1991 to undertake an independent investigation of the environmental and resettlement aspects of the Narmada River Sardar Sarovar dam, a project financed by $450 million in World Bank loans and credits, to be constructed on India's largest westward flowing river.[27] The commission found that "There appears to be a historical numbness . . . at the Bank and in India to environmental issues, a history of omissions, unmet deadlines, and ex post facto revisions." The commission further found that "the Bank is more concerned to accommodate the pressures emanating from its borrowers than to guarantee implementation of its policies."[28]

There appear to be several reasons why the MDBs have been slow to reform their lending practices to promote natural resources. Measures to protect the environment require substantial reforms that conflict with the MDBs' primary mission, which is to move funds as efficiently as possible. Environmental requirements take time to meet, and often slow down projects. Professionals within the banks do not like to see projects delayed.[29] Environmental reforms have occurred on paper, but actual implementation in developing countries is proving to be much more difficult.

The Inter-American Development Bank

The IDB was under heavy pressure from the United States Congress for several years before it started to initiate policy reforms in the mid 1980s. The IDB established an Environmental Management Committee in 1984, ostensibly to evaluate the adverse environmental effects of its projects. However, the committee consisted of existing in-house professional staff, the managers of key IDB divisions, who had a stake in promoting projects. The committee was widely perceived as a political committee of insiders. Its members had no expertise in environmental management. In early 1988 a congressional oversight committee called the IDB's performance in implementing environmental reforms the worst of all of the MDBs.[30] In mid-1988 testimony by United States environmental groups characterized the IDB's inaction as moving "from a posture of recalcitrance and foot dragging on the environment to one of outright resistance."[31] There were two main reasons why the IDB was lagging behind other MDBs in instituting environmental reforms, aside from internal resistance from IDB professionals.

First, there was resistance from two influential IDB members, Brazil and Venezuela, who felt that environmental policies that could hamper project funding should not be imposed (B 44).[32] Second, the United States was sending a message to the IDB that it supported reform in general, but objected to specific measures needed to implement stronger environmental standards in the MDBs. This occurred because the United States Treasury was lukewarm to the idea of environmental reform, despite pressure from the Congress, as such reform could interfere with its ability to contribute to United States foreign policy. Treasury officials expressed this concern when they opposed a requirement that MDBs prepare environmental assessments for their projects, as it "would paralyze our ability to act cooperatively and constructively with other member countries."[33] Treasury was sending a message to the IDB and Congress that it only supported environmental reform up to a point.

The IDB started making reforms in 1987 when a senior environmental specialist was hired to advise its Environmental Management Committee, but this was only one staff position among the IDB's 2,400, a very small commitment. During the same year the IDB held an environmental training seminar for its staff, and invited South American environmental organizations to attend a meeting with finance ministers on natural resource issues. But there was no follow-up and business continued as usual. Congress strengthened its support for MDB reform in 1988 by amending the National Environmental Policy Act (NEPA). The amendment required that environmental impact assessments be prepared for all MDB projects starting in January 1991, to allow bank officers to evaluate the environmental effects of projects. If this information is not provided at least 120 days prior to the presentation of a project to a bank's board of directors, the United States representative has to vote against it. This change in the law requires that environmental concerns be addressed as part of all project evaluations by the MDBs.[34] It is expected that the MDBs will conform to this requirement to avoid forcing the United States to oppose their projects (B 44). As a result the IDB accelerated its effort to reform.[35]

In early 1989 the IDB created a new Environmental Protection Division in the Projects Analysis department, hiring a staff of fifteen specializing in forestry, resource economics, anthropology, water resource management and other environmental specialties. This division, staffed by twenty two professionals in early 1994, is responsible for reviewing all projects and operations of the IDB, and for designing a program for integrating environmental management into its technical cooperation and sector-lending programs.[36] It is has also adopted standard environmental impact assessment (EIA) procedures, classifying projects by the level and type of impact they may generate. But, under the IDB's current standards, the responsibility for implementing the results of EIAs rests with borrowing countries, which will make implementation of environmental protection measures subject to political pressures within borrowing governments that place a strong emphasis on economic growth and investment.

Since 1989 when the Environmental Protection Division was formed, the IDB has continued to integrate environmental protection policies into various operations, projects, and programs. For example, the Bank has approved several loans, totaling one billion dollars in 1992, on projects to support environmental protection. These projects include $22 million to help establish a National Environmental Fund in Brazil, $44.5 million to construct a new sewage system to serve the south coast of Barbados, $450 to initiate a decontamination project for the Tietê River in Brazil and $100 to fund a foreign debt buy-back for ecological conservation in the Mexico City metropolitan area (IDB 1992 Annual Report). But it appears there are weak links in the IDB's efforts to implement its own environmental policies that are very difficult to overcome. The IDB's priority, as a lending institution, is to meet the immediate financial needs of borrowers. The IDB has also shown an inability to strengthen field operations so that in-country staff can carry out monitoring and enforcement of specific measures to protect natural resources. The Bank was revising its environmental guidelines in early 1994. Repeated requests were made of senior staff in the Environmental Protection Division to explain the status of environmental operations in the Bank, and the effect of those revisions, but no response was received.

The United States Agency for International Development

USAID started to adopt environmental reforms in response to a lawsuit filed against it in 1975 by several United States environmental organizations. The suit contended that as an agency of the United States government USAID was required by NEPA to systematically document the adverse environmental effects of its projects. USAID immediately moved to settle the suit and initiated negotiations with environmental groups and the Council on Environmental Quality. As a result, USAID issued an Environmental Policy Determination requiring that it initiate a process to evaluate the environmental consequences of its projects, mitigate any related impact, and assist countries to improve their capability to integrate impact assessment into development projects.[37]

Since the settlement of the NEPA suit the agency has instituted several reforms to integrate environmental protection in its developing planning activities. It has appointed Environmental Officers to its regional mission offices, and allocates a substantial portion of its budget for environmental activities such as preparing national environmental profiles, training to improve the institutional capability of borrowers, major projects such as Development Strategies for Fragile Lands (DESFIL) and Environmental Policy and Training Project (EPAT), and major programs to promote biological diversity, conserve forests, and regulate pesticides.[38]

In 1992 USAID issued "Environmental Strategy," a broad policy statement intended to help establish the agency's agenda for integrating natural resource management within its broader mandate to provide development assistance. The strategy recognized that environmental degradation is a serious and growing problem worldwide, and targeted five categories of major problems: loss of tropical forests and biological diversity, unsustainable agricultural practices, environmentally unsound energy production, urban and industrial pollution, and degradation of water and coastal resources.[39] In late 1993 USAID revised its environmental strategy as part of an overall "Strategy for Sustainable Development." This new strategy attempts to integrate four major components of the overall USAID mission, economic growth, environmental protection, population stabilization, and building democratic societies, into an overall approach to promote sustainable development.[40]

The new strategy is more detailed than the 1992 strategy, and recognizes the importance of linking the major aspects of development assistance, to promote the general goal of sustainable develop-

ment. This integrated approach seems to reflect a major philsoph-
ical shift in USAID, and will no doubt provide a much-needed rhetor-
ical framework for implementing its own existing environmental
policies. But it does not mean that the managerial, technical, and administrative mechanisms in this large agency will simultaneously
shift into a mode that is more responsive to environmental priorities.
USAID, like other donor agencies, has experienced a gap, often large
and glaring, between its stated environmental policies and what actually happens in regional and country missions in the developing
world. Perhaps the recent USAID reorganization will help resolve
this problem.

USAID is undergoing a major reorganization, guided by the following general objectives: to centralize policy initiatives and how
they are communicated to organizational units; to develop a reporting system intended to increase the accountability of managers; to
integrate financial management, budget, and program functions into
the planning process; and to consolidate global programs, field support, and the research bureau. It would seem that centralizing these
key organizational functions will certainly help the agency implement its stated policy objectives, such as environmental protection
and sustainable development practices.[41]

To follow the general recognition of major environmental problems as stated in the overall policy strategies, USAID drafted a specific "Environmental Strategy for Latin America and the Caribbean"
in 1993. The regional environmental strategy discusses some of
problems in the Caribbean that lead to environmental degradation,
such as weak public institutions, lack of education and public awareness, and the general absence of public participation in national policy making in the region. However, when it discusses how to deal
with these problems, the regional strategy is limited to a series of
general recommendations.[42] If implemented, these general policy
and programmatic recommendations will support the agency's efforts to strengthen environmental protection in general. However,
no mention is made of specific strategies that USAID could use to
exert the economic or political leverage with client countries that is
often needed to effectively influence the day-to-day decision-making
process of developing country political leaders, individuals who
stand the most to gain by accepting USAID economic assistance
while ignoring the agency's best-intentioned general advice to protect the natural environment.

Following the "Environmental Strategy for Latin America and
the Caribbean," USAID issued, in cooperation with the World Re-

sources Institute, *Green Guidance for Latin America and the Caribbean: Integrating Environmental Concerns in A.I.D. Programming*.[43] This document is just what its title implies, a general guide to several specific strategies for improving environmental management practices. It offers advice for a variety of programs and projects that are needed to strengthen environmental protection, including democratic initiatives, protection of coastal resources, promotion of ecotourism, tapping indigenous capacity for resource management, promoting biodiversity, forest and watershed management, understanding the linkages between agricultural and land-use practices and resource degradation, and the role of economic policies, trade, and investment on environmentally sustainable development practices. However, this general guide, although it offers prescriptive policy advice, does not explain how this advice can be specifically included in USAID projects, budgets, or managerial, administrative, and technical practices, to enhance the protection and management of limited or scarce natural resources.

Although much progress has occurred to include environmental factors in its overall mission, USAID has had problems implementing some policies. Urged by Congress, the agency initiated an early warning system in the early 1980s to evaluate the environmental effects of projects proposed by other donors. The purpose of this program is to advise United States Executive Directors of the MDBs if bank projects will damage the environment, and to have USAID share this information with other donors. However, this project never was fully implemented, in the absence of a necessary amendment to NEPA requiring that environmental information be developed prior to votes on bank projects.[44]

The Organization of American States

The Department of Regional Development of the OAS sponsors a major technical assistance program that promotes the integration of efficient uses of natural resources. A major objective of the department has been to improve the linkage between natural resources and social and economic development. It has sponsored projects to promote development of renewable energy resources, and to reduce the danger from natural hazards. In the Caribbean the department's recent projects include a natural resource assessment for agricultural development in Antigua, training assistance for small hotels in Barbados, an integrated development project in Grenada, design of a national park system in Trinidad and Tobago, recommendations to establish a parks and protected-area system for Grenada and St. Lucia, a natural resource database in St. Lucia, and tourism projects for several islands.[45] Policy-level initiatives undertaken by OAS in recent years include the formation of an Environment Commission to advise its permanent council and the adoption of the Inter-American Program of Action for Environmental Protection in 1991.

All of the donor agencies have encountered difficulties when attempting to implement policies intended to protect the environment. This failure has been most apparent when large development projects are involved. The history of projects in St. Kitts, St. Lucia, and Barbados shows why this has happened.

Evaluating the Effects of Politics on the Performance of Donor Agencies: The Case Studies

It had been a "long dream of national politicians and landowners to open up the valuable assets" of the 4,000-acre southeast peninsula of St. Kitts (SK 5). The undeveloped beaches and protected bays on the peninsula, a part of St. Kitts that few citizens had ever visited, presented what were perceived as some of the most mouth watering investment opportunities in the Eastern Caribbean. It presented a chance for huge financial returns to the peninsula's thirty or so landowners, and a chance to diversify the sugar-based economy.

Except for a few scattered homes and a small hotel, the peninsula and its abundant natural resources were untouched. In 1980, prior to independence, the government asked the British Development Division (BDD) of the Overseas Development Administration, part of the European Economic Community, to conduct a feasibility study for a new road to connect the peninsula to the main part of the island. Consultants prepared a preliminary road design and completed the feasibility study. The study concluded that a six-mile-long road would pay for itself if accompanied by a diversified development program including farming, salt mining, tourism, and freight hauling across a narrow channel to the sister island of Nevis. However, the BDD believed that the study's economic projections were unrealistic, and that the project was not feasible, so it dropped the project. This decision was based on a road that would cost about $3 million to build, compared to the $17 million USAID eventually spent (SK 1).

After the British refused to build the road, the government of St. Kitts turned to the United States for assistance. In early 1984, shortly after St. Kitts gained independence, its political leaders approached USAID for support. The United States military intervention in Grenada, about 350 miles to the south of St. Kitts, had occurred a few months earlier. The intervention was an indication of the United States' renewed interest in the Caribbean.[46]

Shortly after representatives from St. Kitts met with USAID officials in Washington, D.C., the agency's deputy administrator, its second most powerful official, directed the regional development office in Barbados to "get a project going in the next 30 days" (SK 12). This directive put the project at the top of the agency's agenda, and sent a clear signal to the Barbados office that the project was to proceed without delay. The strong political support that the project got from the leadership of USAID later helped to undercut efforts to protect the fragile natural resources on the peninsula. Following its Congressional mandate to protect the environment, USAID sponsored the completion of numerous detailed studies that cataloged the natural resources of the peninsula, and recommended how to protect them. The studies included an environmental impact assessment, a land use management plan, and a developer's handbook.

Yet, when consultants for USAID were preparing environmental reports for the project in 1989, the environmental officer in the Caribbean office was not allowed event to review them. This was because the Washington, D.C., office had sent word to the regional office "not to make waves on the environmental aspects of the project" (SK 11). Clearly, the timely completion of the project was a priority of Washington, D.C., USAID officials, who are political appointees. The administrator of the agency reports to the secretary of state on matters of policy. It appears that United States foreign policy interests in the region, in the wake of the Grenada intervention, were served by funding a large, high profile project in St. Kitts. This foreign policy interest, and a desire to promote United States business interests during construction of the project and subsequent tourist facilities, pressured USAID regional staff into finishing the project as soon as possible. There was not time to put the environmental policies it had recommended into place, including formation of a National Conservation Commission and a new Environmental Unit, which still do not exist.[47] As a result, the natural resources of St. Kitts are now at great risk, as the government lacks the institutional capacity and political will to protect them. Concern for these resources appears to be well founded, given the recent history of non-implementation of several recommendations made as part of the project by the USAID environmental consulting team. For example, in the last year a large salt pond near Cockleshell Bay, a nursery area for fish slated for protection, has been filled in. Seagrass beds along the sea floor, which provide prime habitat for several marine species, have been cleared with a drag line. A large area nearby has been cleared to provide a storage area for heavy construction equipment. These developments were made in preparation for the construction of a large hotel, which sits unfinished. A small bar and restaurant have been built on the east side of Mosquito Bay without a building permit. A retroactive building permit was later granted for them (SK 20).

Officials of the IDB have said that the Bridgetown Fishing Harbor predated the "environmental period" of the bank, although the IDB often states in official documents that it started incorporating environmental concerns into its operations with the creation of an interdepartmental Environmental Management Committee (EMC) in 1979 (B 34).[48] Given the historical resistance of the bank to instituting environmental reforms, this may be partially true, but it does not tell the whole story.

The Barbados government asked the IDB to fund the Bridgetown Fisheries Harbor in 1982. The project agreement for the design and construction of the harbor was not executed until November 1984. In the same year the IDB established the EMC. The EMC, which can be termed a quasi-political body as its members are also the heads of the bank's main departments, could have required that the environmental impact of the project be evaluated, but it did not, despite the fact that important natural resources were at stake. There are several possible reasons why the IDB did not conduct an environmental analysis of this large project.

First, the IDB did not have formal environmental review guidelines. As a result, environmental review procedures for projects were applied unevenly, with no objective criteria to guide bank staff. It was up to the discretion of the staff, overseen by the EMC, to decide whether and how an environmental analysis should be performed. The lack of formal environmental procedures reflected a general reluctance by the IDB to be held accountable for the environmental consequences of its projects.[49] The historical resistance of key IDB members, such as Brazil and Venezuela, helped create this situation. In addition, political differences between the bank's Washington, D.C., headquarters and the Barbados field office also weakened its capacity for environmental protection.

In 1986 when the Barbados government proposed extending the large breakwater for the harbor, the IDB's technical staff in the Barbados office was opposed. They felt that extending the breakwater could cause sedimentation of the harbor and adjacent river mouth, significantly increasing the long-term cost of the project. The staff also questioned the use of sophisticated technology for the harbor, since a much smaller pilot fisheries project at Ostins on the south coast was "a disaster," with the ice plant inoperable most of the time (B 17).

IDB staff in the Barbados office used the opportunity presented by the redesign of the breakwater to try to address the environmental impact of the project. When the Barbados Ministry of Agriculture, as the sponsor of the harbor, was seeking a permit for the breakwater redesign from national planning authorities, the Barbados IDB staff asked the government to consult the national Coastal Conservation Project Unit (CCPU), which—ironically—is funded by the IDB. The CCPU recommended that additional studies be done to assess the environmental impact of the project, including the effect of increased fishing pressure on the fish population, and possible problems related to sedimentation, water quality, and coastal hydrology. However, the bank's staff in Washington, D.C., apparently did not support this request, which was also opposed by the Barbados government, so the project proceeded without any environmental evaluation.

The history of both the Southeast Peninsula Development Project and the Bridgetown Fishing Harbor showed a resistance among senior officials in USAID and the IDB to including environmental concerns in large projects. There also seems to be a conflict in these agencies between politically appointed professionals whose main goal is to facilitate projects, and technical staff who are concerned with carrying out environmental policies. The influence of the professionals is stronger than that of the technicians, so efforts to protect the environment are not carried out. One reason for this is the lack of formal and meaningful career incentives to implement environmental policies and regulations within the donor agencies.

Lack of Environmental Incentives

The professionals within the donor agencies who are in charge of key departments and offices responsible for choosing and approving projects do not have any formal career incentives to implement environmental policies. When the job performance of career professionals employed within the donor agencies are evaluated, one of the most important criteria is related to how many projects they successfully complete. As a result, upper-level professional staff members aggressively promote projects. Since environmental concerns can interrupt projects and hamper the flow of funding from the donor to the borrower, they are not given a priority as part of the project cycle.

In the case of USAID, mission directors are given job performance ratings based on how efficiently they spend money. With large projects like the Southeast Peninsula Development Project, which cost nearly $17 million, mission directors' job advancement is largely dependent on successfully completing the project. The St. Kitts project was the last major project completed by the mission director for the Caribbean office, who left the region shortly after the road was completed. Clearly, he too wanted the road built without delay.

The IDB has instituted some career incentives for its technical staff who carry out environmental surveys and assessments, but it does not offer any such incentives for professionals such a senior managers, project managers, administrators, and planners in charge of project design, approval, or execution. Since the bank does not reward professionals for integrating environmental concerns into development projects, but does reward them for promoting the flow of project funds, it is unlikely that policies intended to protect natural resources will be implemented. This problem is exacerbated because donors focus on large projects that are planned and implemented using a fixed cycle.

PROBLEMS WITH THE PROJECT CYCLE

The donors all use a similar process, based on an established cycle, to organize and process projects.[50] Policy-based environmental reforms require the strengthening of public institutions in borrowing countries. It is very difficult to strengthen institutions within the constraints of the project cycle. This is a major reason why environmental policies that accompany large projects are not implemented. The project cycle serves as a bias against policy reforms that cannot be easily accomplished within its established structure and limited time frame, which serve to act as disincentives to environmental policy reforms.

In St. Kitts, USAID required that the government adopt a series of environmental policies to protect the natural resources on the undeveloped southeast peninsula. The intent of the agency was to have these policies in place and working by the time the project was completed. But, in the words of an official familiar with the project, USAID "did not see that the environmental planning process established a presence in government, before building the road" (SK 17).

One of the conditions that USAID imposed on the St. Kitts government was that it adopt a new comprehensive national environmental law. The intent of the National Conservation and Environment Protection Act was to replace fragmented, outmoded legislation, and to create a National Conservation Commission to oversee its implementation. A United States–based attorney specializing in conservation law visited St. Kitts and drafted a preliminary law. The purpose of the preliminary draft was to obtain comments from the St. Kitts government. But the government was under pressure to adopt a national environmental policy to avoid a delay in the project. As a result, the government adopted the law without giving the attorney the chance to modify it to fit local political and cultural conditions, which would have increased the possibility that it would be implemented (SK 22). The result was a law that does not work. It does not focus on the practical problems of implementation endemic to the St. Kitts government. The government has yet to enforce any of its provisions. The National Conservation Commission has not been appointed, despite numerous promises of the attorney general to do so. Once it signed the project agreement with St. Kitts, USAID lost any leverage it could use to urge the government to enact environmental reforms, as the funding for the project was guaranteed (SK 12).

Once construction of the road to the peninsula was started, Kittians and USAID environmental staff were shocked at the damage it caused. The original road design, prepared years earlier by a British consultant for the British Development Division, had been replaced by a computer-generated design requiring 50–110 meter vertical cuts and fills exposing over eight acres of earth and bisecting the crown of Timothy Hill.[51] The scarring of the hill, and subsequent risk to nearby coral reefs and mangroves due to sedimentation, was contrary to USAID's stated intent to promote the environmentally sensitive development of the peninsula.[52] What was originally supposed to be a small two-lane road now resembled a highway, out of scale with the island environment, and symbolic of what had gone wrong with the project. USAID simply tried to accomplish too much in too short a time.

Another problem with adhering to the project cycle was the handling of the environmental experts for the project. Originally, the contract for the USAID environmental consulting team, who were responsible for drafting environmental guidelines and staffing the government board that reviews development applications, was to expire in July 1989. But the road was not finished by that time. Without the USAID consultants, no one would be responsible for trying to protect the endangered natural resources on the peninsula. The government still lacked its own professional staff that could have acted as a counterpart for the USAID environmental team, as its Central Planning Unit had basically dissolved the year before, leaving one employee to handle all of the environmental, building permit, and land use review for the country (SK 12). The USAID contract was extended a few months, and the chief of party retained as an independent consultant, but the discontinuity that resulted would not have been necessary if the institution-building aspect of the project, essential to implementing the environmental policies accompanying the project, had been initiated earlier and continued after the road was constructed. As if to underscore its lack of institutional capacity to undertake environmental reforms, the government still had only one person in its national planning office as of late 1993. Similar problems with weak institutional capacity were also a major factor when the IDB sponsored the Bridgetown Fishing Harbor in Barbados.

The Bridgetown Fishing Harbor followed the standard project cycle. The dominance of the single-project model of development was a major reason environmental concerns were ignored, and also poses problems for the current environmental reforms under way at the bank. It is clear that the professional and technical staff of the IDB was under tremendous pressure to complete the harbor. They did not want to tolerate the delay that would occur if the environmental concerns voiced by the regional staff and the Barbados CCPU were examined in detail. There are several reasons why the bank felt pressured to ignore environmental concerns and maintain the predetermined project schedule.

The Bridgetown project was the first major fisheries project undertaken by the IDB (B 17, 31). It wanted to complete it as soon as possible to establish a successful track record for projects of this type. The bank also did not want to deviate from the project cycle because delays could increase the cost of the harbor. Increased costs could not be tolerated because the rate of return for the harbor was estimated at 12.1 percent, characterized by IDB officials as "razor thin" because it barely met the acceptable rate of return of 12 percent established by the bank (B 42). It would take valuable time, not accounted for in the project cycle, to determine whether the project would negatively impact the environment. As a result, environmental studies were not done. The bank's use of the project cycle causes other problems that are also obstacles to environmental reform.

When the IDB reviews the environmental aspects of a project, it does so in the analysis portion of the project cycle. The analysis is done by bank staff in the Washington, D.C., headquarters. This reflects the IDB's focus on analysis at the front end of a project, which results in fewer institutional resources being available for project implementation (35, 42). The bank's field offices are responsible for project implementation, including monitoring and enforcing any environmental requirements handed down by Washington. It is here that the environmental performance of the bank drops off sharply.

Even though the field offices are responsible for implementing projects, including enforcing conditions to protect natural resources, they generally do not have technical staff trained in environmental planning. Personnel in the field offices are usually chosen for other skills, such as engineering, economics, or project management. The result is that staff in the field offices are generally unaware of the IDB's environmental policies, and are not trained to enforce them (B 42). This has caused a real weakness in the ability of the IDB to implement environmental reforms in the field. This problem will still exist even if proposed environmental reforms take place as planned.

As part of the effort to make the IDB more accountable to environmental concerns, it created a new Environmental Protection Division in 1989. This is a very positive step. The bank is instituting new EIA standards and has formalized these standards for all proj-ects. They give the responsibility for implementing environmental protection measures that result from the EIA process to borrowing countries where projects are located (B 44). However, given the tremendous emphasis that political leaders in developing countries place on promoting economic growth, and the control they exert over civil servants, it is very unlikely that countries will make the hard choice to implement environmental safeguards. Yet countries would have to implement their own environmental reforms through this process in order for the bank's environmental reform strategy to be successful. The result is that the bank has announced what seems like an environmental reform strategy, which in reality is almost totally dependent on borrowing countries for its implementation, countries that have no virtually no incentive to implement it.

The IDB is proposing to provide technical assistance to civil servants in its client countries to teach them how to do environmental analysis in the hope they will implement its new environmental policies. However, as my case studies in the Eastern Caribbean show, the missing ingredient in borrowing countries is not technical expertise, but political will and economic incentives that promote conservation, and the bank's policy provides neither.

PROBLEMS WITH LARGE-SCALE DEVELOPMENT PROJECTS

Donors use large-scale projects because they provide the greatest economic impact. While large projects can provide the best opportunity for improving economic conditions, they present their own kind of difficulties. Large projects are complex, often requiring several mid-course corrections before they are successfully completed. Large projects also require the borrowing country to have the institutional capacity to implement them. When institutional capacity is limited, new aspects of the development process such as environmental policies, which place an additional burden on civil servants, do not receive adequate attention.

The proposed Pitons National Park on St. Lucia was a large project that encountered these problems. The objective of the OAS in proposing the park was to promote economic growth while protecting natural resources. This is a very positive goal, and to support it OAS staff prepared an elaborate feasibility study enumerating the benefits of the park. The study showed that the park would generate far greater economic benefit than the private tourist resort which was eventually built in the midst of the proposed park.[53] Although the failed park proposal may have met the same fate regardless of the soundness of the OAS park-planning process, OAS park planners did make some strategic choices that made the project more difficult to implement. One strategic choice was to link the proposed park to a large, complex plan to redevelop the entire waterfront area of Soufriere, the nearby town.

When the OAS presented the park proposal to the government, the Soufriere Development Committee (SDC) simultaneously unveiled its master plan for Soufriere, the nearby town. The SDC is a group of influential businesspeople and community leaders whose goal is to promote economic growth in this remote part of St. Lucia. The centerpiece of the master plan was the proposed Pitons National Park.

The master plan is a multifaceted program to redevelop and revitalize Soufriere. The components of the plan include the national park, cruise-ship facilities, condominiums, a marina, shops, restaurants, bars, offices, several small hotels, and dozens of tourist-related retail businesses, such as a travel agency, a scuba shop, and bicycle rentals. The plan also envisions new community parks, a health spa, and a new road through town to serve the projects.[54] This ambitious plan would involve a complete redevelopment of the waterfront, requiring the relocation of a garbage dump, an oil storage facility, a sewage outfall, and a senior citizens home.

When the OAS and the SDC linked their projects together, they created what would likely be the largest project ever undertaken in St. Lucia. Implementation of this combined project, or the park by itself, requires a long-term planning program. But as has been documented, St. Lucia does not have the institutional capacity for long-term planning.[55] Project implementation would also require a complex series of political decisions and government actions that are difficult to obtain given pressing day-to-day problems in the country, and the limited technical and financial resources within the government (SL 6, 12).

The goal of promoting economic growth while preserving limited natural resources is a good one, and consistent with the projects that the Department of Regional Development sponsors. But the massive size of the project, especially when linked with the Soufriere master plan, is well beyond the capability of the government. The same is true of environmental components of the Southeast Peninsula Project in St. Kitts. In both instances, the donors adopted environmentally sound policies but could not get them implemented. But the lack of local institutional capacity to implement such massive policy initiatives should not have been a surprise to the donors.

Consultants for the OAS and the Organization of Eastern Caribbean States (OECS) have analyzed the institutional capability for natural resource planning in these countries.[56] They have found that public institutions have significant problems implementing existing laws, and have little capacity for long-term planning and public management. As an official familiar with efforts to increase the institutional capacity of the St. Kitts government said, "The country is learning very slowly how to deal with the planning process; this kind of change takes a long time here" (SK 25). If the donors had targeted additional resources for institution building, and designed smaller-scale projects that were easier to implement, it would have helped these small countries to pursue environmentally sound development projects.

SUMMARY

International development assistance agencies have been under increasing political pressure, mainly from United States-based environmental groups and the United States Congress, to institute environmental reforms. There are several competing objectives that are part of the development process, including the need for economic growth and the use of development assistance to carry out foreign aid policies, that have slowed environmental reform. In particular, the dependence of many countries on donor agencies for foreign investment has made it especially difficult to implement environmental reforms because of these countries' desperate need for investment capital.

Since the early 1980s when the United States passed the Caribbean Basin Initiative and sponsored a military intervention in Grenada to oust a pro-Leninist government, it has reasserted its foreign policy interest in the region. As a result, the amount of development assistance from the United States has greatly increased. Two agencies that the United States uses to promote development and continue its program of unification with the Caribbean and Latin America are the IDB and USAID. These agencies spend millions of dollars each year in the Eastern Caribbean. Both agencies are attempting to implement environmental reforms required by the United States Congress, but have had mixed results.

USAID has effectively integrated environmental concerns into a wide range of activities, but has trouble carrying out its own environmental policies in the field because of overarching political interests that control the agency. In the case of USAID and its Southeast Peninsula Development Project on St. Kitts, a 1984 directive from the agency's deputy director to "get a project going in the next 30 days" sent a clear signal to the Caribbean Regional Development Office to complete the project without delay. The project was accompanied by several new environmental policies, included in the project by the regional staff, that have been only partially implemented, placing the abundant natural resources of the peninsula at great risk. The agency did not allocate sufficient resources to build the institutional capacity for environmental reform in the government prior to building the project. USAID also failed to plan "beyond the road," and underestimated the time and money it would take to enact change in the government.

In 1984 when the IDB undertook the Bridgetown Fishing Harbor it totally neglected the possible environmental impact of the project. The 12.1 percent rate of return for the harbor barely met the 12 percent minimum required by the bank, so delays to conduct environmental research were not tolerated. Recent reforms within the Bank may improve its environmental accountability, but the current plan to delegate responsibility to recipient countries to carry out their own environmental assessments is not likely to result in the protection of limited or fragile natural resources. The political pressures in developing countries are too great for anyone to carry out objective, complete, and accurate environmental studies there, and national governments lack the resources to implement any policies that might result from such studies.

Other major problems that prevent donor agencies from implementing their own environmental policies include an excessive dependence on large-scale projects that overwhelm the institutional capacity of governments, a lack of career incentives for professionals within the agencies to implement environmental policies, and constraints of the standard project cycle that prevent these professionals from carrying out long-term programs to protect natural resources.

What does the record of the development assistance agencies tell us? In combination with the failure of many developing countries to successfully undertake environmental reforms, this record tells us that there is definite room for improvement. But improving the implementation of environmental policies, as we have seen from the case studies, is exceedingly difficult. If there is to be any opportunity for improving the record of environmental protection in development assistance agencies and developing countries, their collective approach to decision-making must change. The first step in this needed change is to shift from a closed decision-making process to a more open one that can account more fully for environmental concerns.

Chapter Seven

SUGGESTIONS FOR STRENGTHENING ENVIRONMENTAL POLICY IMPLEMENTATION

We have seen why environmental policies fail. In general terms, there are two main reasons for this failure. First, even with the best intentions, the underlying complexities that affect decision making in both donor agencies and developing countries make policy reform very difficult to achieve. The combination and interdependence of conflicting political, cultural, and economic conditions make it particularly hard to implement environmental policies in an effective manner. Second, environmental concerns are treated as tangents to the development process; policies, laws, and regulations intended to preserve limited natural resources are treated as add-ons to it, and as a result, are given a low priority by many donor agencies and developing countries. Policies intended to protect natural resources are seriously constrained by the temporal limitations of the standard project cycle and the lack of political will within donor institutions and countries to embrace procedural reforms that threaten the way they do business.

Environmental policies and the natural ecosystems they are supposed to protect do not fit neatly into existing institutional niches. There is a limit to the responsiveness of policies that are imported, ignore local culture, and exclude key stakeholders. I believe that in order for environmental polices to be effectively implemented, all of the major stakeholders need to participate in a policy-making process that is more open. An open process is needed to design strategies for environmental policy implementation that integrate politics, economics, and culture, transcending the barriers erected by the traditional approach to development that treats them as separate, unrelated components. An open process needs to account for the interests of all of the stakeholders affected by development, including donor agencies, national politicians, civil servants, resource users, and environmental NGOs. If any one of the stakeholding groups is left out, it will leave a gap the others will use to pursue their own policies, counteracting the best efforts to strengthen and promote environmental reform. This type of reform will also strengthen local and national institutions in general, making them more accessible and accountable to the diverse needs of the public, as should be the case in democratic societies.

Programs to improve environmental policy implementation must account for four key factors: politics within national governments, politics within donor agencies, the role of national culture, and a near-total reliance on short-term economic development strategies. Any attempt to improve the way that environmental policies are implemented has to systemically account for these factors on a country-by-country basis. Efforts to improve environmental policies have to originate in three key groups: donor agencies, national governments in developing countries, and non-governmental agencies specializing in environmental policy.

CHARACTERISTICS OF THE CLOSED DYSFUNCTIONAL APPROACH TO POLICY MAKING

Environmental policies, especially those that are required by donor agencies as a condition of development projects, are created by a decision-making process that is basically closed (see Figure 2).

This closed process reflects the priorities within donor agencies and borrowing countries that promote development without seriously considering the environmental damage that will result. This process is dysfunctional because it excludes key stakeholders and ignores several vital elements of policy making, such as the culture of decision making in developing countries and the political behavior of donor agencies. Top policy makers in donor agencies and borrow-

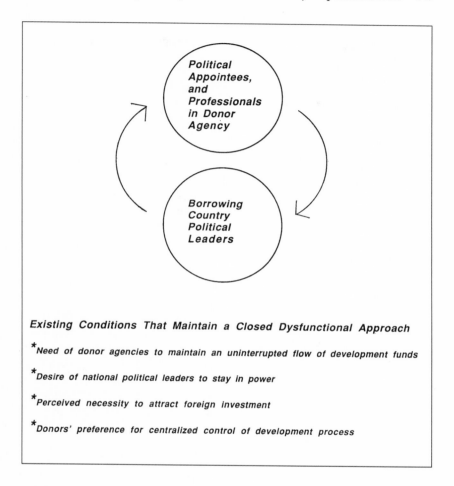

FIGURE 2
The Closed Dysfunctional Approach to Decision Making

ing countries are motivated to promote development that causes environmental damage because of four main factors: the need to maintain the flow of development funds, the desire to stay in power, a preference for centralized control of the development process, and a perceived necessity to attract foreign investment. The result is a closed, dysfunctional approach to development decisions that promotes the degradation of limited natural resources.

This closed approach promotes environmental degradation in several ways. When civil servants within government agencies that are responsible for natural resource management (i.e. forestry, agriculture, fisheries, etc.) are excluded from development decisions, invariably so are resource users whose livelihoods depend on the health of the environment. Information about the environment, such as whether a development will impair the stability of a local fishery or the productivity of agricultural land, is not considered by decision makers. Environmental NGOs, which have the expertise to promote economic stability by training resource users how to produce more efficiently while protecting the natural resources they depend on, are also excluded. The exclusion of these two groups increases the likelihood that fragile natural resources will be damaged.

Perhaps the most important element of this closed approach is how it reflects the behavior of the key decision makers who are involved. National political leaders know that the primary interest of political appointees and professionals in the donor agencies is to keep projects moving and to complete them as quickly as possible. Political appointees and professionals in the donor agencies know that political leaders in the countries control the political process, and that their highest priority is to attract foreign investment by approving big development projects.

The behavior of policy makers in both the developing countries and the donor agencies is mutually reinforcing. Both groups realize that if environmental policies are enforced, projects will probably be delayed. Decisions to ignore or downplay environmental concerns set precedents that influence civil servants and environmental technicians, who know that their superiors will not look favorably on their efforts to enforce policies intended to protect natural resources.

The mutually reinforcing behavior of policy makers within donor agencies and developing countries is exacerbated by the procedural constraints of the standard development process, epitomized by the standard project cycle. The steps in the development process are predetermined. There is not enough flexibility within the project cycle to accommodate major new policy initiatives such as environmental laws and regulations. Environmental reforms are usually included in the development process by slightly modifying the existing project cycle, rather than instituting new procedures that are tailored to the special characteristics of environmental problems. It can take several years to implement new environmental policies, especially when they represent a major shift in the way that a country makes decisions. Public institutions need to be reformed, personnel hired and trained, and funds provided to pay for them. It is difficult to complete these tasks within the temporal and financial constraints of the standard project cycle.

For example, environmental impact assessments are now being done by several donors in an attempt to protect natural resources, but they have limited influence on how measures to protect natural resources are actually implemented. By the time that a project is identified, a tentative financing package assembled, and a funding commitment obtained, the momentum that has been created prevents the recommendations in an environmental analysis from being followed. This happened with the Southeast Peninsula Project on St. Kitts. Despite extensive, expensive, and complex efforts by USAID to promote environmental reforms in the country, most of these reforms have not been implemented because of the tremendous economic and political pressure to simply approve and build projects. In the case of the Bridgetown Fisheries Harbor in Barbados, environmental concerns were ignored entirely, because of the political pressure to build the project as quickly as possible. These cases appear to support the proposition that environmental reforms cannot be fit into the straitjacket of the project cycle.

The existing closed development process is also unable to account for the importance of the culture of decision making in developing countries. Even if legitimate environmental investigations are prepared for projects, subsequent recommendations to protect natural resources are not implemented because they do not conform to local cultural norms. The public policy process in developing countries is based on personal relationships, family ties, and party loyalty. Political leaders often lack the necessary political will to carry out environmental reforms. The standard project cycle does not allow for allocating sufficient time or financial resources to design and carry out a multiyear program of institution building to address these issues.

Even though donor agencies are subject to varying degrees of government oversight, their decision-making process is heavily weighted towards promoting development and maintaining a flow of projects. This philosophy is consistent with recent budget increases in the World Bank and the IDB, which are intended to provide funding for an increasing number of development projects each year. While the banks are under pressure from United States environmental groups and the United States Congress to accelerate environmental reforms, they are simultaneously funding more and more projects. These two objectives are in conflict, and this conflict has motivated the banks to adopt environmental reforms in a way that causes the least disruption to the project cycle and subsequent flow of funds.

Thus far, countries and donor agencies have attempted to adopt policies using a fragmented approach that reflects their own short-term economic and political interests. In addition, the nature of most large-scale environmental problems that are occurring in developing countries, such as depletion of fisheries, forests, and agricultural soil, water pollution, and widespread health problems, require long-term solutions. Environmental damage shows up years after projects have been approved and built. There is no accountability for environmental damage in less-developed countries that are dominated by short-term political and economic interests.[1] The combination of economic, political, and cultural factors that prevent environmental policies from being implemented effectively can be accounted for in a more open approach to development and policy making.

CHARACTERISTICS OF AN OPEN FUNCTIONAL APPROACH TO POLICY MAKING

In order for environmental policies to be effectively implemented, I believe that the public policy process needs to open up, to become more accessible. To do this, a new model of decision making needs to be implemented that integrates the essential elements of the implementation process and involves all of the affected stakeholders. This more open approach to policy implementation, which integrates environmental protection with the development process, cannot be accommodated within the constraints of the existing development paradigm. One way to implement a more open policy-making process is to have the stakeholders participate in a collaborative dialogue that uses a negotiation process.

A NEGOTIATED PARTNERSHIP FOR SUSTAINABLE DEVELOPMENT

The parties involved in international development can improve environmental policy implementation by participating in a collaborative negotiation process. A negotiation model needs to be created to reflect the specific needs of the development process, to fit within a framework that is acceptable to the participants, while improving the effectiveness of environmental policies on the national and international levels (see Figure 3). At the beginning of the process, projects suitable for a negotiation process need to be carefully chosen using three criteria: (1) the parties involved in the pro-

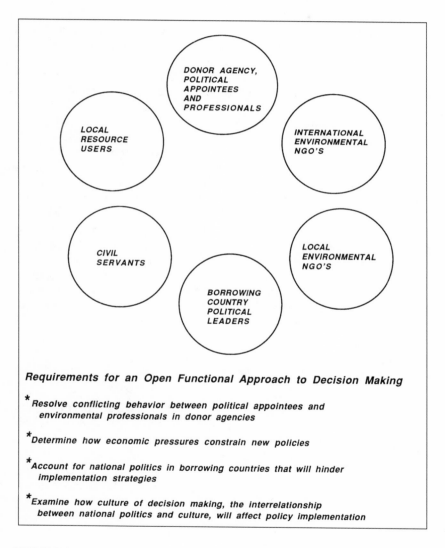

Requirements for an Open Functional Approach to Decision Making

*Resolve conflicting behavior between political appointees and environmental professionals in donor agencies

*Determine how economic pressures constrain new policies

*Account for national politics in borrowing countries that will hinder implementation strategies

*Examine how culture of decision making, the interrelationship between national politics and culture, will affect policy implementation

FIGURE 3
An Open Functional Approach to Decision Making

jects are willing to sit down to cooperatively design an approach to protect natural resources; (2) the parties possess the financial and political resources to make this approach work; (3) at least the first projects chosen have a high likelihood of success. Projects should be selected that will allow cooperative learning to take place among all of the parties involved.

The negotiation model needs to be based on similar cooperative efforts that have been undertaken to protect the environment. Different negotiations that have addressed international environmental concerns include the Convention on International Trade in Endangered Species, the Montreal Protocols for reducing chlorofluorocarbon emissions, the Treaty for the Protection of Migratory Birds and Game Mammals, and recent agreements to swap debt for nature in South America.[2]

These agreements were reached using the single-text model of negotiating. The parties reached a consensus by slowly modifying a single text that was ultimately transformed into a final agreement. This approach was used because the purpose of the negotiations was for the parties to reach an overall agreement on one basic issue, although several sub-issues existed that made the negotiations very complex. The model I am proposing must create a negotiation process that will be continually repeated with each project, compared to a negotiation model that deals with one monolithic issue at one time. Several preconditions have to be met to establish a creditable negotiation process designed to integrate environmental policy implementation into the development process.

PRECONDITIONS OF THE NEGOTIATION PROCESS

Several preconditions need to be met before a negotiation process can commence. Similar preconditions would be necessary for any negotiation that involves many parties and several issues, but in this instance they account for the specific complexities of the international development process, and the political and cultural conditions that are found in most developing countries. The first precondition relates to who will participate in the negotiation process.

Precondition 1: Participation

It is essential to establish who will take part in the negotiation process, as a stable result requires that all of the parties who are affected by it have a voice at the bargaining table. A negotiation can only be successful if it involves all of the stakeholders who have an interest in the outcome. In the context of environmental disputes in developing countries, the issue of participation is complicated by the high stakes generated by large donor-funded development projects.

Each of the stakeholders has a different motivation to participate in this open decision-making process. Donor agencies will benefit from a development process that accounts for environmental factors as it helps create a more certain investment climate, promoting long-term economic growth that is environmentally sustainable. Donors are also motivated by the need to implement their own environmental policies, as mandated by the United States Congress and their own governing boards. By taking part in a more open approach to policy making, donors will fulfill their mandate to promote development that meets basic human needs and promotes long-term self-reliance.

National political leaders also are motivated by several factors to participate in a more open development process. International pressure on the donor agencies will eventually force them to stop funding projects that cause environmental problems. Unless political leaders encourage changes in the development process that lead to better protection for natural resources, at some point they may not be eligible to receive development assistance. This in turn will create serious political problems at home for national leaders.

In addition, by preventing key stakeholders from participating in the public policy process, politicians have generated resentment that will cause long term political instability, contrary to their own primary self-interest, which is to stay in power. National politicians need to create a greater degree of political stability in their governments, by increasing each government's institutional capacity to implement public policies, which will enhance its self-reliance and reduce political and economic dependency on outside parties.

In many instances, civil servants in borrowing countries have taken the initiative to take a more active role in development decisions, but have been stopped by political leaders who exert near-total control over the political process. Civil servants who are responsible for natural resource management (i.e. in forestry, fisheries, agriculture, land-use planning, etc.) have often invested in a specialized college education to train for their work, and have made a personal and professional commitment to express their environmental values when participating in the public policy process. The positive motivation of civil servants is also shown by their involvement in political reform movements that attempt to open up the policy dialogue in countries where political leaders place strict limits on who can participate in decision making. Two examples of reform movements that civil servants participate in are environmental interest groups in St. Lucia and Barbados that are attempting to influence political leaders.

Environmental technicians in the donor agencies are motivated to take part in a negotiation process by the same basic factors as civil servants: a desire to place environmental concerns higher on the agenda of the policy process, so that administrators will be persuaded to allocate additional institutional resources to environmental reform. Being able to participate in a negotiated dialogue that places environmental concerns higher on the policy agenda, in essence creating a level playing field for the stakeholders, is a major motivation for both civil servants and environmental technicians to take part in a more open process.

Local resource users, such as farmers, fishers and charcoal producers, are motivated to take part in a negotiation process because it will give them the access to the political system that has been denied them. In addition, it is a way of tapping their specialized knowledge of the local natural environment. If this special knowledge is included in the design and implementation of development projects, environmental damage could be reduced. In turn, this will keep the local resource base intact, enabling resource users to continue their livelihoods.

International and local environmental NGOs are motivated to participate because they will gain political influence by being brought into the mainstream of the public policy process. It will allow international NGOs to efficiently target where their limited resources can best be used, in countries where environmental policies are integrated into the development process. Local NGOs will be able to form coalitions with international NGOs to receive financial and technical assistance, while providing crucial insights about the operation of national political systems. Local NGOs will become stronger as they use the framework of a formal negotiation process to work more closely with resource users, increasing the political influence of both groups.

Participation also involves how the right stakeholders will be chosen to take part in the negotiation process. It is important that all parties that have a legitimate interest in the outcome of a project be included, in order for the outcome to be stable. At the foundation of all democratic societies and their political institutions is the idea of fair and open decision making. The closed system of environmental decision making now in place in many donor agencies and developing countries in inherently undemocratic. This alone is reason enough to find a way to open up environmental policy making as a function of the development process. An essential element of democratic decision making is the issue of who takes part in decisions and whose interests they represent.

Precondition 2: Representation and Assistance for Weak Parties

After the stakeholders have been chosen, the negotiation process has to be designed to make sure they are adequately and equally represented. This is necessary because of the severe power imbalances between key stakeholders within the closed policy-making process. Civil servants are routinely overruled by political leaders. Resources users are often poor and uneducated. They lack access to political leaders and do not know how to participate in the public policy process. In donor agencies, environmental technicians are often overruled by professionals or political appointees. If these parties attempt to participate in a new, more open policy dialogue, they are subject to political retribution and personal persecution by more powerful stakeholders.

To help ensure a successful negotiation, guarantees have to be made to protect stakeholders who are politically and financially weak. Civil servants who fear political retribution may require legal guarantees to protect their jobs, careers, and families. Resource users are usually poorly organized and may not be comfortable with the formal surroundings in the urban capital in which negotiations usually take place. Resource users and other stakeholders may need technical and financial assistance as they are at a disadvantage because they lack scientific resources, are illiterate, or are simply not willing to attend public negotiating sessions. For example, resource users often depend on each day's catch or harvest to feed their families, and may need to be paid compensation to attend negotiation sessions.

The party that convenes the negotiation should be responsible for initially determining what type of assistance each stakeholder will need in order to take part. In turn, this implies that a successful negotiation may depend on long term institution building to improve the capacity of weak parties to take part in a public policy dialogue. Efforts to increase the institutional capacity of NGOs and resource users may have to be undertaken before these parties can take part in the negotiation process. Institution building can include training in basic administrative skills (e.g. bookkeeping, fund raising, use of the media), policy analysis, and conflict resolution. Once the institutional capacity of the weak parties is improved, subsequent negotiations can be initiated more easily.[3]

Guarantees that give legal protection to weak stakeholders, provide compensation for lost wages, or establish a program for institution building can be part of a prenegotiation agreement among all of the parties. However, even if the weak stakeholders are guaranteed that they will be legally protected, they may be unwilling to participate openly in the negotiation. Fear of retribution can be quite strong, especially in countries where environmental advocates have been labeled as anti-government, or imprisoned, or publicly denounced. Such actions often silence the most ardent critic of government policy. If parties are unwilling to participate even with guarantees, it is the responsibility of the convener and the neutral party that organizes and manages the negotiation process to ensure that the interests of parties who are not physically present will be adequately represented. The party that convenes the negotiation has other responsibilities as well.

Precondition 3: Legitimacy, Sponsorship, and the Neutral Mediator or Facilitator

The issue of legitimacy is particularly important in the context of political systems that are not highly developed, or where the public policy process lacks a tradition of public participation. The participants in a negotiation have to believe that the process they are engaged in is valid and genuine. If the stakeholders do not believe in the legitimacy of the negotiation process, or that it should be used to resolve a specific conflict, a formal negotiation will probably not work.

A negotiation process should include several key elements to gain legitimacy in the eyes of its participants. First, a successful negotiation has to account for the attitudes and perceptions of the stakeholders.[4] Second, the negotiation process has to represent the interests of all of the key stakeholders. Third, the stakeholders have to be shown how they can gain from participating in the negotiation process. This is particularly important in developing countries, given the anticipated skepticism of weak parties who have historically been excluded from the public policy process or strong parties who are afraid that they will lose power if they participate.

All of the stakeholders are responsible for creating legitimacy in the negotiation process. Donor agencies have the financial resources that give them the leverage that may be needed to convince other stakeholders to participate. The capital that donors bring to the development process may be needed to convince national politicians that a participatory approach to development is needed to protect natural resources. Conversely, borrowing countries may want to initiate a negotiation so they can convince donors to fund projects that meet local needs. NGOs can lend legitimacy to a negotiation by agreeing to provide technical support and scientific information about natural resources to be affected by a particular project. By showing a willingness to initiate or participate in a negotiation, all of the stakeholders can help legitimatize the process.

For a negotiation process to have the required sense of legitimacy, it needs to be convened by a legitimate party. There are several ways that a negotiation can be convened. Any stakeholder that has the institutional capacity and motivation to improve environmental policies can act as the convener. This could be a donor agency, a government ministry, a quasi-government organization such as a trade association or professional group, a private foundation, a university, or a local NGO. Donor agencies have the financial and technical resources that a negotiation requires, and are motivated by a need to promote environmental reforms as part of the development process. This makes them a likely candidate to act as the convener for a negotiation process. National governments can also convene a negotiation. They possess the political leverage to convince other stakeholders to come to the bargaining table, and can benefit from institution-building programs that accompany the negotiation process. Local NGOs have several advantages that enable them to act as conveners. They are familiar with the national public policy process, possess knowledge about natural resources, and often have existing relationships with donor agencies that sponsor projects.

To be legitimate, a negotiation process also has to account for the cultural differences of the parties involved. Negotiations about development projects will usually involve parties from different cultures. Representatives from a donor agency are often from the United States or Europe, and may be relatively new on the job because of the job rotation most agencies use. Representatives from international NGOs, probably have a similar background, while those from the national government, local NGOs, and resource users in the country are from the local culture. To account for cultural differences, the convener can use an elicitive feedback process which is described in step 4 of the negotiation process in the following section.

A legitimate negotiation process should also include initial ground rules to protect stakeholders who are politically weak.

Ground rules can include commitments to protect weaker parties from political retribution, an agreement to depersonalize the debate so parties can focus on their real interests, and the responsibilities of the chairperson.[5] These provisions also relate to the accountability of the stakeholders, and their ability to keep commitments made during the negotiation.

The parties may also benefit from a pre-negotiation condition that governs how they will communicate with the media. The parties can designate a media subcommittee and establish written guidelines describing who, how, and when the media will be informed of the progress or results of the negotiation. Establishing media guidelines as a precondition of negotiation can also help prevent the negotiation process from being used by the opposition party to attack the majority party. This step may be needed to convince the majority party to approve the government's participation in the negotiation process. Allowing a member of the opposition party, especially one who is knowledgeable about environmental issues, to take part in the negotiation will often be necessary to create a negotiated outcome that is politically stable.

To be legitimate, a negotiation should be assisted by a neutral helper. Different negotiations usually require different types of help. There are several different methods of dispute resolution that can be used. The two types that are usually appropriate for complex negotiations involving environmental policies in developing countries are facilitation and mediation.

A facilitator is a neutral person whose primary role is to organize the negotiation, to make sure that it gets started, and to help participants understand the process they are engaged in. The facilitator is concerned more with the procedural aspects of the negotiation than its substance. A mediator is also an outside neutral party, but takes a more active role in the negotiation process than a facilitator. The mediator is skilled in identifying areas of potential agreement, helps the participants discuss the substance of their differences, and assists them in creating a packaged agreement that advances the interests of all of the parties.[6] The convener, whether it is a donor agency, the government, or an NGO, needs to examine the needs of the negotiating partners and determine whether a facilitator or a mediator is needed. Because of the complex nature of environmental disputes, it may be desirable to chose a neutral helper who is qualified to serve as both a facilitator and a mediator. Negotiations that initially need process-oriented help often need substantive assistance as they progress. A facilitator should be capable of making the transition to mediation during a negotiation, as he or she gains trust from the stakeholders.

It is crucial that the helper be perceived as neutral by all of the parties. Even if the convener perceives itself as being neutral, if other stakeholders perceive it as having a vested interest in the outcome of the negotiation, it needs to bring in an outside party to act as a neutral helper, rather than supplying the helper from its own staff. There are several professional organizations that specialize in negotiation who can advise the convener how to find a suitable helper.

The qualifications of the neutral helper are very important. The credibility of the entire negotiation program depends on the sensitivity the convener exhibits when choosing a neutral who both meets the needs of the stakeholders and is someone they trust. I believe that a mediator in this context has to possess two major qualities.[7] First, the mediator needs to have substantial expertise in issues related to environment-development conflicts, in addition to expertise in the procedural aspects of a negotiation process. Second, the mediator has to have experience in cross-cultural negotiations, and be able to design a negotiation strategy that reflects the cultural norms of the stakeholders.

Once a mediator has been chosen who possesses the necessary qualifications, it usually will be necessary to find a co-mediator from the borrowing country who is an expert in the local culture, including the indigenous language and the culture of decision making within the political system. A multi-cultural mediation team will give a negotiation the credibility and substantive expertise that it needs to deal effectively with the complexities of environment-development disputes and their underlying cultural component, while providing accountability to the parties.

Precondition 4: Accountability

In societies where key stakeholders have been largely excluded from the public policy process, the negotiation process has to include provisions to assure the accountability of the participants. Accountability relates to the capability and willingness of the participants to be held answerable for their actions, during and after the negotiations. To address these concerns in the negotiation process, the convener should help the participants understand their duties and responsibilities to the process, and to each other. This is especially important in situations where stakeholders have not had the benefit of legal protection.

An example of how the lack of legal protection can inhibit stakeholders from participating in a policy dialogue is the way that planning legislation is not effectively implemented in many developing countries. The duties and jurisdiction of planning authorities are often ambiguous. Planning legislation is generally unclear and lacks precise language that would empower civil servants to carry out planning laws. Permit systems are typically full of loopholes and inconsistencies. Civil servants are commonly hesitant to promote environmental reforms within this uncertain framework, as the legal system does not afford them legal protection from political retribution. The convener can help the parties devise ground rules or legal protection in the prenegotiation stage.

The concept of accountability also includes the need to use objective criteria in a negotiation process. In developing countries, policy decisions are often made without fully considering how development will impact the environment. The environmental impact process is an attempt to remedy this shortcoming. However, an environmental analysis is only effective if it is translated into a binding commitment. Guarantees that borrowing countries will implement the findings of environmental assessments need to be linked to conditions contained in their lending agreements with donor agencies. A negotiation process that accompanies each project can provide the framework for establishing agreements that improve the accountability of the environmental assessment process, and its use of objective criteria to strengthen implementation of environmental protection measures.

The convener should consider who can best represent the stakeholding groups during the negotiation. This relates to the ability of the representatives to make binding commitments on behalf of their constituencies. Deciding who the representatives will be is of particular importance in developing countries because of the intensely personal nature of the political process, and the difficulty that may be encountered by outside parties, such as donor agencies, when they try to convince governments to enforce the specific elements of an agreement, such as new environmental policies. For a negotiation to be successful, the agreement that comes out of it has to be implemented. The ability of the parties involved to follow through on commitments they make on behalf of the organizations they represent, such as politicians who represent the government, is crucial. If agreements are not kept, trust between the parties can be severely damaged. It is particularly important that this tendency to break agreements be guarded against when parties are involved in a formal negotiation process for the first time.

The convener, with the advice of the neutral helper, can identify individuals from each stakeholder group who have the authority
to speak for the organization they represent. From the donor agency,
this should include representatives from the headquarters who are
responsible for project design and finance, and staff from its field office who are responsible for project implementation and environmental protection. It is important that both groups participate on
behalf of the donor.

For the government, representatives should include senior civil
servants from key ministries, such as finance and planning, who
have close personal relationships to political leaders and are aware
of the institutional capacity within the government to implement
different aspects of the negotiated agreement. Whenever possible,
permanent secretaries should be selected. Officials from ministries
that are responsible for implementing environmental policies should
also be present. The possibility that governments will change after
national elections has to be accounted for, so that new political leaders are bound by agreements made by a previous administration.
Representatives from NGOs and resource users will probably be evident as these groups are small and do not have many members to
serve as negotiators.

If the resource users or other stakeholders are not sufficiently
comfortable to be physically present at the negotiating sessions, the
neutral helper needs to determine how their interests can be represented at the bargaining table in their absence. Their interests can be
represented by a coalition partner who shares the same interests and
is willing to speak for them during the negotiations. The neutral
helper can represent a party who is not present by reminding the
other stakeholders of the importance of considering the interests of
all parties to create an outcome that is durable and stable. The convener should start to think about which strategy is appropriate before the negotiations start.

After the preliminary steps for a successful open policy dialogue are taken, the actual negotiation process can start. The negotiation process itself can be organized in a series of steps.

STEPS NEEDED TO PROMOTE EFFECTIVE ENVIRONMENTAL REFORM

To strengthen and promote environmental reform, several
steps can be included as part of a negotiation process. They are offered here as one way to address the constraints to environmental

policy implementation that exist in borrowing countries and donor agencies.

The following steps can be initiated at many places in the project cycle, depending on when the stakeholders decide that a negotiation process is needed. If the objective of the stakeholders is to develop a coordinated strategy to implement environmental policies that accompany a development project, they may want to initiate negotiations at the beginning of the project cycle when a project is still in the conceptual stage, before the parties have developed firm ideas about it that can hinder the environmental policy implementation process.

These steps for strengthening and promoting environmental policy implementation do not have to be followed exactly. There are many ways to promote effective environmental reform. The following steps are one way.

1. Evaluate the institutional capability of host country
2. Conduct a culturally sensitive stakeholder analysis
3. Choose the facilitator or mediator
4. Design an "elicitive model" for the negotiation process
5. Initiate negotiations to create an implementation strategy
6. Create performance standards to link the implementation plan with the project agreement
7. Agree on a time frame and procedure for post-project evaluation of the implementation plan

Evaluate the Institutional Capacity of the Borrower

Evaluating the institutional capacity of the borrower is necessary to determine the likelihood that environmental policies accompanying projects will be implemented. This can be done by a donor, an NGO, or the country itself. To evaluate institutional capacity, several tasks need to be carried out. As with the other steps in this process, these tasks can be undertaken by any qualified analyst, usually working for the convener or neutral helper. Throughout the following discussion of the steps, I will use the word *analyst* to describe the person who carries them out.

First, the analyst should conduct interviews with civil servants in the borrowing country and with environmental NGOs in the region to determine whether existing environmental laws and regulations are being implemented. If a preliminary analysis shows that these policies are either wholly or partially unenforced, the analyst should identify where the bottlenecks are in the local political process. Bottlenecks typically include a closed public policy process, lack of public participation, political limitations placed on national planning agencies, unclear and conflicting environmental statutes, and laws that lack administrative guidelines for implementing them. Once bottlenecks are identified, the stakeholders can start to develop linkages between the project and an institution-building program to improve the chances that project-specific environmental protection measures will be carried out.

An important goal of this initial step is for the stakeholders to start to understand how the national and local cultures of decision making affect the public policy process of the borrower. This includes the pivotal role that political leaders play in policy implementation, how they depend on traditional social relationships to make decisions, and the sustained effort the donor must make to build the personal relationships with national leaders that are needed to effectively promote environmental reform.

Conduct a Culturally Sensitive Stakeholder Analysis

Conducting a cultural stakeholder analysis involves identifying all of the parties that will be affected by the proposed project. It provides a detailed road map of how the political system includes and excludes parties affected by development projects. This analysis requires formal consultations with NGOs that are familiar with the political system and the culture of decision making in the borrowing country. Many stakeholders, especially resource users who are typically excluded from the public policy process, are hard to find. They may be politically or socially alienated, and unwilling to participate. But they possess valuable information about fragile natural resources—information that project planners need.

As part of the cultural stakeholder analysis, the analyst should identify who the stakeholders are, their interests in the project, who represents their interests, and how their interests are in conflict. This will show who makes policy decisions, and whose interests they represent. By identifying the most powerful stakeholders, it will become clear which parties have to take part in the negotiation to secure a binding commitment for the negotiated agreement.

The stakeholder analysis will also show who is excluded from the decision making process. Often the interests of unorganized stakeholders, such as resource users who provide vital services for the society, are not represented by the political system. The analyst can use this information to design a process for including stake-holders who have not been part of the public policy dialogue; such inclusion is also needed to reach an agreement that is enforceable.

Choose the Facilitator or Mediator

The convener, who has already been identified as part of the precon-ditions to negotiation, should choose an outside party to serve as the neutral facilitator or mediator, in consultation with the stakehold-ers who will take part in the dialogue. Having assessed the institu-tional capacity of the borrower and identified the interests of the stakeholders, the convener can now assess, in cooperation with the neutral helper, whether facilitation or mediation is needed.[8]

Given the complexity of environmental disputes, and the widely varying interests of the stakeholders, the neutral helper should be capable of acting as a facilitator or as a more active medi-ator. To maintain the accountability of the negotiation, the neutral helper should be approved by all of the parties who are taking part. The donor agency should have a list of qualified neutral helpers that can be circulated to the parties, so that one person can be chosen by consensus. If the mediator is not from the local culture, he or she should select, in consultation with the stakeholders, a co-mediator.

At this point the convener and mediator will normally start to design the specific elements of an organized negotiation process. This will typically include a set of ground rules or protocols that bind the negotiating parties to a set of rules governing communica-tion, how to reach consensus, and the behavior that will be ex-pected during all discussions. Ground rules can also spell out how technical and scientific information will be developed to help the negotiators reach a decision. This process is commonly called "joint fact-finding" and helps to provide high-quality, objective in-formation for the negotiators to consider when making decisions. The ground rules can also address the responsibility of each nego-tiator to keep their constituencies informed of the progress of the negotiation, so that they will be able to make binding commit-ments on behalf of the organization they represent. Finally, the ground rules should discuss the timing and work products of the ne-gotiation process. For example, it is often wise to design a negotia-tion process so that the negotiators reach at least one mini-agreement at each meeting, rather than trying to create a sin-gle grand accord near the end of the negotiation. A series of mini-agreements help maintain the interest and participation of the negotiators and are more easily understood. Using this approach, the collection of mini-agreements collectively comprise the overall agreement that the negotiators make by the end of their discussions.

Another crucial element of the negotiation process is how to set the agenda for negotiation, so that the stakeholders can see their concerns represented in the discussions. It is very important that the neutral helper continually stress that the negotiation process is owned by the participants; he or she is present to help the parties craft their own unique agreement. This sense of ownership will translate to a tangible asset of the policy implementation process when the energy, resources, and commitment of the negotiators are called upon to implement various aspects of the agreement after formal discussions are over.

Next, the convener and mediator will need to design a strategy to motivate the stakeholders to take part in the actual negotiation.[9] The convener may have to provide incentives to the stakeholders to get them to participate in the negotiation. The neutral helper can assist with this step by identifying the benefits that each party is likely to derive from the negotiation process, such as providing increased institutional capacity for the government or giving the donor a method of implementing mandated environmental policies. It is likely that environmental NGOs will already want to participate, as this may be the first time they have had a voice in strengthening environmental policies.

Design an Elicitive Model for the Negotiation Process

The negotiation model most often used in the United States depends heavily on a top-down approach that can bias the proceedings to favor the convener or the parties with the most sophisticated communication skills. To account for this, the convener should incorporate an elicitive feedback process into the negotiation model. To use this approach, the convener elicits from the participants how they deal with conflict, acting as a catalyst, rather than recommending a standard top-down method of dealing with conflict. This will help to frame the negotiation process within the setting of the local culture.[10] The mediator elicits stories from the stakeholders about what has happened to past environmental policies, whether they succeeded or failed, and why. This work can be started in the pre-negotiation stage before formal negotiations commence, and continued in the actual negotiation sessions.

The elicitive approach should recognize the difference between formal and informal authorities, and how they need to be included in an implementation process that reflects local cultural norms. For example, informal authorities, such as church leaders and village elders, may be able to exert social pressure to encourage compliance with environmental protection policies more effectively than government officials, who are limited by a lack of training and by a flawed regulatory system.[11]

The benefit of this approach is that it elicits the experiences of the participants to identify bottlenecks in the policy implementation process, in the context of the local culture of decision making. It will allow the implementation plan for environmental policies that results from the negotiation to be based on local conditions, opportunities, and constraints. To properly use an elicitive approach, the mediator may need to have a co-mediator from the local culture, especially if the stakeholders include indigenous people or residents from a rural community.

Initiate Negotiations to Create an Implementation Strategy

The convener, with the assistance of the mediator, initiates the actual negotiations, whose purpose is to design an implementation strategy for environmental policies or specific project-related measures to protect natural resources. Negotiations can take place in any location agreed to by the stakeholders, but in general it is desirable to hold them in the country where the project is located. The first step in the actual negotiations are for the neutral helper to explain the protocols, or ground rules, that govern the proceedings. The protocols should be agreed to by all of the participants to establish a procedural context for the discussions.[12] The mediator should tell the parties in clear language what the purpose and expected outcome of the negotiations are, namely, to reach a binding agreement linking development and the protection of natural resources.

Two important elements of the negotiation process that should be given special consideration relate to the culture of decision making. First, all of the stakeholders should participate in the negotiation sessions, and be able to represent their constituencies. This could cause a problem for national political leaders, who may want to send civil servants to represent their interests, and then be able to change the position of the government without being accountable to the rest of the stakeholders.

The second element of the negotiation process that deserves special attention is how to account for the importance of informal and formal authorities in policy making. Typically, negotiation sessions take place in the setting of a modern office. If the culture has an indigenous population, who are often the resource users who have special knowledge about natural resources, they may wish to conduct discussions among their constituents in a traditional setting. For example, in New Zealand when the indigenous Maori engage in negotiations with the politically dominant European culture, they take part in the primary negotiation sessions with other stakeholders, but also sponsor their own informal negotiations on the *marae*, their traditional meeting place, to gain consensus among members of the local community. This is known as the "two table" model of negotiation.

If indigenous people are among the stakeholders, the negotiation process should make allowances for them to conduct discussions in their own community throughout the negotiations. The mediator should pay special attention to these informal proceedings, as they may show how informal authority figures in the society can help implement the final negotiated agreement.

Create Performance Standards to Link the Implementation Plan with the Project Agreement

Once the stakeholders have agreed on how to design and enforce environmental policies, they need to negotiate performance standards. Performance standards are a tool that allows the parties to objectively evaluate the success of the final negotiated agreement, and provide guidelines for enforcing it. The final agreement typically consists of a series of actions to be taken by each of the parties to strengthen environmental policies. Each action that is agreed to should be accompanied by an objective standard that can be reviewed to determine whether a specific party is implementing it.

For example, the government may be required to establish a procedure for civil servants to review permit applications by developers, so they can prepare an objective analysis for the cabinet before it approves a project. The accompanying performance criteria could specify a date by which the cabinet will start using a specific method of objective analysis, and require the government to show the donor each year how development decisions have been affected by the new procedure. Or, the donor may require the government to include unorganized resource users as participants in development decisions. Such a requirement could be monitored by an NGO that prepares a required annual report, based on interviews with fishers, farmers, and other individuals, documenting whether and how they were contacted by the government when projects were being reviewed, and if any mitigation measures resulted in actions that actually protected natural resources.

Additional elements of an agreement might require the donor to provide funds to increase the institutional capacity of local environmental NGOs or ministries responsible for natural resource management prior to a project being built, while the government would agree to let these organizations take part in the planning process as projects are reviewed. This type of agreement is called a *contingent agreement*, where one party agrees to fulfill a commitment, triggering a second reciprocal commitment from a second party. These interlocking commitments often form the basis of complex multi-party multi-issue agreements, and are commonly used in international diplomatic negotiations. Again, annual reports prepared by a neutral party can accompany each action that is agreed to.

It is crucial that the performance standards be realistic, and conform to the cultural norms of the borrower. It is common for the parties involved in implementing environmental policies, even those from the country, to be think that they can increase institutional capacity in a year or two. Performance standards should account for the tendency to make unrealistic time estimates by using a multi-year schedule that extends over three to five years.

The final agreement will be stronger if it is linked to the project agreement between the borrower and the donor. The parties may choose to include provisions that tie fulfillment of the agreement to a phased payment schedule. When specific actions are taken as specified in the agreement, funds are then released for the development project. This will create direct financial incentives for the parties to carry out their responsibilities under the agreement.

Agree on a Time Frame and Procedure for Post-Project Evaluation of the Implementation Plan

The final agreement should include clear language that describes how the parties have agreed on a time frame and procedure for post-project evaluation of the implementation plan. This is essentially a summary of the performance criteria that accompany each action agreed to by the parties. To avoid miscommunication between the parties, and to make sure that each one knows what is expected of it, the final agreement should include a separate section summarizing the actions and performance standards agreed to by each party, and the penalties to be assessed if they fail to live up to the agreement.

To design an effective model for protecting natural resources in developing countries, the agendas for the stakeholders have to integrate four major elements of public policy implementation: national politics, the culture of decision making, economic conditions, and the behavior of donor agencies. It is the connections among these four elements of policy implementation, and the involvement of the major stakeholders, that will enable a collaborative negotiation process to succeed.

An integrated system to implement environmental policies or environmental protection measures is based on the active participation of four main parties: donor agencies, national politicians, resource users, and environmental NGOs. By following steps to open up the decision process, the stakeholders can work cooperatively to help resolve several of the problems that prevent environmental policies from being implemented. The open system of decision making will have a better chance to succeed if the major parties take the following actions.

ADVICE TO DONOR AGENCIES

There are several actions that donors can take during the negotiation process to help make it work, to help ensure that a more open system of decision making is put into place that will help preserve natural resources. The first action relates to starting the negotiation process.

Start Slowly: Select Candidate Projects for Negotiation

Organizing and carrying out a negotiated dialogue can strengthen the protection of natural resources for several reasons. A negotiation process provides a forum for diverse stakeholders to express their interests, needs, and concerns in a manner that can be translated into public policy. It provides an organized and disciplined structure to deal simultaneously in a stepwise fashion with several complex issues that otherwise would be overwhelming and nearly impossible to integrate. It strengthens existing decision-making forums by improving relationships between organizations and individuals, creating a positive precedent for cooperatively finding solutions to exceedingly complex problems. But while all this is true, negotiation is not a panacea, and can fail if preparation or execution of the mediation process is weak.

When first using an organized negotiation process, it is imperative that the parties initiating it carefully select projects on which to use it first. It is critical that a positive precedent be set with the first few mediated negotiations. The success of complex negotiations can be increased if a set of selection criteria are used to screen possible candidates for mediation. Selection criteria can include the willingness of the parties to enter into a mediation process, the availability of financial resources to fund the cost for the mediator to prepare and carry it out, the openness of the parties to pool technical and scientific information to properly inform the negotiators, and the availability of a well-trained mediator to design and execute the negotiation process. One approach is to choose for an initial negotiation process a pilot project that meets all of these criteria.

Provide Start-up Resources

Donor agencies possess financial and technical resources that they can bring to the negotiating table. In many instances, the other stakeholders will need these resources to be able to take part in a negotiation process, due to the general shortage of staff and money in developing countries. If these resources are made available to other stakeholders, in return for agreements to participate in a collaborative negotiation, they can be used as incentives to open up the environmental policy process. Donors may find that this is more effective and less risky than making massive one-time policy interventions which often overwhelm the institutional capacity of the borrower.

Create Linkages to Build Institutional Capacity

Donor agencies can help to support a more open decision-making process by allocating more resources to increase the institutional capacity within countries and their own agencies. Countries need to improve their performance in three areas: policy analysis, natural resource management, and long-term planning. Institution building for countries is needed on both the local and national levels as well as regionally. Regional organizations, such as NGOs and quasi-governmental organizations, and regional coordinating bodies, such as regional economic common markets, can serve as conduits to increase international learning between countries. Donors should target regional organizations as well as national governments and local

NGOs for institutional support. Donors can help an open policy-making process work by providing support to stakeholders through regional organizations when governments resist making changes on the national level. This can include funding regional training centers that specialize in teaching skills such as conflict resolution, environmental leadership, and project management.

To support the negotiation process, donors should make sure that the borrower has sufficient institutional capacity to provide a trained counterpart during the actual negotiations, someone who will available to help implement the final agreement. This is crucial given the shortage of trained personnel in many countries. In most instances, this counterpart will be from a ministry dealing with planning, land use, or economic development.

Donor agencies also need to build their own capacity for environmental planning. In many instances, field offices that are responsible for getting projects built and policies implemented do not have staff trained in natural resource management. As a result, it is almost impossible to enforce policies, or a negotiated agreement, intended to protect the environment. In addition to hiring properly trained personnel in field offices, donors should pay special attention to whom they assign as their representatives to a negotiation. It is important that they include field staff who are responsible for project implementation. It is critical that the negotiation process be linked with the implementation process of both the donor and country.

The donor should be aware that a negotiation for implementing environmental policies linked to a single project may need to be tied to a multi-year program to build the institutional capacity in the borrowing country. It may often take three to five years to increase the institutional capacity of local environmental NGOs and selected ministries within the borrowing country before a negotiation can be successfully carried out. If a country is hesitant or unwilling to be involved in a negotiation, out of fear that it will cause unwanted political change or upset the status quo, the donor may be able to overcome this resistance by offering long-term assistance to build up its institutional capacity for policy analysis and development planning, which will increase the self-reliance of the borrower.

Adopt Formal Career Incentives

Donors can help motivate their employees to initiate a negotiation process to implement environmental policies by offering them career incentives. When donors evaluate the job performance of their employees, they do not use specialized criteria to formally and consistently rate how effectively the employees have worked to implement environmental policies attached to individual projects. Instead, the normal job performance criteria that donors currently use reward employees for completing projects and moving funds as efficiently as possible; this method of evaluating job performance acts as a disincentive for implementing new environmental policies.

Career incentives could be added to promote the acceptance of environmental reforms. This may include evaluating how effectively employees incorporate environmental reforms into projects using the collaborative negotiation process. If the negotiation model is incorporated into the project cycle as a way to improve cooperation between the stakeholders and strengthen environmental policy implementation, employees should be financially rewarded. This is part of the institution building that donors need to undergo to increase their own capability to protect limited natural resources affected by development projects.

Invent Economic Incentives That Promote Environmental Protection

In most instances, environmental policies will remain unenforced unless they are tied to economic incentives. The most direct way that donors can link economic and environmental policies is to make the negotiation process part of the project cycle. If this is done, direct economic incentives can then be created to tie implementation of negotiated agreements to project cost/benefit. One approach would be to estimate the cost of carrying out all of the actions agreed to during the negotiation process, and add it to the overall project budget. This is essentially a way of accounting for the environmental cost of a project. If the project is not profitable enough to pay for the environmental policy implementation package, it should not be funded. This will provide a direct economic incentive to protect natural resources.

The donor can use contingent agreements as part of the negotiation process to link a comprehensive institution-building program to one project or a series of individual projects it sponsors, as it is common for a donor to fund multiple projects in the same country. A contingent agreement could use performance standards to link the successful completion of a series of several finite steps in an institution-building program for the funding of individual projects. As the government completes each step of the program, the donor then funds another project. This could provide the capital the borrower needs and the economic incentive to carry out long-term environmental reforms.

Account for Cultural Constraints in Implementation Plans

A combination of cultural constraints makes it very difficult for donors to implement environmental policies in developing countries. The negotiation process needs to take cultural conditions into account or, despite everyone's best efforts, environmental policies will in all likelihood remain largely unenforced. There are several kinds of cultural constraints that require the special attention of donor agencies. To overcome these constraints requires a clear understanding of the culture of decision making in a country, the inseparable link between culture and political decision making.

In general, policy changes occur slowly in developing countries, especially by the continental standards used by donor agencies and their consultants. For example, the transition from environmental laws to guidelines is very important. This transition represents the progression of an abstract concept into public policies that affect people's lives. In all societies, especially less-developed societies that have a high degree of interdependency, people notice this kind of change and take a long time to accept it. Culturally based habits and traditions exist for a reason and can take a long time to understand and be integrated into policy changes. Political leaders, who control every aspect of the policy-making apparatus, reflect the hesitancy of the culture to change. Personal relationships have to be developed between political leaders and those advocating change, for it to actually take place. Often there is no institutional memory left in countries when transient expatriate experts are in charge of designing or implementing environmental protection measures. Time is not spent in the field soliciting the participation of local and regional environmental NGOs.

Key Questions to Help Understand the Cultural Constraints. When involved in a negotiation process to implement environmental policies, donors, as well as other stakeholders, can account for cultural factors by addressing the following questions.

1. How will the slow rate of change in a borrowing country, where new policies may take several years to take effect, be accounted for in the implementation strategy and conditions for a project?
2. How will the implementation program be designed and translated so it can be understood by political leaders?

3. How will the donor's representatives create personal trust with senior civil servants and political leaders to build the informal yet essential one-on-one relationships needed to influence the political process?
4. How will the donor's representatives overcome the tendency of individuals and organizations in the country to treat them as outsiders? This may require building long-term relationships with regional NGOs who can advise donors on how to design an implementation strategy that is compatible with the culture of decision making in the country.
5. How will policy reforms be translated into a form of the local written and spoken languages that political leaders can easily understand, instead of relying solely on planning techno-speak? Local experts can be hired to perform the translation, so that recommendations are presented one small step at a time, consistent with local cultural norms.
6. What needs to be done as part of the negotiation process to overcome the fears of local stakeholders, including alienation and exile from the political process and a general distrust of risk taking and innovation?

ADVICE TO NATIONAL POLITICAL LEADERS IN DEVELOPING COUNTRIES

National political leaders are faced with tough choices. If they promote economic development in a manner that excludes efforts to preserve natural resources, such as fresh water, fisheries, agricultural soils, and forests, large-scale environmental degradation will continue, and their economic and political dependency on western industrialized nations will grow. If they promote environmental reforms too aggressively, they may scare off foreign investors, which can lead to a slower rate of economic growth.

It is important that national political leaders take part in the negotiations to design an effective strategy to implement environmental policies. The largest donor agencies, including the World Bank, USAID, and the IDB, are under immense pressure from environmental groups and the United States Congress to stop funding programs that damage natural resources. If countries continue to propose projects that cause environmental damage, donors may have no choice but to reduce or eliminate their level of funding, which would result in substantially less direct foreign aid. To avoid this situation, political leaders can support a series of steps that are needed to increase the institutional capacity of their governments to promote development projects that are both profitable and environmentally sustainable.

Allow Stakeholders to Participate

First, to send a clear message to the donors that they support projects that are environmentally sound, political leaders should empower their governments to fully participate in the negotiation process. This will accomplish several objectives. It will build local institutional capacity for policy analysis and long-term development planning, maintain the flow of money from the donors for future development, and protect the natural resources that are needed to support development. By participating in a collaborative policy dialogue, and giving legal protection to local stakeholders, politicians will in turn gain the leverage to ask donors to provide long-term funding for institution building that cannot be accomplished in a single project cycle.

Slowly Open Up the Public Policy Process

Political leaders should slowly open up the national policy-making process. Environmental interest groups are growing in developing countries. It is just a matter of time before they become strong enough to mount effective challenges to the government. But political leaders can turn the opposition of environmental groups to their advantage by using their own leadership to initiate environmental reforms.

An initial step in this process could be to delegate authority to civil servants to provide an objective analysis of development proposals. Political leaders often approve projects without the benefit of an objective policy analysis. Civil servants should be allowed to objectively compare development proposals with national environmental policies before the cabinet makes any decision to support a project, such as granting landholding licenses or financial concessions to developers.

The second step that is needed to open up the policy-making process is to allow civil servants who work in different offices to openly and directly communicate with their counterparts in other ministries when they are dealing with common issues related to natural resource management. One way to do this is to form local natural resource planning groups, made up of civil servants who are responsible for different aspects of natural resource management and environmental planning. The offices that typically would be included are planning, land use, finance, fisheries, agriculture, forestry, and water resources. These groups could also help the government coordinate national policy making, creating consistency and clarity that would help when the government takes part in the negotiation process.

Promote Self Reliance through Institution Building

In return for participating in the negotiation process, national political leaders could make a side agreement with the donor agencies, requesting multi-year assistance that is necessary for institution-building to improve their indigenous capacity for development planning and policy analysis. If governments make the case that efforts to improve their institutional capacity cannot be successfully completed within the constraints of the single project cycle, they may be able to convince donors to provide soft loans and grants to complete these improvements. By improving the quality of decision making in their public policy processes, governments will reduce their dependency on outside experts who are not familiar with political and cultural conditions in the developing world.

ADVICE TO ENVIRONMENTAL NGOS AND RESOURCE USERS

These groups can have the greatest impact on the public policy process if they form a coalition to promote reforms in both donor agencies and national governments. Participation in the negotiation process offers the opportunity to form a coalition. These stakeholders need to work together to create a common agenda that makes the most efficient use of limited resources so they are not at cross purposes.

There are two types of environmental NGOs to which I am offering advice, international groups, often headquartered in Washington, D.C., and the small local and regional organizations that exist in most developing regions. Each of these groups needs to understand how its particular strengths and weaknesses have to be accounted for when it engages in a negotiation process to promote environmental reform.

The strengths of international NGOs include political access to the United States Congress, which they can use to promote environmental reforms in donor agencies; their ability to obtain funding; and the practical experience they have obtained by participating in conservation projects all over the world. Their weaknesses include a lack of credibility with political leaders in developing countries, who are often distrustful of outsiders; the difficulties inherent in operating in countries that possess many different cultures; and the troublesome First World bias they bring to conservation.

Environmental NGOs located in developing countries are able to operate effectively in the local political system and are aware of cultural norms that underlie the public policy process. They are weak because they are small, lack adequate financial support, and often do not have the direct access to political leaders that is needed to influence development decisions. By combining their efforts, international and local NGOs can use each other's strengths to compensate for their weaknesses.

Identify and Train Environmental Leaders

The environmental protection and related policy implementation process in many instances is greatly influenced by a few people with strong personalities who have developed the skills needed to operate successfully within the political system. One way to influence public decision making is to train individuals who are likely to assume leadership positions in their countries. No one knows local political and culture conditions as well as those who have grown up and worked in a country. For example, only local people really understand the subtleties and opposition politics with any particular government, and how the local culture of decision making influences political leaders.

To train future leaders who are likely to place environmental problems higher on the national agenda, local NGOs can identify civil servants and political leaders that show exceptional promise. Local NGOs are familiar with local people and conditions, and in most instances are able to judge the likely candidates for advanced training. Once candidates for environmental leadership training are selected, international NGOs, in cooperation with supportive donor agencies, can use their expertise in administering and funding training programs to train the candidates. Training could include conflict resolution techniques, communication skills, project administration, and policy analysis. This should be an ongoing program, part of an institution-building effort in selected regions. Ideally, it would take the form of a permanent training center, perhaps a joint effort of more than one NGO, with field offices where training would take place.

It is important that the training be designed specifically for the political and cultural conditions encountered in developing countries. In addition to training future leaders, this approach would build coalitions between future decision makers, NGOs and donors, as well as promoting learning between governments. This is a form of technology transfer from industrialized countries to developing nations that supports economically and environmentally sustainable development.

Link Environmental Reform to the Negotiation Process

International NGOs should use their access to national political bodies, such as the United States Congress or the British Parliament, to urge donors to open up their decision-making process, to make it accountable for the environmental damage caused by development projects, and to build the institutional capacity for environmental reform in both donor agencies and developing countries—by adopting the model of collaborative negotiation. The negotiation process could be carried out as part of the standard project cycle, to be completed before donors make funding commitments for projects. International groups can also pressure donors to provide more soft loans and grants to fund multiyear programs to increase the institutional capacity of governments, to enable them to participate in a negotiation process.

Strengthen Relationships between NGOs and Resource Users

Local NGOs should develop programs to strengthen their relationships with resource users such as farmers, fishers, foresters, tourist guides, and charcoal producers. There are two ways to do this. First, NGOs can talk to resource users to educate them about the environmental damage caused by traditional forms of development, such as large tourist resorts that often damage fishing grounds or close off public access to the coastline. Second, NGOs can work with resource users to help make them more efficient producers. This can be done by sponsoring programs to examine how resource users operate, and then designing a strategy to increase the efficiency of their operations in a manner that is environmentally sustainable.

This could include observing the habits of local fishers that may be environmentally harmful, such as dynamiting reefs or over-

harvesting certain species. The NGO could work with fisheries bi-
ologists to identify species that can be safely harvested, and train
fishers in the techniques needed to catch them. Then the NGO could
act on behalf of a fishing community to seek funding from a donor
agency to build facilities for storing, processing, and marketing the
fish that are caught.

By creating this kind of downward linkage with resource users,
NGOs will generate economic and political leverage for both groups.
This can translate into stronger political influence with the government, which in turn will strengthen both stakeholders during the negotiation process.[13] If international NGOs participate in this effort,
coalitions will be formed between local NGOs, international NGOs,
and resource users, increasing the political leverage and influence of
all three parties.[14]

OTHER APPROACHES FOR STRENGTHENING
ENVIRONMENTAL POLICIES

I believe that the integrated negotiation model that I have presented will be the most effective way to open up the decision-
making process so that it includes unrepresented stakeholders and
integrates political, economic and cultural issues in way that is
needed to resolve complex environmental problems. This model reflects the important role that cultural, political, and economic conditions play in the development process, and it can be tailored to meet
the specific needs of different countries. However, there are other
methods for resolving international environmental problems, many
of which are compatible with the mediated negotiation approach.

Several environmental problems cut across national boundaries. These include air pollution, acid rain, the greenhouse effect,
and depletion of the earth's protective ozone layer. During international negotiations to stabilize the earth's climate, developing countries have formed the Group of 77 to bargain with industrialized
nations as a block. The Group of 77 believes that by agreeing to an
international treaty to reduce emissions of chlorofluorocarbons and
hydrocarbons, developing countries may have to reduce industrial
production processes, which in turn will slow down economic
growth. They argue that countries that have already developed have
caused the most global pollution, and should bear most of the burden for resolving the problem. This is just one recent development

in the North v. South debate that has marked international environmental negotiations since the 1972 Stockholm conference on the environment.

Developing countries believe that industrialized nations should compensate them for their efforts to reduce air pollution. Compensation would be in the form of cash payments for foregone economic opportunities and assistance in developing new technologies to substitute for ones that are causing the most pollution. The Montreal Protocols specifically called for developed nations to accelerate their efforts to provide new technologies to the developing world. This is starting to happen, as the United States and other countries agree to provide some technical and financial assistance to developing nations. However, Caldwell and others believe that existing international institutional arrangements are not adequate to deal with the complexities of global environmental problems.[15]

Countries seem to value national sovereignty more than environmental stability. Many international treaties and conventions have been adopted, as transboundary problems require international solutions. But the international community has been slow to promote the institutional and legal reforms that must accompany these complex agreements. In addition, international agreements take too long to implement, lack formal mechanisms to achieve compliance, and address problems on an ad hoc basis.

In response to the difficulties of implementing international agreements, it has been suggested that regional negotiation centers be established to address transboundary problems on a scale that is easier to grasp. Regions often share similar cultures, languages, and political systems. One possible model is for countries to sign global environmental treaties, and delegate implementation to regional centers or quasi-governmental organizations. This could combine the strengths inherent in international cooperation, while accounting for the weakness in implementing agreements on an international scale. This approach would decentralize environmental policy implementation to the regional level, but it is unclear how a regional strategy can secure a binding commitment without violating the national sovereignty of countries that participate.

Another model of implementation would take decentralization one step further. It is based on the assumption that countries have too many differences to cooperate effectively, and that international interventions infringe on national sovereignty. An example would be the differences among the island nations in the Caribbean. Even though these countries seem to have much in common, they have different languages (English, French, Spanish, and Dutch, plus many creolized versions), political systems (socialism in Guyana, communism in Cuba, many parliamentary democracies and several countries still administered from the United States and European capitals), cultures, and legal systems. Under a decentralized model, it is assumed that countries will support the indigenous change needed to reform environmental policies. Solutions could include local people organizing a Green Party to pressure the political leaders to undertake reform. But, in developing countries that lack a tradition of public participation and open political dialogue, this approach may not work.

Summary

The current approach that donor agencies and developing countries use to design and implement environmental policies is not working because it relies almost entirely on a closed decision-making process. Closed decision making does not adequately account for the interests of several key stakeholders, including resource users, local and international environmental NGOs, civil servants, and environmental technicians. It also fails to account for the role that four elements of the public policy process play in environmental policy implementation. The four elements are national politics, the culture of decision making, economic necessity in developing countries, and the behavior of donor agencies.

Political appointees and policy makers in both donor agencies and developing countries behave in a manner that is mutually reinforcing and allows development that damages limited natural resources. To account for the interests of stakeholders that are now excluded from environmental policy making, and to integrate the crucial four elements of the public policy process into decision making, a new open system of decision making should be adopted. This new open system can be implemented using a negotiated partnership for sustainable development. It will be hard for the closed system of decision making to become more open, but this has to be done to preserve limited natural resources for future economic growth.

An organized and well-thought-out negotiation process can be designed to open up the public policy process, but the first obstacle that has to be overcome is the reluctance of borrowing countries and donor agencies to participate in a more open policy dialogue. There are significant incentives for both parties to participate. Donor agencies will be subject to more and more political pressure from the United States Congress, European governments, and international environmental organizations to implement environmental reforms that work. If the donors fail to adopt more effective strategies for protecting natural resources, their funding may be curtailed.

Similarly, borrowing countries may not be eligible for development assistance unless they promote effective environmental reforms. By accounting for environmental factors in development decisions, national political leaders will blunt the growing opposition from pro-environmental interest groups at home and abroad, creating political stability that will allow them to stay in power. By increasing the institutional capacity within their own governments for policy analysis and environmental planning, as an element in the development process, politicians will enhance national self-reliance and reduce political and economic dependency on outside parties. National governments and donor agencies will benefit from integrating economic and environmental factors in a manner that promotes sustainable development, which in turn will create a more certain investment climate.

As major stakeholders, donor agencies and borrowing countries possess the political and financial leverage to convince the other to take part in a more open process. Once a decision is made to open up the policy dialogue, a collaborative negotiation process can be convened by any one of the stakeholders, as long as certain preconditions are met and specific steps followed.

National politics and the culture of decision making in developing countries present obstacles that will be hard to overcome. National political leaders often have close ties to developers and make decisions to support their projects in private, without public participation. The exclusion of the public from policy making in many instances has included the absence of an open press and media, with the government controlling the flow of information that reaches its citizens. Political leaders exert control over civil servants using party loyalty and family ties as leverage to enforce their pro-development policies. This discourages civil servants from working to enforce environmental policies that Parliament has passed, often as a condition of approval to receive funds from donor agencies.

Local environmental groups, NGOs, and resource users do not have the personal access to national political leaders that is needed to influence the public policy process. Policy decisions are made based on personal trust, political loyalty, and intense communication based on traditional social relationships that outsiders, such as donor agencies attempting to implement environmental policies, simply do not understand. Cultural differences are complicated by the role of informal authorities in decision making, a resistance to innovation, and a general distrust of outsiders attempting to intervene in the political system, because of a history of economic and political dependency. In short, outside parties trying to make policy interventions are hindered because they do not understand the cultural norms and political practices that combine to create national culture of decision making. But there are ways to manage these differences in a new open decision-making process.

These concerns can be accounted for in the prenegotiation phase of an open process by meeting a series of preconditions, and in the second phase by following a series of steps. The convener of a negotiation, whether it is a donor agency, a country, or an NGO, can design the process to include stakeholders that are excluded from the political process, such as local resource users and NGOs. Ground rules can be established to protect civil servants in the countries and environmental technicians in the donor agencies. These can include legal and procedural protection to shield them from political retribution for participating in an open dialogue. Weak stakeholders can be provided with financial and technical resources, including training in economic development and conflict resolution, to place them on an equal basis with more powerful stakeholders. The convener, working with a neutral facilitator or mediator, can create protocols to help the participants in the negotiation understand their responsibilities to each other and the process, and show them the importance of using objective criteria in their arguments instead of relying on subjective judgments that favor parties who traditionally have been the most powerful.

The mediator can choose a co-mediator from the local culture to help in designing a negotiation process that accounts for the culture of decision making. The mediation team can carry out several specific steps, such as conducting a culturally sensitive stakeholder analysis and using an elicitive model of communication that is weighted towards local cultural norms, to account for cultural biases. If donors include the funds and technical expertise needed to support long-term institution building in countries where they sponsor development, several culturally related constraints to implementing effective environmental policies can be resolved. Long-term institution building is needed to promote the personal trust, one-on-one communication and cultural awareness that is necessary to design and carry out policies that work.

The difficulty of accounting for economic factors when designing environmental policies can also be addressed in a negotiation process. Local NGOs can strengthen their coalitions with local resource users who provide vital services for their societies. Resource users are generally not organized. If NGOs promote downward linkages with resources users, and help them to become more efficient producers, both groups will gain more political and economic leverage, giving them a greater voice in development decisions. If donors promote long-term institution building in borrowing countries, it can help harmonize conflicting economic and environmental policies, and promote economic incentives to protect natural resources.

The behavior of donor agencies that prevents environmental policies from being enforced can also be accounted for in a negotiation process. Negotiations should include representatives from the field offices and environmental units of the donors, so that the policy dialogue includes their viewpoints. These parties are responsible for designing and implementing strategies to protect natural resources, but are often overruled by political appointees who do not want to interrupt the flow of development funds. By including all of these parties in a collaborative negotiation, implementation strategies can be created that incorporate the environmental reforms that donors are supposed to be carrying out.

The stakeholders can also undertake initiatives outside of the negotiation process to help make it more effective. Donor agencies can take the leadership in promoting effective environmental policies by creating economic incentives that protect natural resources. They can use contingent and reciprocal agreements that link institution building with the approval of individual projects. As a country builds its capacity for protecting natural resources, the donor can then provide funds for development projects. This provides an incentive for countries to increase their own capacity for environmental protection. Donors should also provide formal career environmental incentives for their employees to reward them financially for creating and promoting environmental reform, including use of the collaborative negotiation process. NGOs should coordinate their efforts to identify and train talented individuals who will serve as the next generation of leaders in their governments. This could take the form of a permanent training center to build skills in conflict resolution, interpersonal communication, and policy analysis.

APPENDIX

RESOURCES AND METHODS

To prepare for field work in each country, I conducted a series of background interviews with researchers and professionals involved in environmental planning and economic development in the Caribbean. Contacts within various donor agencies and NGOs gave me access to public and private documents discussing the status of the public policy process in the Eastern Caribbean. I used these documents, the background interviews, my experience in the region, and several published references focusing on politics, culture, anthropology, economics, public administration, and natural resources to formulate an approach for carrying out the field work. All of the background and reference material that I used is cited in the notes to the book.

The approach I used to create the case studies is described by Robert K. Yin in *Case Study Research: Design and Methods* (Beverly Hills: Sage, 1984). Cases were chosen in three different countries with similar political systems to illustrate the different obstacles to implementing environmental policies. The cases have several common elements: they all involve large development projects designed and funded by donor agencies; fragile natural resources are at stake; and efforts to protect the resources have generally failed.

After I identified the cases in each country that I wanted to examine, it was necessary to obtain access to politicians, civil servants, and other key sources who possessed the special knowledge I needed to create these case studies. This was crucial as public policy decisions in all three countries are difficult to document, since many cabinet decisions and other major deliberations of government offi-

187

cials are not a matter of public record. In most instances, my affilia-tion as a Research Associate with the Centre for Resource Manage-ment and Environmental Studies (CERMES) at the University of the West Indies, Barbados, and as a Fellow of the Organization of Amer-ican States was sufficient to convince my sources that I was an ob-jective party. However, in St. Lucia I was told that access to key sources would not be granted unless I registered as a researcher with the National Research and Development Foundation, agreeing to sign a contract that guaranteed the foundation access to my findings. Thus, finding suitable institutional affiliations was an essential ele-ment of preparing for the actual field research.

The field research was designed so that I would serve as a participant-observer, relating the story of each case from the vantage points of key parties who played integral roles in them. Multiple sources of evidence were used to prepare the cases. To establish mul-tiple sources of evidence, I compiled a collection of written evidence to form a database for the cases. Written evidence included papers from the archives of the University of the West Indies, Barbados, and several types of documents from the collections of national libraries in Barbados and St. Lucia, including national plans, newspaper arti-cles, planning documents, and special studies related to natural re-sources, economics, and culture, including agriculture, forestry, anthropology, coastal planning, tourism, and land-use control. All of the sources I used are cited in the notes to the book. The library at the National Research and Development Foundation in St. Lucia was a valuable source of local information.

Several national and international NGOs also provided back-ground information to prepare me for field work and in-country interviews. The library of the Island Resources Foundation in Wash-ington, D.C., compiled and managed by Edward and Judith Towle, was invaluable. Staff at the OAS provided several reports prepared for the Economic Base Resource Management Plurinational Project sponsored by the OAS and the Organization of Eastern Caribbean States (OECS) Natural Resources Management Project (NRMP). These reports discuss the capabilities of St. Lucia and St. Kitts to un-dertake development control and physical planning activities, and include several recommendations to improve institutional capacity in these areas.

A series of reports describing the status of national legislation relating to natural resources management in St. Lucia and St. Kitts, sponsored and provided to me by the OECS-NRMP, provided excel-lent summaries of the status of environmental planning in these two countries. A comprehensive review of coastal-related legislation in Barbados, by Kenneth Atherley of the Coastal Conservation Project Unit, was also helpful.

Before traveling to each country to conduct interviews, I also had a series of discussions, over a period of two years, with a range of people who have long experience working and living in the Caribbean. The Towles of the Island Resources Foundation, Janos Zimmerman and Mervin Williams at the OECS-NRMP in St. Lucia, Victor Williams in St. Kitts, David Staples in Barbados, Dr. Euna Moore at CERMES and Richard Meganck, formerly with OAS and former director of the United Nations Caribbean Action Plan office in Jamaica, all provided me with the benefit of their experience in the Eastern Caribbean.

Once the background data for each case were collected, I formulated a series of questions to ask of my sources in each country. Each source was asked essentially the same set of questions. The questions were designed to establish a chain of evidence for each case. I wanted to find out how each project was initiated, who sponsored it, paid for it, and supported it politically. The key decisions leading up to project approval, made by officials from both national governments and donor agencies, as project sponsors, were generally not in a written record. The only way to obtain this information was to conduct interviews with a wide variety of people in each country. In total, I interviewed 78 people in four countries, including the United States, and had about 150 total contacts with them.

A wide range of people were interviewed who had a diverse set of opinions on the environment-development dialogue. These included elected and appointed officials, such as an attorney general; permanent secretaries and senior civil servants in ministries of development, agriculture, tourism, fisheries, planning, coastal management, and finance; the heads of national planning authorities; the director of a national development corporation; members of the port authority; staff from a national sugar corporation; and the chairmen of national advisory boards for conservation, development, and historical preservation.

Several officials from the donor agencies—USAID, the IDB, and the OAS—were also interviewed, in their headquarters in Washington, D.C., and in regional offices in the Eastern Caribbean (the USAID regional office in Bridgetown, Barbados, the IDB representatives' office in Barbados, and the OAS field office in St. Lucia). These sources included the managers of the three projects: the Southeast Peninsula Development Project in St. Kitts, the Bridgetown Fisheries Harbor in Barbados, and the proposed Pitons National Park in St. Lucia, and specialists from the donor agencies in economic development, environmental planning, engineering, and rural development.

Research officers from several quasi-governmental agencies were interviewed, including the officers of Caribbean Tourism Organization, Barbados, who provided information about the importance of the regional tourist economy. The USAID-funded planning team in St. Kitts gave me numerous planning studies and background documents for the Southeast Peninsula Road Project. Directors from various chambers of industry and commerce briefed me on the economic status of each country, and gave me insights into the local political system. Officials from the St. Lucia National Trust explained the history of conservation activities in the country, and members of the Barbados Association for the Environment described the history of their attempts to influence national conservation policy.

The president of the Barbados Fishing Cooperative, staff from the Folk Research Centre in St. Lucia and the director of the West Indies/USAID Caribbean Justice Improvement Program, Barbados, provided data on the regional fishery, the importance of the Pitons to the culture of St. Lucia, and the legal and judicial framework in individual countries and the Eastern Caribbean region. The technical Advisor to the Caribbean office of the European Development Fund in Bridgetown, Barbados, provided vital information about the history of the Southeast Peninsula Development Project in St. Kitts. The vicar general of the Archdiocese of St. Lucia was extremely helpful in explaining how senior civil servants in that country have attempted to reform the national public policy process, and how the reform movement related to the Pitons controversy.

In addition to members of official organizations, I also spent considerable time interviewing lay people, to ensure that the cases reflect the viewpoint of resource users. I had long conversations with fishers, farmers, and forest guides in all three countries. These conversations were unstructured, and yielded useful insights into the way that politics, economics, and culture intertwine to form an informal framework for natural resource management.

Almost all of the interviews were initially conducted in person, with multiple follow-up conversations with key sources via telephone for three years after the field work, to ensure that the cases reflect current events. In all instances, in person and when using the telephone, I took notes by hand, and did not use a tape recorder. There are two reasons for this. First, I felt that this method was essential to establishing personal trust with my sources, given the informality of interpersonal dialogue in the countries. This informality reflects the dominance of the oral tradition in the region, which as I mention in chapter 4, contains the elements of intense person-to-person dialogue and requires an acute awareness of the surroundings and cultural ambiance in which the interview is conducted. By taking notes, I was forced to tune in to the surroundings, and carefully listen to the person being interviewed, to know when to push for more information, usually of a politically sensitive nature, and when not to.

The second reason I depended on handwritten notes was that all of the cases were the subject of intense political debate in the countries, and within the donor agencies. This included the sensitive nature of the environmental reform movement among the donors. I felt that my informants would be unwilling to discuss elements of the cases that were clearly of a politically sensitive nature with a tape recorder in front of them. I am sure that one reason why I successfully elicited candid comments on the political aspects of the cases was the confidentially promised to my sources. Hence, in the body of the book, interviews are cited with a letter followed by a number (e.g. B 12, SK 7, SL 1), signifying the country where the case is located (B = Barbados, SK = St. Kitts, and SL = St. Lucia), and who the source is. Each number refers to a person interviewed.

My descriptions of the key events in the cases were mainly derived from the interviews, newspaper articles, and project-related documents on file in government offices and donor agencies. In almost all instances, key events, such as a decision by a cabinet or a donor agency, were confirmed by more than one source. The environmental consequences of the projects were documented by field visits in each country, accompanied by local residents or officials from the government or donor agency. My experience as a land-use planner and environmental analyst helped me understand what I was seeing (e.g. the cause and extent of beach erosion, degradation of offshore reefs, deforestation, results of intensive coastal development).

I did encounter difficulties during the field research. These included logistical problems, such as a shortage of operable telephones, understanding local dialects, and finding out how to get around in each country. Gaining physical access to the three project sites was often difficult. Sympathetic officials, landowners, and local guides accompanied me to all of the sites, to explain to me the elements of each project, and to help me avoid encountering problems with legal trespass.

Precautions were taken to avoid intervening in the outcome of each case. If participants asked me for advice about how to create a strategy to strengthen environmental policies, I explained that it was not my role to provide that kind of information. This approach, coupled with my association with local and regional research institutions, allowed me to remain neutral.

After the initial interviews were completed, and all of the background materials summarized, I prepared three documents for each case: an annotated chronology of key events, and summaries of the major themes and lessons. Next, I analyzed these documents to develop new, specific propositions that the evidence would support. The resulting propositions relate to the relationship of mandated environmental policies to four major themes: national politics, the culture of decision making, economic conditions, and the behavior of donor agencies. Chapters 2 through 6 describe these relationships in the context of specific events and conditions within each case.

The criteria for the findings in each chapter related to the effectiveness of environmental policies. In all instances, fragile or limited natural resources were identified by governments, outside experts, or donor agencies, and policies were adopted to protect them. In general these policies failed. When adopted policies were compared to the actual or likely environmental damage generated by the projects, these inconsistencies were interpreted as the findings for the cases and, specifically, how the four major factors identified contributed to the degradation of natural resources.

NOTES

CHAPTER ONE

1. I use the terms *donor agencies* and *development assistance agencies* interchangeably, referring to bilateral foreign assistance agencies such as the U.S. Agency for International Development, and multilateral agencies such as the Inter-American Development Bank and the World Bank.

2. The developed nations I refer to here comprise the North Atlantic countries that are the source for many of the international initiatives for environmental protection and economic development, including the United States and Canada, as well as countries in central and northern Europe. I do not examine the substantial involvement of Japan in international development and conservation.

3. I am not proposing that Eastern European countries, known as the Second World nations, are developing countries per se, only that they share many of the same problems as developing countries, problems that have intensified with these countries' recent break with the former Soviet Union. This break has brought them political independence and decentralized economic planning, and has required that they assume responsibility for their own severe environmental problems.

4. For a series of discussions of various environmental problems in developing countries, especially those related to rapid population growth, modern agricultural practices, loss of biological diversity, and the utilization of non-renewable energy resources, see the Worldwatch Institute's annual reports: Lester R. Brown et al., *State of the World*, New York: W.W. Norton and Company, 1984–93. For an overview of the relationship between human resources, managing common global resources and sustainable development, see The World Commission on Environment and Development, *Our Common Future*, (New York: Oxford University Press, 1987). Francis R. Thibodeau and Hermann H. Field, eds., *Sustaining Tomorrow: A Strategy for*

World Conservation and Development, Hanover: University Press of New England, 1984, describes the purpose and need for a world conservation strategy, the relationship between ecological processes and life support systems, and the nexus of food, nutrition, and population.

5. Department of International Economic and Social Affairs, "World Population Prospects: Estimates and Projections as Assessed in 1984," New York: United Nations, 1986, as reported in The World Commission on Environment and Development, *Our Common Future.*

6. See *Coastal Resource Management: Development Case Studies,* Coastal Publication No. 3, Renewable Resources Information Series, ed. John R. Clark (Washington, D.C.: National Park Service and U.S. Agency for International Development, 1985).

7. United Nations Food and Agricultural Organization, *Yearbook of Fishery Statistics* (Rome: UN Food and Agricultural Org., various years).

8. Thomas E. Lovejoy and Alexander R. Brash, "Tropical Forests and Genetic Resource Areas," in *Sustaining Tomorrow: A Strategy for World Conservation and Development.* (Hanover: University Press of New England, 1984).

9. Lloyd Timberlake, *Africa in Crisis: The Causes, the Cures of Environmental Bankruptcy* (London, International Institute for Environment and Development, 1985).

10. Sierra Club, *Bankrolling Disasters: International Development Banks and the Global Environment* (San Francisco: Sierra Club, 1986).

11. Taken from the statement of Bruce M. Rich, Senior Attorney, Environmental Defense Fund, in a hearing before the U.S. Senate Committee on Appropriations, 102nd Congress, First Session, 1992.

12. Ibid.

13. James Q. Wilson, *American Government: Institutions and Policies* (Lexington, MA: Heath and Company, 1986).

14. Various political scientists talk about the relationship between interest groups and government as a subgovernment or "issue network," but I believe that the access to power and political capital that this collection of individuals and institutions possess should cause them to be thought of as an interest group by themselves. For an explanation of the more traditional depiction of a subgovernment, see Carl E. Van Horn, Donald C. Baumer, and William T. Gormley, Jr., *Politics and Public Policy* (Washington, D.C.: Congressional Quarterly Press, 1972).

15. While I believe that this portrait of environmental policy making in both developing countries and donor agencies is accurate, change is un-

der way. As countries develop economically and mature politically the policy-making process tends to become more open. There are several reasons for this: citizens become active in policy making by creating nongovernmental organizations that press for government reform and challenge traditional interest groups; political leaders grow more sophisticated and are able to handle and manage conflict more effectively; and international environmental groups learn how domestic decision making works and are able to influence it. Donor agencies are responding, albeit slowly, to similar pressures, gradually increasing their institutional capacity for more effective natural resource management. See chapter 6 for a discussion of how specific donor agencies are improving their environmental policy making.

16. All acronyms and abbreviations used in this book are listed and explained on page xv.

17. Please refer to the Appendix for additional explanation of the sources of information for the cases, and the research design and methods that were used.

CHAPTER TWO

1. For a discussion of natural resource conditions and problems that are unique to oceanic islands, and alternate approaches to natural resource management, see U.S. Congress, Office of Technology Assessment, "Integrated Renewable Resource Management of U.S. Insular Areas" (Washington, D.C.: June 1987).

2. J. S. Beard, *The Natural Vegetation of the Windward and Leeward Islands*, Oxford Forestry Memorandum No. 21, (Oxford, U.K.: Clarenton Press, 1949).

3. The countries that are the focus of the case studies are considered "democratic" when viewed from a distance. Certainly, on a continuum of models of governance ranging from centrally controlled autocratic or dictatorial regimes to the open and accessible democracies of the United States, Canada, and many European nations, the island states of the Caribbean are somewhat closer to the democratic end of the continuum. However, these countries often lack what can be considered some of the basic requirements of an open and accessible democracy, such as open media, frequent public hearings sponsored by the government, and the freedom to conduct public assemblies. Thus, the term *democracy* should be carefully considered in the context of how each government behaves and the responsiveness of its institutions, both of which factors vary widely.

4. Refer to Caribbean and Central American Association, *Caribbean and Central American Databook* (Washington, D.C.: Caribbean and Central American Association, 1988) and Jamal Khan, *Public Management: The*

Eastern Caribbean Experience (Providence: Foris Publications, 1987) for a thorough description of how the political system in St. Kitts has evolved.

5. The Economist Intelligence Unit, *Country Profiles: Guyana, Barbados, Windward and Leeward Islands, 1991–92* (London: The Economist Intelligence Unit, 1992). Statistics for unemployment are from the 1986 World Bank Economic Report. During my field work it was evident that the large influx of capital for the Southeast Peninsula Development Project has lowered the unemployment rate considerably. The actual unemployment rate appears to be much lower than 20 percent, and some observers indicate the workforce is near full employment, considering the large number of Kittians who work in the informal sector and would not appear in official statistics as being employed.

6. The World Bank, *St. Christopher and Nevis Economic Report* (Washington DC: The World Bank, 1986).

7. Robert Norton, *Resource Management Plans: Wildlife Resources* (Gainesville, Florida: Southeast Peninsula Board, St. Kitts, and Tropical Research and Development, Inc., 1988). Norton gives a full description of natural resources on the peninsula, and recommends management alternatives to assist preservation efforts as the peninsula develops.

8. Information about the history and status of older laws relating to different aspects of natural resource management is contained in Organization of Eastern Caribbean States Natural Resource Management Project, *Description of National Legislation Related to Natural Resource Management, Report 1SKN,* (St. Lucia: OECS, November, 1986).

9. Ibid.

10. When conducting confidential interviews to gather evidence for this study, I promised informants that their identities would be protected. As a result, in the text where a statement is directly attributed to an official in a country, an alphanumeric symbol, such as SK 13, is used in place of the name of the person interviewed. The letter refers to one of the three countries where the case studies are located SK = St. Kitts, B = Barbados, and SL = St. Lucia. The number after each set of letters was randomly chosen, and is keyed to my original interview notes. If an interview was conducted in the United States, such as conversations with officials from development assistance agencies in Washington, D.C., their comments are also cited using one of the three country abbreviations, depending on which case they commented on.

11. The proceedings of the workshop are summarized in; John K. Gamman, *Report on the St. Kitts–Nevis Coastal Resource Management Project* (St. Lucia: Organization of Eastern Caribbean States Natural Resource Management Project, August 1987).

12. Fernaldo Soler, *Development Control and Physical Planning: The Case of St. Kitts and Nevis* (West Indies: Organization of American States Department of Regional Development and the OECS Natural Resource Management Project, 1988). This report summarizes the administrative structure of the physical planning process in St. Kitts and problems that it has encountered due to the lack of a clear mandate from the political leadership. It also predicts how these problems will increase with the added responsibility of the Southeast Peninsula Development Project.

13. Regional Development Office/Caribbean (RDO/C) St. Kitts–Nevis Country Supplement to the Caribbean Regional CDSS, 1986–90 (Bridgetown, Barbados: USAID, June, 1985). The CDSS outlined USAID's strategy for developing the project. It was intended as a way to diversify the economy by expanding it into non-sugar agriculture, tourism, and light manufacturing.

14. USAID, *AID Policy Paper: Environment and Natural Resources* (Washington, D.C.: USAID, The Bureau for Program and Policy Coordination, 1988). The U.S. Congress amended the Foreign Assistance Act in 1981 to require that USAID prepare environmental impact assessments.

15. Island Resources Foundation, *Environmental Assessment Report on the Proposed Southeast Peninsula Assess Road, St. Kitts, West Indies* (Washington, D.C.: Island Resources Foundation, 1986).

16. Ibid., Executive Summary: 5.

17. Soler, *Development Control: St. Kitts and Nevis.*

18. Refer to Gordon K. Lewis, *The Growth of the Modern West Indies* (New York: Monthly Review Press, 1968) and J. H. Parry and Philip Sherlock, *A Short History of the West Indies* (London: MacMillan, 1971). These two books trace the growth of the West Indies, including the early colonial period, the relationship between fierce land wars in the region as related to power struggles in the metropolitan capitals of Europe, and the transition of colonial political systems into modern democratic governments.

19. The Economist Intelligence Unit, *Country Profiles;* Caribbean and Central American Association, *Caribbean and Central American Databook* (Washington, DC: Caribbean and Central American Association, 1989) and The World Bank, *St. Lucia; Economic Performance and Prospects,* A World Bank Country Study, (Washington, DC: The World Bank, 1987). Both of these reports contain detailed information about current economic conditions and trends in St. Lucia, and contain data on the political system, international trading partners, and a summary of economic conditions in the last decade.

20. For a description of all of the environmental legislation in St. Lucia, refer to *Description of National Legislation Related to Natural Re-*

sources Management for St. Lucia, Report 1 SLU, (St. Lucia: Organization of Eastern Caribbean States Natural Resources Management Project, November 1986).

21.   Taken from Mark Eckstein and Felix Finisterre, *Short Run Gain–Long Term Pain.* St. Lucia: National Enviromental Commission, 1987. This report discusses several types of environmental problems in St. Lucia and recommends ways to help resolve them.

22.   Organization of Eastern Caribbean States Natural Resources Management Program, 1986.

23.   Fernando Soler, *Development Control and Physical Planning: The Case of St. Lucia* (OAS and OECS Natural Resource Management Project, 1988). This report outlines the administrative framework of the national planning process and makes several recommendations about how to improve it.

24.   Organization of American States; *Proposal for the Development of the Pitons National Park* (Department of Regional Development, Executive Secretariat for Economic and Social Affairs, General Secretariat, OAS, 1989).

25.   Earl Bousquet, "Changing the Face of the Pitons," *St. Lucia Star,* 31 March 1990.

26.   The World Bank, *Barbados Economic Memorandum* (Latin America and the Caribbean Regional Office, 16 January 1984). Barbados has a trade deficit of about $300 million, as it must import food, fuels, building materials, chemicals, and machinery. Its external public debt grew from $987 million in 1990. The Economist Intelligence Unit, *Country Profiles.* The unemployment rate is estimated at about 18 percent. Like other islands in the region, Barbados is adopting economic policies to diversify agriculture, strengthen manufacturing, and increase tourism to expand and stabilize the economy. Barbados has no industrial raw materials, apart from small quantities of oil and natural gas. Its primary natural resources are fertile soil, fresh water, a tropical climate, and white sand beaches.

27.   See Kenneth Atherley, *A Review of Coastal Related Legislation in Barbados* (Barbados: Coastal Conservation Project Unit, March 1987). Sea eggs are taken from sea urchins and are a delicacy in the West Indies.

28.   Wayne Hunte, *Short Term Perspectives and Marine Resources in the Caribbean* (West Indies: University of the West Indies, 1989). Dr. Hunte is Director of the Bellairs Research Institute in Barbados. This paper summarizes several environmental problems related to the coastal zone and marine environment that exist in Barbados and throughout the region.

29.   Leonard Nurse, "The Barbados Coast: A Planning and Management Evaluation," Paper given at the OAS Workshop on Coastal Zone Man-

agement, Miami, Florida, December 12–16, 1988. Dr. Nurse is project manager of the Coastal Conservation Project Unit.

30. In 1982 the United Nations Food and Agricultural Organization issued the "Report of the Barbados Fisheries Development Project," sponsored by the United Nations Food and Agricultural Organization (FAO) Investment Center. The report included a "quick and dirty" estimate of the sustained yield of the Barbados fishery. It estimated that an annual yield of 20,000 tons can be sustained. This is more than three times the peak fish catch, which occurred in 1983. There was no scientific evidence to support the estimate (B 24).

31. See Caribbean Conservation Association, *St. Lucia Country Environmental Profile* (USAID: Island Resources Foundation, 1991).

CHAPTER THREE

1. Jeffrey M. Barry, *The Interest Group Society* (Boston: Little, Brown & Co., 1989). Barry discusses the roles and functions of interest groups, including the roots of a group theory of politics. This work was based on experience in the United States but contains a good overview of interest-group theory.

2. George E. G. Catlin, *A Study of the Principles of Politics* (London: George Allen and Unwin, 1930) as discussed in *Interest Groups in American Society*, L. Harmon Zeigler and G. Wayne Peak, 1972, Englewood Cliffs, NJ: Prentice Hall. Catlin describes interest groups as a political concept within the context of democratic societies.

3. See Catlin, *Principles of Politics*, 371–75, for a discussion of how the desire for personal power often influences the behavior of individuals involved in the policy-making process. Catlin describes the thirst for power as one where political goods are valued more than peace and order in society, a corollary to how the desire for power motivates politicians to make development decisions that damage the environment.

4. Warren F. Ilchman and Norman Thomas Uphoff, *The Political Economy of Change* (Berkeley: University of California Press, 1969). The field of political economy has been developed to examine aspects of the public-policy process that are not clearly identified by standard analytic research methods.

5. Jamal Kahn, *Public Management*.

6. Ibid., 43–44, 76. Khan describes the importance of personal ties between elites and politicians and the importance of these ties within the informal decision-making mechanisms that influence public policy implementation.

7. Ibid, 43.

8. Lawrence Susskind and Jeffrey Cruikshank, *Breaking the Impasse: Consensual Approaches to Resolving Public Disputes* (New York: Basic Books, 1987), 11, 13, 25, 103–4, 239–40). The authors discuss how to identify stakeholders, the need to involve all stakeholders in the decision-making process, and how to include stakeholder attitudes and perceptions in negotiations and policy making.

9. The judiciary and courts have not played a significant role in the development or implementation of public policy in the eastern Caribbean region. The reasons for this are discussed in chapter 4.

10. Kahn, *Public Management*, 50, 51, 76. Khan also discusses the work of Simey, who cautions that management issues in the West Indies tend to become submerged in a welter of conflicting personalities (T. S. Simey, *Welfare and Planning in the West Indies* (Oxford: Clarendon Press, 1946), Also see Monte Palmer, *Dilemmas of Political Development: An Introduction to the Politics of the Developing Areas* (Itasca, Il: Peacock Publishers, 1946). Palmer describes the role of charismatic politicians in political development, including how such leaders operate outside the boundaries of traditional authority.

11. Khan, *Public Management*. He discusses the dominant factors in the relationship between politicians and civil servants, factors that were confirmed by my field work. In all of the countries studied, it was found that civil servants working in planning agencies feel pressured to promptly review and approve development proposals, often ignoring time-consuming environmental requirements (B 2, 22, 30; SL 5).

12. Ibid., 76.

13. "NWU Backing for Jalousie" St. Lucian Weekend Voice, 13 May 1989.

14. John Forester, *Planning in the Face of Power* (Berkeley: University of California Press, 1989). Forester discusses, in chapter 3, how the exercise of private economic power combines with politics to counteract the implementation of plans. He describes how this contributes to the intensely political nature of the planning process.

15. Peter Bartelmus, *Environment and Development* (Boston: Allen and Unwin, 1986). Bartelmus describes the major stages in the national planning process and how the potential for ecologically sound development is affected at each stage. He cites a report prepared in 1976 by the United Nations Environment Program, titled "Ecodevelopment," which recommends that "the style and rate of development . . . be determined by those people most affected." However, this recommendation did not account for the political realities of existing power structures and the difficulty of gaining access to them.

16. G. E. Mills, "Educating and Training for the Public Services in the West Indies," *Journal of Administration Overseas*, 1966 (5 July):. Also see Edwin Jones, "Bureaucracy as a Problem Solving Mechanism in Small States: A Review in Terms of the Current Literature," in *Size, Self-Determination, and International Relations: The Caribbean*, ed. Vaughan Lewis (Mona, Jamaica: Institute of Social and Economic Research, 1976).

17. See Island Resources Foundation, *Summary Report on Eastern Caribbean Nongovernment Organizations* (Washington D.C. and the U.S. Virgin Islands: Island Resources Foundation, June 1987). This report lists all of the NGOs in the region in each country that have or could have an interest in promoting environmental protection, and discusses the limitations NGOs face when trying to affect national public policies.

18. Max Weber, "Politics as a Vocation," *From Max Weber: Essays in Sociology*, Gerth and Mills (eds.), (Philadelphia: Fortress Press 77–128, 1968). Weber talks about the "flame of pure intentions" and the "ethic of responsibility" in relation to political decision making.

19. For a more detailed history of St. Kitts, St. Lucia, and Barbados see Parry and Sherlock, *History of the West Indies*, or Eric Williams, *From Columbus to Castro: The History of the Caribbean* (New York: Random House, 1984).

20. Robert Norton, *Resource Management Plans: Wildlife Resources* (Southeast Peninsula Board, St. Kitts and Tropical Research and Development, Inc., 1988). Norton gives a full description of natural resources on the peninsula, and recommends management alternatives to assist preservation efforts as the peninsula develops.

21. Government of St. Kitts and Nevis, *National Development Plan of St. Kitts and Nevis: 1986–1990.*

22. J. Beekhuis, *Preliminary Outline of a Tourist Strategy for USAID and the English-Speaking Eastern Caribbean* (Bridgetown, Barbados: USAID, the Regional Development Office for the Caribbean, 1985).

23. Organization of American States, *Proposal for the Development of the Pitons National Park* (St. Lucia: Department of Regional Development, Executive Secretariat for Economic and Social Affairs, February 1989). The St. Lucian government, through the Soufriere Development Program, requested technical assistance from the OAS in 1985. This report summarizes the results of the planning process for the proposed national park, and includes economic conditions, natural and cultural resources, how the project would be executed, and an assessment of its financial benefits. The OAS plan is accompanied by a master plan for the redevelopment of Soufriere, prepared by the Soufriere Development Program. It includes a resort hotel closer to Soufriere as an alternate the Jalousie project, a waterfront market mall, restaurants, hotels, commercial facilities, condominiums, a spa, and an anchoring area for large cruise ships.

24. Earl Bousquet, "Soufriere—The Jalousie Story: Iranians say 'M. Group's Project not Tenant's" (St. Lucia; The Voice, 18 February, 1989). This article summarizes the elements of the proposed resort. Official information from the government about what the project includes was not available. Several local newspaper stories were pieced together to help understand key elements of the case.

25. Government of St. Lucia, *St. Lucia National Plan: Development Strategy* (St. Lucia, 1980). The plan promotes the development of tourism, but also notes that it can disrupt "the socio-economic balance, aggravated by the fact that the sector is extremely susceptible to external influence at times of international boom and recession." The plan also states that "a more specific social problem requiring close monitoring concerns local participation and interaction of tourists and residents." On 11 April 1989, the prime minister addressed Parliament regarding the Pitons controversy. He indicated his commitment to developing the resort facility while supporting the park proposal. It is important to note the public position taken on this controversy by the prime minister. A public pronouncement from this top political official and leader of the majority party is at least as important as the objectives contained in the National Plan.

26. In *Growth of the Modern West Indies,* Lewis describes how the attitude of West Indians towards outsiders was formed by the involvement of colonial English interests as the region developed. He tells a story about how England appointed a commission in 1956 to recommend a list of sites for a new federal capital in the West Indies. The commissioners knew nothing of life in the West Indies, and "brought with them the social values of Englishmen for whom the West Indies have traditionally been a promising employment agency or pleasant vacation spot." Lewis tells of an incident in Grenada, reporting the remarks of a Dr. Groome, who said that "the Federal House of Representatives surely did not need an audience of gilded tourists to applaud its deliberations." He mentions the attitude of the British towards the colonies, "which has always had something of a chauvinistic paternalism about it."

27. Caribbean and Central American Association, *Caribbean and Central American Databook,* (Washington, DC: Caribbean and Central American Association, 1989).

28. Taken from Derek Walcott, "Jalousie Argument Borders on Prostitution" (St. Lucia Star, 26 August 1989).

29. Rick Wayne, "Is Compton Muzzling the DCA?" (The St. Lucia Star), 30 April, 1988.

30. Taken from the transcript of the Annual Address to Parliament by Prime Minister John Compton (Government of St. Lucia, Office of the Prime Minister), 11 April, 1989.

31. The *St. Lucia Star* editorial of 22 April 1989 was titled "Must We Always Choose Sight Unseen?" It mentioned that the government had not taken any public position on either the resort or park, and concluded by saying "It would do us all a world of good if the government came clean with all the facts of the matter. We should not be required yet again to make our choices in the dark of ignorance." The editorial in the *St. Lucia Voice* of 29 April was titled "Piton Confusion." It said that the resort and park cannot both be located in the same area, and declared "It is high time that the government make its position clear."

32. Vincent Lewis, "DCA Says Pitons Hotel Project Far from Approval: No Jalousie OK Yet" (The Weekend Voice) 20 May, 1989.

33. When the Southeast Peninsula Development Project was initiated in the early 1980s, its 4,000 acres were divided into twenty-two parcels owned by about 30 private parties. The peninsula was left in private ownership after the government formed the National Sugar Corporation in 1975 and nationalized all of the sugar plantations in the country. No working plantations existed on the peninsula at the time.

34. The full purpose and jurisdiction of the board is contained in the Southeast Peninsula Land Development and Conservation Act passed by Parliament in late 1986. The act was required by the Loan and Grant Agreement executed by St. Kitts and USAID in Article 5, Section 5.1(a).

35. Ibid.

36. The Barbados National Development Plans for the years 1979–83, 1983–88 and 1988–93 describe how the fishing industry will be improved, with the intent of decreasing food imports, lowering the balance of payments deficit, and providing additional food protein for the population.

37. There was a national election in May 1986, four months after the project was approved. In interviews, civil servants said that ministers push large projects through the planning process when national elections are coming up, to convince voters that they are productive. This means that large projects which normally require the most careful planning, often receive the least attention from planning technicians.

38. The Chief Forestry Officer was the first civil servant to advocate environmental reform in St. Lucia. He retired in 1990.

39. Soler, *Development Control: St. Kitts and Nevis.*

40. "Jalousie Project Under Scrutiny: Concern Over the Pitons," (Catholic Chronicle) No. 4, April, 1989.

41. Earl Bousquet, "Changing the Face of the Pitons," *St. Lucia Star,* 31 March 1990.

42. In "Overt Militarism and Covert Politics in St. Kitts–Nevis," Whitman Browne mentions that while the government of St. Kitts–Nevis was once a proponent of ideological pluralism, there is a present trend to limit political debate. Browne relates this shift to a more closed political system to the Caribbean Democratic Union, a conservative-oriented organization founded by several Caribbean leaders. Browne also examines how the St. Kitts military has grown in recent years, and relates this to a military attack made on St. Kitts from Anguilla in 1967, and the subsequent effect on St. Kitts politics, which has included threats of military intervention from rival political parties. Browne's essay is included in ed. Beruff, Figueroa, and Greene, *Conflict, Peace and Development in the Caribbean* (London: MacMillian Academic and Professional Ltd., 1991).

43. Three of the best known radio call-in shows were Tell It Like It Is, Getting Down to Business, and Gottaerperk (which roughly means to catapult or to shout directly). These shows are a good example of "bottom-up" participation in the public policy process.

CHAPTER FOUR

1. Edward T. Hall, *Beyond Culture*. (Garden City, New York: Anchor Books, 1976).

2. Michael Weiss, *Negotiation and Culture: Some Thoughts on Models, Ghosts, and Options* (Washington, D.C.: Dispute Resolution Forum, National Institution for Dispute Resolution, September 1987).

3. Edward T. Hall and Mildred Reed Hall, *Hidden Differences* (New York: Anchor Press, 1987). The Halls discuss the importance of several elements of culture and how they affect human relationships, including time, space, personal space, and time as structure.

4. Ibid., Pierre Casse, *Training for the Cross-Cultural Mind* (Washington, D.C.: The Society for Intercultural Communication, 1981).

5. Sally Engle Merrie, *Cultural Frameworks of Mediation* (University of Hawaii: Workshop on Transcultural Issues in Dispute Resolution, June 1987). Merrie discusses how conceptions of conflict and dispute resolution, often needed when new public policies are adopted, are embedded within cultural frameworks. How people view conflict, and traditions for resolving it, develop in response to conditions that can be unique to a specific culture. Since the adoption of new public policies—such as environmental policies—changes the status quo, conflict will result. Knowing how the members of a society deal with conflict can help an intervenor gain credibility and design an implementation process that fits local conditions.

6. See David Olsen, "From Utterance to Text: The Bias of Language in Speech and Writing" *Harvard Educational Review*, 47(1977); and David

Olsen, Nancy Torrance, and Angela Hildyard, eds., *Literacy, Language and Learning: The Nature and Consequences of Reading and Writing* (New York, Cambridge University Press, 1985). This book discusses the differences between written and spoken language, how these two kinds of discourse vary with oral and literal competency, and the ways that culture can affect communication when a native language is used.

7. Mervyn C. Alleyne, "A Linguistic Perspective on the Caribbean," in *Caribbean Contours*, ed. Sidney W. Mintz and Sally Price (Baltimore: Johns Hopkins University Press, 1985).

8. Parliamentary Commissioner for the Environment, *Environmental Management and the Principles of the Treaty of Waitangi* (New Zealand: November 1988). This report discusses how the Treaty of Waitangi has affected environmental management decisions, and the miscommunication that has occurred over the different language versions of the treaty. New Zealand has created an independent Waitangi Tribunal that deliberates to resolve conflicts arising from language in the treaty, but basic misunderstandings about how it should be applied to environmental conflicts persist.

9. Susan Goldstein, *Cultural Issues in Mediation: A Literature Review* (Manoa, Hawaii: University of Hawaii Program on Conflict Resolution, 1986). Goldstein discusses how cultural factors such as attitudes towards conflict and confrontation, verbal and non-verbal communication, self-disclosure, reason, logic, and self-perception within the larger cultural context need to be understood to resolve conflicts between different cultural groups.

10. Ron Scollon and Suzanne B. K. Scollon, *Narrative, Literacy and Face in Interethnic Communication* (Norwood, New Jersey: Ablex Publishing, 1981). The Scollons discuss how interethnic communication is affected by communication styles, and how the content and structure of information affects exchanges between people from different ethnic groups. They also discuss the concept of discourse as politeness phenomena, and offer suggestions for improving interethnic communication by incorporating politeness in cross-cultural dialogue.

11. Laura Nader and Harry F. Todd, Jr., eds., *The Disputing Process: Law in Ten Societies* (New York: Columbia University Press, 1978). This book focuses on the anthropology of law by examining ten actual disputes from different countries, and discusses why certain types of outcomes take place based on the relationship between the formal legal system and localized, informal styles of resolving conflict.

12. Max Gluckman, *Politics, Law and Ritual in Tribal Society* (Oxford: Basil Blackman, 1965). Gluckman discusses the application of social anthropology to political struggles and social order, especially in relation to rights to land and property, which are comparable to control over natural resources.

13. In *Public Management*, Khan summarizes the pre-colonial history of the region, and how political power gradually shifted from the metropolitan capitals to the islands. In *From Columbus to Castro: A History of the Caribbean* (New York: Random House, 1970), Eric Williams discusses how power struggles between European colonialists were fed by a world economy fueled by monopoly control of gold, sugar, and slaves in the Caribbean, and the resulting impact of European cultures in the region.

14. In "The Caribbean as a Socio-Cultural Area," *Journal of World History* 9(1966): Sidney W. Mintz argues that the mix of historical traditions, diverse origins of Caribbean populations, and complicated history of European cultural impositions make it useless to assign a single definition of culture to all Caribbean societies.

15. H. Hoetink, " 'Race' and Color in the Caribbean," in *Caribbean Contours*, ed. Sidney W. Mintz and Sally Price (Baltimore: Johns Hopkins University Press, 1985). Hoetink describes how the meaning attached to skin color and ethnicity evolved in the Caribbean, and why it is tied to the colonial history in the region. He quotes David Lowenthal, *West Indian Societies* (London: Oxford University Press, 1972), regarding the relationship between skin color and political control of St. Kitts and St. Lucia.

16. During my field work several Barbadians observed that a black middle class is emerging on that island, and in St. Kitts, perhaps one of the most stratified societies in the region, recent economic opportunities support several small and mid-sized black-owned businesses.

17. Mintz hypothesizes that a distinct quality of Caribbean social organization, especially in local cultures with a long plantation era such as those of the Eastern Caribbean, is the heavy emphasis on individual dyadic ties, rather than membership in larger social groups based on family. He proposes that this is an adaptive response to the intense westernization, long colonial history, heterogeneous population origins, and special economic history of the Caribbean (*The Caribbean as a Socio-Cultural Area*).

18. In the West Indies this has included several prime ministers, including Vere Bird, Sr., Antigua; Dr. Eric Williams, Trinidad and Tobago; Errol Barrow and the Adams family in Barbados; and John Compton, St. Lucia, who all served for many years (Bird and Compton were still in office in the early 1990s).

19. See Khan, *Public Management*, chapter 3, for a psychological-attitudinal profile of the Eastern Caribbean. He describes these societies as experiencing perceived powerlessness and incapacity for self-governance, so that "policy makers tend to create an impression of being powerful," and "decisions on all ranges of questions tend to be made by them personally." The observation of W. A. Lewis, in *The Industrialization of the British West Indies* (Port-of-Spain, Trinidad: Ministry of Industry, Com-

merce and Tourism, 1957), that "West Indians wait for something to happen" helps to explain how people in the region do not take the initiative to create social change, leaving the responsibility for policy change to a few strong individualistic political leaders who also often prefer not to take the initiative.

20. Neville C. Duncan, *Political Systems and Constraints on Cultural Sovereignty in the Anglophone Eastern Caribbean.* (Grenada: Conference on Culture and Sovereignty in the Caribbean, 20–23 November 1982). Duncan says "A consideration of the concept of alienation is vital because development is essentially a process that restores man to himself." He goes on to quote Marx, that all developments in human history tend "toward a single goal of eliminating alienation among men and, thus, revealing to them that they are masters and creators of their own social world."

21. From the poem "A Far Cry from Africa," by Derek Walcott, in *Derek Walcott: Collected Poems, 1948–84* (New York: Farrar, Straus and Giroux, 1986).

22. Mintz, *The Caribbean as a Socio-Cultural Area.* Mintz states that the plantation system has contributed to the development of a national identity in some Caribbean societies, but in many others has retarded their development. He mentions that the elements of the plantation system that have created this situation are forced labor and forced immigration.

23. See Paget Henry, "Decolonization and Cultural Underdevelopment in the Commonwealth Caribbean," in *The Newer Caribbean: Decolonization, Democracy and Development,* ed. Paget Henry and Carl Stone (Philadelphia: Institute for the Study of Human Issues, 1983). Henry describes how Africans brought to the Caribbean sought to define a new West Indian identity to replace the cultural heritage left behind on the Ivory Coast. Anglicization was brought into the Eastern Caribbean with the plantation system, further suppressing the development of a regional culture based on the African experience.

24. United States Bureau of the Census, *Statistical Abstract of the United States* (Washington, D.C.: U.S. Printing Office, 1984).

25. See Stephen Koester, "A Close Encounter of the Third World: West Indian Fishermen and Supertankers," *Cultural Survival Quarterly* 11(1987): Koester documents how the new Hess oil refinery at Cul de Sac Bay on St. Lucia has displaced several fishermen who can no longer fish. They cannot move to other sites as it would result in war with other fishermen who already have claimed them. The fishermen who are displaced depend on artisanal techniques that they can no longer use. In Gros Inlet on St. Lucia, a resort destroyed two fishing beaches. These and similar developments threaten artisanal fishers throughout the region, who use fishing techniques their ancestors brought from Africa.

26. Lindel Smith, "Elections and Politics in the Eastern Caribbean," *Caribbean Quarterly* 27 (March 1981): Smith discusses St. Kitts as being one of the true plantation economies in the Eastern Caribbean, with a socio-economic structure that lends itself to an extreme form of paternalism. He mentions how low levels of political and economic development in the region lead to a highly personalistic form of government, with primary importance placed on leaders, and that because of the small size of the islands this is likely to continue for some time. The observation about leaders being re-elected despite obvious corruption is based in part on the 1987 re-election of Vere Bird, Sr., long-time prime minister of Antigua, even after it was publicly revealed that a contract to pave the airport had included large side-payments to his son, also a government official, who then was given the nickname "Runway."

27. The "one person–many hats" phenomenon can by seen by looking at the career of two individuals on St. Lucia. Clem Bobb is an influential businessman who owns an insurance company, a television station, is a former member of the DCA, is founder of the Soufriere Development Committee, and is a member of the Tourist Board and School Board. Gabriel Charles was the CFO, founder of the Environmental Commission, chairman of the Parks and Protected Areas program, vice-chairman of the Beaches and Parks Commission, and on the governing board of the National Trust.

28. Interviews with current and former officials in the region revealed that public forums are not encouraged in general in the Eastern Caribbean. Political leaders feel that politically sensitive issues "could generate too much interest among the public and stretch out the process too long" (SK 4). Public forums can also be used by opposition groups to undermine the government.

29. Barbados has its own judicial system, while St. Lucia and St. Kitts are part of the Organization of Eastern Caribbean States judicial system. The two systems are similar. The first level of judicial review is the High Court followed by the Court of Appeal. Decisions made by the Court of Appeal may be appealed to the Privy Council in London.

30. See Yves Renard, ed., *Perceptions of the Environment: A Selection of Interpretative Essays* (Bridgetown, Barbados: Caribbean Conservation Association, 1979). This collection of articles focuses on different ways that small communities of resource users use and think about the environment.

31. When asked to explain this, a former Peace Corps worker on St. Kitts who worked with fishermen for several years said that they are generally described as "someone with an empty stomach and a wet ass" (SK 19).

32. Hurricanes in 1979 and 1980 wiped out the banana crop in St. Lucia, the largest earner of foreign exchange. In June 1987 a rain storm caused widespread damage on Nevis and knocked out a main power plant in St.

Kitts. In 1989 Hurricane Hugo destroyed or damaged half of the buildings on Nevis and caused heavy damage on St. Kitts. Local residents say that it takes months to recover from the psychological effects of these disasters, and for life to resume a normal pattern, because of the severe disruption they cause.

33. See Khan, *Public Management*. This finding is consistent with Khan's research, which found that a belief in organized life and long-term planning is limited in the region.

34. Robert Devaux, *St. Lucia Historical Sites* (Castries, St. Lucia: St. Lucia National Trust, 1975).

35. This was reflected in comments made to me in the streets of Soufriere by local residents during the annual carnival, and in the words of the song "Jalousie's Wedding" sung by the 1989 Calypso King, Alman. The lyrics of this Calypso tune talk of the "wedding" between the developers of the resort and politicians, that the Jalousie Estate has been lost to outsiders, the people of Soufriere have nothing to say about it, and will gain nothing from it.

36. See Lindel Smith, "Elections and Politics." Smith hypothesizes that politics in St. Kitts are less sophisticated than in other countries in the region because of its low level of political development, which leads to a highly personalized brand of public policy.

CHAPTER FIVE

1. For a description of the sugar and slave trades, see Parry and Sherlock, *History of the West Indies*.

2. See Khan, *Public Management*.

3. Dr. Colin Clarke, *Sovereignty, Dependency and Social Change in the Caribbean*. In South America, Central America and the Caribbean (London: Europa Publications, 1988).

4. Lewis, *Growth of the Modern Indies*. Lewis describes why political and economic reform was so late in coming to the West Indies, and how England in particular contributed to this retardation of development. Reforms leading to independence were slow and piecemeal, and it was not until the end of the colonial era in the 1960s that West Indians were appointed to important administrative posts, in lieu of the British who had historically been assigned to important positions in the region.

5. Richard Fletcher, "Resources and Expectations in the English-Speaking Caribbean," in *The English-Speaking Caribbean: Current Conditions and Implications for U.S. Policy* (Washington, D.C.: Congressional Research Service, 1975).

6. Robin Chapman, "Latin America and the Caribbean: Economic Problems," in *South America, Central America and the Caribbean, 1988* (London: Europa Publications, 1988).

7. While the national economies in the Eastern Caribbean have grown and generally stabilized, many other countries in the wider Caribbean have experienced negative economic growth. Negative growth has tended to occur in countries dependent on exporting oil, certain agricultural products, and minerals (e.g., Trinidad-Tobago, Jamaica, Haiti, and Guyana). For a description of economic trends in the Caribbean as a whole, see Carmen Diana Deere et al., *In the Shadows of the Sun: Caribbean Development Alternatives and U.S. Policy* (San Francisco: Westview Press, 1990).

8. See DeLisle Worrell and Compton Bourne, eds., *Economic Adjustment Policies for Small Nations: Theory and Experience in the English-Speaking Caribbean* (New York: Praeger, 1989). This book discusses macroeconomic conditions and trends in the region, including the important role of trade, capital movements, and fiscal and credit policies. Also see David L. McKee and Clem Tisdell, *Development Issues in Small Island Economies* (New York: Praeger, 1990), in particular chapter 13, which discusses how most island economies are dependent on international trade and the problems associated with this dependency.

9. See U.S. Congress, House, Committees on Foreign Affairs and Ways and Means, and Senate, Committee on Foreign Relations and Finance, "Country Reports on Economic Policy and Trading Practices" (Washington, D.C.: U.S. Government Printing Office, February 1993).

10. For a description of current and past economic conditions in the Eastern Caribbean, refer to The Economist Intelligence Unit, *Guyana, Barbados, Windward and Leeward Islands: Country Profile, 1991–92* (London, 1992).

11. World Bank, *Caribbean Countries: Economic Situation, Regional Issues and Capital Flows* (Washington, D.C.: The World Bank, 1988).

12. Wendell A. Samuel, *Foreign Assistance in the Caribbean: Another View* (Barbados: University of the West Indies, 1988). Samuel proposes that even though the debt service ration of Eastern Caribbean countries is fairly low, their lack of resiliency to variations in the world economy makes them particularly vulnerable. Evidence of this is that most of the foreign debt of the islands is owed to international aid organizations because the islands lack the economic stability to attract commercial loans.

13. Ransford W. Palmer, *Problems of Development in Beautiful Countries: Perspectives on the Caribbean* (Lanham, Maryland: North-South Publishing Company, 1984). Palmer describes the reasons for underdevelop-

ment relating to small-resource poor islands in the region, and why early strategies to reduce unemployment through industrialization have failed to live up to expectations.

14. Kempe Ronald Hope, *Economic Development in the Caribbean* (New York: Praeger, 1986). Hope describes the effect of unemployment and underemployment on the economies of the region, and the relation of these factors to a fast-growing population.

15. Ibid.

16. *South America, Central America and the Caribbean* (London, Europa Publications, 1988).

17. The figures on the tonnage of sugar produced in 1988 and 1989 are from West Indian Committee, *Caribbean Insight*, 13(3) (London, March, 1990). A shortage of cane cutters was noted in 1989 field interviews with sugar estate managers who have to use imported labor to supplement local workers.

18. Latin American Monitor, *The Caribbean* (6(10), London, Latin American Monitor Ltd., December 1989).

19. Taken from The Economist Intelligence Unit, *Country Profiles* and The Economist *A Survey of the Caribbean* (London, 6 August 1988).

20. World Bank, *Barbados Economic Memorandum* (Latin American and Caribbean Regional Office, the World Bank, Washington, D.C., the World Bank, 1988).

21. Carmen Diana Deere et al., *Caribbean Development Alternatives*, 149.

22. See Economist Intelligence Unit, 1992, page 43.

23. See Scott B. MacDonald and Georges A. Fauriol, eds., *The Politics of the Caribbean Basin Sugar* (New York: Praeger, 1991). In chapter 6, titled "Sugar in the Commonwealth Caribbean," Mark H. Bidua and Daniel J. Seyler discuss why many countries are trying to move away from sugar production. Among the reasons they cite are a steady decline in the efficiency of sugar production in the region, international market pressures on sugar exporters as global competition for sugar production and sales have increased, and the poor standard of living in rural areas that depend on sugar production for jobs.

24. World Bank, *Caribbean Countries: Economic Situation, Regional Issues and Capital Flows* (World Bank, Washington, D.C., 1988).

25. Hope, *Economic Development in the Caribbean*.

26. Caribbean Tourism Research and Development Centre, *The Contribution of Tourism to Economic Growth and Development in the Caribbean* (St, Michael, Barbados: CTRC, 1988).

27. The Economist Intelligence Unit, *Country Profile*, page 46.

28. The World Bank, *Barbados Economic Memorandum* (Washington, D.C.: Latin American and Caribbean Regional Office, the World Bank, 1984): The World Bank, *Caribbean Countries: Economic Situation, Regional Issues and Capital Flows* (Washington, D.C.: The World Bank, 1988).

29. *The Latin American Monitor, The Caribbean.* 6(10), (London, Latin American Monitor Ltd., December, 1989).

30. The World Bank, *Caribbean Countries.*

31. Worrell, *Economic Adjustment Policies for Small Nations.*

32. Palmer, *Problems of Development in Beautiful Countries.*

33. World Bank, *Caribbean Countries.*

34. Europa Publications, South America, Central America and the Caribbean. CARICOM was founded in 1973 for the purpose of promoting economic integration through a common market. Headquartered in Guyana, CARICOM brings together Caribbean heads of state to foster regional cooperation in economic, health, educational, communication and industrial relations. Island Resources Institute, *Organizational Profiles: A Guide to Donor Organizations and Technical Assistance Agencies* (Washington, D.C.: Island Resources Institute, 1989).

35. The Economist Intelligence Unit *Country Profile 1989–90* (London: The Economist, 1990).

36. World Bank, *St. Lucia: Economic Performance and Prospects* (Washington, D.C.: A World Bank Country Study, 1985).

37. Orlando Patterson, "The Emerging West Atlantic System: Migration, Culture, and Underdevelopment in the United States and the Circum-Caribbean Region," in *Population in an Interacting World,* ed. William Alonso (Cambridge: Harvard Press, 1987).

38. Neville C. Duncan, *External Development Aid: New Policy Considerations* (Barbados: University of the West Indies, Cave Hill Campus, 1986). Duncan mentions that the islands in the Eastern Caribbean were eager to accept foreign aid from the United States in light of the relatively small contributions the British made to the region after independence. He mentions the "paltry independence assistance to each of the EC states as a grant and another 5 million pounds sterling as aid."

39. Clarke, *Sovereignty, Dependency and Social Change.*

40. Richard Brown, *U.S. Relations with the Commonwealth Caribbean* In "The English-Speaking Caribbean: Current Conditions and Implications for U.S. Foreign Policy." (Washington, D.C.: Congressional Research Service, 1985).

41. Kenneth I. Boodhoo, "Economic Dimension of U.S. Caribbean Policy," in *The Caribbean Challenge: U.S. Policy in a Volatile Region*, ed. H. Michael Erisman (Boulder, Colorado: Westview Press, 1984).

42. Caribbean Basin Information Center, *CBI Business Bulletin*, 7(2), February, 1989. William Demas, "Situation and Change," in *Caribbean Economy*, ed. G. Beckford.

43. Richard Brown, *The English-Speaking Caribbean: Current Conditions and Implications for U.S. Policy*, Proceedings from a workshop held on December 11, 1984 (Washington, D.C.: U.S. Government Printing Office, 1985).

44. World Bank, *Caribbean Countries*.

45. See U.S. Congress, House, Committee on Foreign Affairs, Subcommittees on International Economic Policy and Trade and Western Hemisphere Affairs, "Beyond the Northern Free Trade Agreement: Chile, the Caribbean and Administrative Views," Hearings before the Subcommittees 102nd Cong., 2nd sess., 12 May and 1 July 1992 (Washington, D.C.: U.S. Government Printing Office, 1993).

46. Worrell and Bourne (eds), *Economic Adjustment Policies for Small Nations*.

47. Clarke, *Sovereignty, Dependency and Social Change in the Caribbean*.

48. Lewis, *Growth of the Modern West Indies*.

49. W. Andrew Axline, *Caribbean Integration: The Politics of Regionalism* (New York: Nichols Publishing, 1979). Axline describes how the special characteristics of the political systems in the Caribbean make regional integration difficult. He discusses the pattern of regional negotiations and how coalitions shift in the midst of a multinational dialogue.

50. Lewis, *Growth of the Modern West Indies*.

51. In 1987 several political leaders in the Eastern Caribbean initiated a movement to create a political and economic federation by strengthening the Organization of Eastern Caribbean States. But other leaders said in response that a new unitary state was a kind of colonialism, and would promote the influence of foreign powers. These differences are typical of the current obstacles to regional integration. See Gary Brana-Shute and Rosemary Brana-Shute, "The Anglophone Eastern Caribbean and British Depen-

dencies," in *Latin America and the Caribbean Record* (New York: Holmes and Meier, 1989).

52. Anthony Payne and Paul Suttar, *Dependency Under Challenge: The Political Economy of the Commonwealth Caribbean* (Manchester, U.K.: Manchester University Press, 1984).

53. Worrell and Bourne (eds.), *Economic Adjustment Policies for Small Nations.*

54. World Bank, *Caribbean Countries;* The Economist Intelligence Unit *Country Profiles.*

55. Khan, *Public Management.*

56. The Alliance of Small Island States (AOSIS) has recently formed as a political coalition to create an international voice that can express the needs and concerns of island nations. AOSIS is a group of forty-one island states gathered into an "ad hoc coalition of developing countries which share common objectives on environmental and sustainable development matters." AOSIS members, using their status as members and observers of the United Nations, are drawing attention to the special needs of island countries, especially needs related to environmental problems, resource management, and institution building (*The Independent Sectors' Network* (Geneva: Switzerland: The Centre for Our Common Future, April 1993).

57. Island Resources Foundation, *Organizational Profiles: A Guide to Donor Organizations and Technical Assistance Agencies* (Washington, D.C.: IRF, 1989).

58. Lynton Keith Caldwell, *International Environmental Policy: Emergence and Dimensions* (Durham, North Carolina: Duke University Press, 1990).

59. United Nations Environment Programme, "Report of the Meeting of Experts for the Development of a Protocol Concerning Specially Protected Areas and Wildlife in the Wider Caribbean," St. Croix, U.S. Virgin Islands, October 24–26, 1988.

60. Details of the case are taken from interviews with Yves Renard, coordinator of the Southeast Coast Project and co-founder of the Caribbean Natural Resource Institute, and from World Wildlife Fund, "Conservation and Development in St. Lucia," Letter no. 3 (: WWF, 1988).

61. Data on 1985 land values taken from a consulting report prepared for USAID, titled *Potential for Recovery of Public Investments and Costs: Southeast Peninsula, St. Kitts* by Robert R. Nathan Associates, Washington, D.C., May 28, 1986. Data on 1990 land sales are from personal interviews conducted in St. Kitts.

62. *Weekend Voice,* St. Lucia, February 18, 1988; and *Caribbean Insight,* 13(3), (London: the West Indian Committee, March, 1990).

63. Organization of American States, *Proposal for the Development of the Pitons National Park* (Washington, D.C.: The Department of Regional Development, OAS, 1989). The operating income for the park needed to create the 500–1,200 jobs would be derived from admission fees and proceeds from its concessions (restaurant, bar, botanic garden, fruit and spice plantation, mini-zoo and glass-bottom boat) and the sale of tourist souvenirs.

64. Ibid. To build the park the government would risk at least EC$4.5 million for initial expenses, and probably much more as the owners of the Jalousie Estate would not be willing sellers, plus an estimated EC$700,000 a year for operating expenses. The return on this substantial public investment depends on the continued strength of the world tourism market.

65. Soler, *Development Control: St. Lucia.* Soler evaluates the capacity of the government to support projects that require long-range planning, and finds that it lacks the institutional capacity to do so.

Chapter Six

1. Michael Todaro discusses why economic indicators are not a reliable measure of development. It is common for countries to experience an increase in economic growth while showing little or no improvement in unemployment and equality, as measured by examining an increase in income or wealth for the poorest 40 percent of the population. For a complete discussion of the different theories and models of development see Michael P. Todaro, *Economic Development in the Third World* (New York: Longman, 1985).

2. Ransford Palmer, *Problems of Development in Beautiful Countries: Perspectives on the Caribbean* (Lanham, Maryland: North-South Publishing Co., 1984). Palmer describes the problems of peripheral development shared by the island economies of the Caribbean. The historical dependence on metropolitan centers in the plantation era is being succeeded by a continued dependence on foreign investors and donor agencies because the region lacks the domestic resources to develop on its own. But it is my observation that integrated development strategies are showing positive results in lessening dependency somewhat. Whether this continues to happen will depend on the strength of the tourist economy and what happens to preferential import quotas for agricultural crops in the United States and the European Community in the 1990s.

3. For a discussion of the need for outside investment and how it relates to national growth strategies in the Eastern Caribbean, see Ransford

Palmer, "The Commonwealth Caribbean: Crisis of Adjustment," in *The English Speaking Caribbean: Current Conditions and Implications for U.S. Foreign Policy* (Washington, D.C.: Congressional Research Service, 1985).

4. Caribbean Development Bank, *Basic Information* (Bridgetown, Barbados: CDB, 1988).

5. General information on the operation and organization of the IDB is derived from Eurofi, Ltd., *Development Aid: A Guide to National and International Agencies* (London: Butterworths, 1988).

6. R. Peter DeWitt, Jr., *The Inter-American Development Bank and Political Influence* (New York: Praeger, 1977).

7. M. Margaret Ball, *The OAS in Transition* (Durham: Duke University Press, 1968). Ball discusses the organization and functioning of the OAS, including how its numerous specialized agencies work.

8. O. Carlos Stoetzer, *The Organization of American States—An Introduction* (New York: Praeger, 1965); and "The Annual Report of the Secretary General, 1987–88," General Secretariat of the OAS, Washington, D.C.

9. The word *environment* was added to the name of the department in 1989.

10. Taken in part from *Summary of Services Provided by the Department of Regional Development, General Secretariat of the OAS, 1989–90* (Washington, D.C.: OAS, 1989–1990).

11. Organization of American States, "Final Report: Cultural Patrimony and the Tourism Product—Towards a Mutually Beneficial Relationship," proceedings from a conference organized by the OAS International Trade and Tourism Division and the Caribbean Tourism Research and Development Centre in conjunction with the Caribbean Conservation Association and the OAS Department of Cultural Affairs, held in Barbados, July 18–22, 1983. These proceedings include papers on how to create beneficial linkages between tourism and culture, tourism and historical architecture, tourism and craft development, and the performing and the literary arts, with recommendations for each area.

12. OAS, *Minimum Conflicts: Guidelines for Planning the Use of American Humid Tropic Environments*. Washington, D.C.: Organization of American States, Lima: Government of Peru and, Washington, D.C.: United Nations Environment Programme, 1987. This work examines how legal, governmental, and institutional authority in Peru affects natural resource management. It also discusses major factors that fuel natural resource conflicts in the humid tropics, such as water resources, wildlife, human health, human settlement patterns, agriculture, forestry, ranching, fisheries, mineral development, transportation, and energy use and production. Several

recommendations are included for strengthening integrated planning and resource management, but specific in-country actions that are needed to implement these suggestions are fairly general.

13. OAS, *Integrated Regional Development Planning: Guidelines and Case Studies from OAS Experience* (Washington, D.C.: OAS, 1984).

14. OAS, *The Optimum Size and Nature of New Hotel Development in the Caribbean* (Dept. of Regional Development, OAS, Washington, D.C., 1987) and OAS, *Plan and Policy for a System of National Parks and Protected Areas in Grenada and Carriacou* (Grenada Forestry Department with the OAS, Washington, D.C., 1988).

15. John Horberry, "Development Assistance and the Environment: A Question of Accountability" (Ph.D. diss., Massachusetts Institute of Technology, 1984).

16. Wendell A. Samuel, *Foreign Assistance in the Caribbean:* USAID uses double-tiered aid; it requires the recipient to use development funds to buy exports from the United States, including equipment, professional services, and raw materials. This requirement helps insure that funds are used for the purpose they are intended, but it can also prevent recipients from using them to achieve development objectives that they prefer. However, recipients need hard currency, so they accept these terms in project agreements as the alternative may be no project at all.

17. USAID Regional Development Office for the Caribbean, "Summary of Expenditures in the Caribbean" (Bridgetown, Barbados: USAID, 1990).

18. For a full description of USAID's programs, funding procedures, and scope of activities, see Eurofi, Ltd., *Development Aid: A Guide to National and International Agencies* (London: Butterworths, 1988).

19. Eugene Bardach, *The Implementation Game: What Happens When a Bill Becomes a Law* (Cambridge: MIT Press, 1977).

20. Deborah Stone, *Policy Paradoxes and Political Reason.* (Boston: Scott, Foresman and Co., 1988). Stone describes how personal qualities such as emotion, passion, irrationality, self-interest, shortsightedness, and raw power motivate people, such as entrenched bureaucrats, during their involvement in the policy-making process.

21. Albert O. Hirschman, *Development Projects Observed* (Washington, D.C.: The Brookings Institute, 1967).

22. Ignacy Sachs, *Development and Planning* (New York: Cambridge University Press, 1987).

23. Sierra Club, *Bankrolling Disasters*.

24. Statement of R. Augustus Edwards III, Deputy Assistant Administrator for External Affairs, U.S. Environmental Protection Agency, in a hearing before the Subcommittee on Hazardous Wastes and Toxic Substances of the Senate Committee on Environment and Public Works, June 16, 1988.

25. Statement of James A. Baker III, Secretary of the Treasury, and Progress Report in Implementation of Environmental Reform in Multilateral Development Banks, presented during hearings before a Subcommittee of Appropriates, United States Senate, March 30, 1988.

26. Taken from the *Statement of Bruce M. Rich, Senior Attorney, Environmental Defense Fund* before the Senate Subcommittee on Foreign Relations at a hearing on Foreign Operations, Export Financing and Related Programs Appropriations, 102d Congress, First Session, Fiscal Year 1992, pp. 217-241.

27. Information about the Morse Commission is taken from Bruce Rich, *Memorandum on The Role of the World Bank After UNCED: The Need for Institutional Reform* (Washington, D.C.: Environmental Defense Fund, 1992). Mr. Rich has been examining the environmental performance of the World Bank and other development assistance agencies for several years, documenting case studies of World Bank actions and recommending how reforms should be instituted to change World Bank policies and procedures to protect limited natural resources more effectively. Also see Statement of Bruce M. Rich on Behalf of the Environmental Defense Fund, National Wildlife Federation and Sierra Club Concerning Fiscal Year Appropriations for the World Bank, Global Environmental Facility, African Development Bank, United Nations Environment Program, World Heritage Fund, Inter-American Foundation, Appropriate Technology International and Other Related Issues, presented to the Subcommittee on Foreign Operations, Committee on Appropriations, United States Senate, June 15, 1993. `

28. Bradford Morse et al., *Sardar Sarovar: Report of the Independent Review* (Ottawa: Resources Future International, Inc., 1989), 36.

29. See John Horberry, *The Accountability of Development Assistance Agencies: The Case of Environmental Policy. Ecology Law Quarterly,* 12 (4), (Berkeley, CA: University of California, 1985).

30. Taken from a comment made by Senator Kasten to Mr. Malpass, Deputy Assistant Secretary for Developing Nations, Department of the Treasury, during a hearing before the Subcommittee of the Committee on Appropriations, hearing transcript, United States Senate, 30 March 1988.

31. Statement of Stephan Schwartzman before a hearing of the Subcommittee on International Development Institutions and Finance of the Committee on Banking, Finance and Urban Affairs, hearing transcript, House of Representatives, June 1988.

32. The opposition of IDB members to environmental reforms is re-lated to the larger North-South debate over environmental reform. Many de-veloping countries believe that they should not have to sacrifice economic growth if they agree to protect natural resources. Developing nations have formed the Group of 77 to negotiate as a block with developed nations on global environmental issues. For example, several rapidly industrializing na-tions, such as Brazil, India, and Mexico, believe that restrictions on hydro-carbon emissions to mitigate the greenhouse effect will constrain their use of energy and thereby slow industrialization. They are seeking compensa-tion in exchange for pollution controls. See United Nations Environment Programmes, *North America News* 5 (February 1990).

33. Statement of David Malpass before the Subcommittee on Haz-ardous Wastes and Toxic Substances of the Committee on Environment and Public Works, United States Senate, 16 June 1988. This statement reflected the resistance of Treasury to a suggestion that the MDBs be required to con-duct detailed environmental impact assessments on their projects. Treasury apparently felt that this would give environmental concerns a higher prior-ity than economic factors, which are a key element of United States foreign policy. As a result, foreign policy initiatives based on economic cooperation could be compromised.

34. U.S. Senate, "An Amendment Extending the Requirements of the National Environmental Policy Act to Recommendations for the United States Vote in International Financial Institutions" (Washington, D.C.: U.S. Senate Calendar No. 918, 100th Congress, 2nd Session, Report 100-498).

35. The IDB does fund some environmental improvement projects such as reforestation in Haiti, coastal conservation in Barbados, soil conser-vation in Jamaica, and an integrated natural resource management program in Paraguay. These projects make up a very small part of the IDB's overall budget. (Inter-American Development Bank, *The IDB and the Environment* [Washington, D.C.: IDB, 1988]).

36. See "Proceedings of the Third Consultative Meeting with Public Agencies and Nongovernmental Organizations Concerned with Environ-mental Protection and Conservation of Natural Resources," sponsored by the Inter-American Development Bank Environmental Management Com-mittee, Caracas, Venezuela, June 17-19, 1991.

37. Horberry, *The Accountability of Development Assistance Agencies.*

38. USAID, *AID Policy Paper: Environment and Natural Resources* (Washington, D.C.: Bureau for Program and Policy Coordination, USAID, 1988).

39. USAID, June, 1992. "Environment Strategy: Policy." This policy statement also discusses general strategies for addressing environmental

problems in the developing world, including strengthening institutional capacity and encouraging private sector participation in promoting environmentally sound development practices.

40. USAID, *Draft USAID Strategy Papers* (Washington, D.C.: 5 October 1993). This new strategy, intended to form the basic policy for worldwide USAID operations, places a strong emphasis on the importance of measuring the results of USAID projects and programs. It discusses the desire to build indigenous capacity, using Private Voluntary Organizations (PVOs) and NGOs to extend influence in the developing world. The Environmental Strategy is linked with Agenda 21 of the Earth Summit's guidelines for ecologically sustainable development, and stresses as major priorities climate change, biodiversity, improving land use practices, and strengthening public policies in the developing world. However, like the previous strategy, this one does not include specific recommendations for how USAID can strengthen public policies and institutions in countries where it develops large projects that are most likely to cause environmental damage.

41. USAID, *A Draft Reorganization Proposal for A.I.D. Washington*, accompanied by a memorandum for USAID Staff from J. Brian Atwood, USAID Administrator, Washington, D.C., August, 1993.

42. USAID, *Environmental Strategy for Latin America and the Caribbean.* (Washington, D.C.: USAID Bureau for Latin America and the Caribbean, January, 1993).

43. USAID, *Green Guidance for Latin America and the Caribbean: Integrating Environmental Concerns in A.I.D. Programming* (Washington, D.C.: Bureau for Latin America and the Caribbean and the Center for International Development and Environment of the World Resources Institute, January 1993).

44. During testimony before the Senate Subcommittee on International Economic Policy, Trade, Oceans and the Environment in mid-1988, the National Resources Defense Council reported that only one of eight projects rejected by United States MDB directors appeared on a USAID list, and that the information used did not influence non–United States directors, who approved the projects despite being aware that they would cause environmental damage.

45. Organization of American States, Department of Regional Development, 1989. *Summary of Services Provided by the Department of Regional Development.*

46. The United States has expressed a strong interest in supporting the tradition of parliamentary democracies that exists in the Eastern Caribbean. Its invasion of Grenada in 1983—after ultra-leftist Leninists massacred 100 innocent people, including Prime Minister Maurice Bishop—reflected a statement made by Sally Shelton, a former Ambassador to the Eastern Caribbean, in 1980 and repeated on several occasions: "(the)

U.S. will support progressive forces . . . who are committed to economic and social development and who respect democratic processes." See Anthony Payne, *Change in the Commonwealth Caribbean* (London: The Royal Institute of International Affairs, 1981). After Bishop had taken office by a bloodless coup in 1979, he suspended the constitution and canceled elections, to the consternation of the United States government. See Wendell Bell, "The Invasion of Grenada: A Note of False Prophecy," *The Yale Review* 1986.

47. USAID has played a major role in promoting United States business interests in St. Kitts, in both the planning and construction of the road, and the facilitation of investment opportunities in tourist projects that will follow the road. In May 1986 the agency organized a "hotel investment mission" in St. Kitts. Attending were top corporate officers from the hotel industry including representatives of Hilton Inns, Club Med, Divi Hotels, Ramada International, Resorts International, and several real estate companies. The contractor for the road was from Puerto Rico, a United States territory, the engineer was from a United States company, and over $1 million was spent on United States environmental consultants.

48. For example, several Annual Reports issued by the IDB have made this assertion.

49. In mid-1990, the IDB's new Environmental Protection Division issued new procedures for carrying out an environmental impact assessment process. The Division now employs several experts in various aspects of environmental management. It is still overseen by the EMC.

50. The basic steps in the project cycle are (1) designing the project concept; (2) examining and helping refine a national growth strategy; (3) creating a financial package that is feasible; (4) analyzing and documenting technical issues, including environmental concerns; (5) approving the financial package, usually a loan and smaller grant; and (6) building the project (Inter-American Development Bank, "The Programming, Processing and Approval of IDB Loans" [Washington, D.C.: IDB, 1983]).

51. USAID, *Amendment to the Environmental Assessment Report for the St. Kitts Southeast Peninsula Development Project* (Washington, D.C., 1988).

52. Joshua C. Dickenson, "Environmental Impact Assessment" (An informal paper presented to USAID and the DESFIL planning team, 1989). Dr. Dickenson is president of Tropical Research and Development, Inc., a major participant in the environmental planning process for the peninsula. His brief paper summarizes some of the difficulties of implementing environmental reform in developing countries, and integrating them into USAID projects.

53. Organization of American States, *Proposal for the Development of the Pitons National Park*. Chapter 4.0, Financial and Economic Assessment.

54. Nick Peter Troobitscoff and Frank Alfred Hamilton, "Master Plan for Soufriere Regional Tourism Maximization Strategy" (Commissioned by the Soufriere Development Program, 1988).

55. Soler, *Development Control: St. Lucia.* Soler points out that "when forward planning is done it reaches a plateau and never goes further ahead. What's more, whatever forward planning is done is strongly oriented to urban design or to critical issues which are already in themselves a problem." (p. 29)

56. Fernaldo Soler analyzed the planning capability of St. Kitts and St. Lucia in 1988 for OAS and OECS. The Natural Resource Management Project of OECS has documented the inability of both countries to implement environmental laws in its series of reports on "Harmonization of Environmental Legislation" (St. Lucia: OECS, 1986).

CHAPTER SEVEN

1. John L. Seitz, *The Politics of Development: An Introduction to Global Issues* (New York: Basil Blackwell, 1988), 143.

2. Lynton Keith Caldwell, *International Environmental Policy: Emergence and Dimensions* (Durham, North Carolina: Duke University Press, 1990). Caldwell discusses conventions, treaties, and regional agreements that were reached by negotiation.

3. See Janet M. Chernela, *The Role of Indigenous Organizations in International Policy Development: The Case of an Awa Biosphere Reserve in Colombia and Ecuador* (Miami: Florida International University, the State University at Miami, 1989). Chernela mentions that international funding agencies attached conditions that required the government in Ecuador to include an NGO representing an indigenous tribal group, which strengthened the bargaining positions of both indigenous and environmental groups in the negotiations for a new biosphere reserve.

4. Lawrence Susskind and Jeffrey Cruikshank, *Breaking the Impasse: Consensual Approaches to Resolving Public Disputes* (New York: Basic Books, 1987). See pages 25 and 101–3 for a discussion of stakeholder attitudes and perceptions, and the need to include all stakeholders in a negotiation.

5. Susan Carpenter and W. J. D. Kennedy, *Managing Public Disputes* (San Francisco: Jossey-Bass, 1988), 118–24.

6. The roles of the facilitator and the mediator are derived from "Dispute Resolution Methods" (Washington, D.C.: National Institute for Dispute Resolution,). Also see Susskind and Cruikshank, *Breaking the Impasse*, who differentiate between assisted and unassisted forms of negotiation, and describe what each entails.

7. There are other qualities that any good mediator should possess, such as good communication skills, and the ability to analyze a conflict, design a strategy for dealing with it, and manage a process filled with conflicting personalities and large amounts of data. See Carpenter and Kennedy, *Public Disputes*, 191–3.

8. See Susskind and Cruikshank, *Breaking the Impasse*. In chapters 4 and 5 the authors discuss under what circumstances facilitation and mediation should be used.

9. Susskind and Cruikshank, ibid., discuss the typical tasks that a mediator will carry out when assisting the negotiating parties. These tasks include helping to set the agenda for the negotiating sessions, helping the parties summarize the issues they are most concerned with, and structuring the discussion so that all of the parties are given a voice in the proceedings. See pages 142–3 of *Breaking the Impasse* for a description of other responsibilities of the mediator.

10. John Paul Lederach, *Summaries of The Transfer Model and the Elicitive/Catalyst Model* (Akron, Penn.: Mennonite Conciliation Service, 1988).

11. Ibid.

12. See Susskind and Cruikshank, *Breaking the Impasse*, and Carpenter and Kennedy, *Public Disputes*, for discussions of what type of protocols and ground rules should be established.

13. Carpenter and Kennedy, *Public Disputes*, 216–8. Carpenter and Kennedy discuss the value of being able to reward the other side for cooperation, the importance of a sound alternative, and the ability to cause harm by increasing a cost. Stakeholders who are excluded from development decisions can offer all of these incentives to political leaders in exchange for their participation in decision making.

14. See H. Jeffrey Leonard, *Environment and the Poor: Development Strategies for a Common Agenda* (New Brunswick: Transaction Books, 1989). Leonard describes strategies that combine environmental protection with improving the quality of life for poor resource users; see pages 31–43. David Pitt, " ," in *The Human Dimension in Environmental Planning*, ed. Jeffrey A. McNeely and David Pitt (London: Croom Helm, 1985), 283, discusses the effectiveness of linking resource users to national environmental planning programs.

15. Lynton K. Caldwell, *International Environmental Policy*, chapter 9.

Bibliography

In order to write this book I spent considerable time in several countries, visiting with a wide variety of people, taking the time to build personal relationships in order to hear the stories of individuals involved in all aspects of environmental policymaking. It is the collection of these stories that forms the backbone of this book, its assumptions, reflections and recommendations. Yet, I have attempted to build on existing theoretical research that touches on and interconnects the fields of international development, public policy, environmental studies, international conservation and cross cultural communication. Because I have mainly focused on gathering evidence from people actually involved in the cases I describe, I have not been as specific when tying my findings to existing theory. However, I continue to conduct research and practice professionally in this area, and invite individuals conducting similar research to contact me if they have questions about any of the work that appears in this book.

Public Policy and Politics

Allison, Graham. *Essence of Decision.* Boston: Little, Brown, and Co., 1971.

Bardach, Eugene. *The Implementation Game: What Happens After a Bill Becomes a Law.* Cambridge: MIT Press, 1977.

Barry, Jeffrey M. *The Interest Group Society,* Boston: Little, Brown and Co., 1984.

Catlin, George E. G. *A Study of the Principles of Politics.* London: Allen and Unwin, 1930.

Caldwell, Lynton K. *Science and the National Environmental Policy Act: Redirecting Policy Through Procedural Reform.* University, Alabama: University of Alabama Press, 1982.

Cooper, C. *Economic Evaluation and the Environment.* London: Hodder and Stoughton, 1981.

Daly, Herman E. "The Steady-State Economy: Toward a Political Economy of Biophysical Equilibrium and Moral Growth." In *Economics, Ecology and Ethics,* Herman E. Daly. San Francisco: W. H. Freeman, 1980.

Douglas, Mary, and Aaron Wildavsky. *Risk and Culture.* Berkeley: University of California Press, 1982.

Etzioni, Halevy. *Political Manipulation and Administative Power: A Comparative Study.* London: Routledge and Kegan Paul, 1979.

Fischer, Frank. *Politics, Values and Public Policy: The Problem of Methodology.* Boulder: Westview, 1980.

Fisher, B. Aubrey. *Small Group Decision Making.* New York: McGraw Hill, 1980.

Forester, John. *Planning in the Face of Power.* Berkeley: University of California Press, 1989.

Gamson, William. "Political Discourse and Political Action." In *From Structure to Action and Social Movement Participation Across Cultures.* Edited by Bert Klandermans, Hanspeter Kriesi, Sidney Tarrow. Greenwich, CT: JAI Press, 1986.

Hufschmidt, Maynard M., et al. *Environment, Natural Systems and Development.* Baltimore: Johns Hopkins University Press, 1983.

Huntington, Samuel P. and Jorge I. Dominguez. "Political Development." In *Macropolitical Theory,* Edited by Greenstein and Polsby. The Handbook of Political Science, vol. 3. Boston: Little, Brown and Co., 1975.

Ilchman, Warren F., and Norman Thomas Uphoff. *The Political Economy of Change.* Berkeley: University of California Press, 1969.

Kellerman, Barbara. *Leadership: Multidisciplinary Perspectives.* Englewood Cliffs, N.J.: Prentice-Hall, 1984.

Kingdon, John W. *Agendas, Alternatives and Public Policies.* Boston: Little, Brown and Co., 1984.

Kuhn, Thomas S. *The Structure of Scientific Revolutions.* Chicago: University of Chicago Press, 1970.

Lowi, Theodore J. *The End of Liberalism: The Second Republic of the United States*. New York: W.W. Norton, 1981.

McAllister, Donald. *Evaluation in Environmental Planning: Assessing Environmental, Social, Economic and Political Tradeoffs*. Cambridge: MIT Press, 1981.

Majone, Giandomenico. *Evidence, Argument and Persuasion: Analysis and the Policy Process*. New Haven: Yale University Press, 1988.

———. *Regulatory Policies in Transition*. Jahrbuch fur Neve Politische Okonomie, 1985.

Olsen, Mancur. *The Logic of Collective Action*. Cambridge: Harvard University Press, 1965.

Page, Edward. *Political Authority and Bureaucratic Power: A Comparative Analysis*. Brighton: Wheatsheaf, 1985.

Pfeffer, Jeffrey. *Power in Organizations*. Boston: Pitman, 1981.

Rein, Martin. "Frame Reflective Policy Discourse." Working Paper No. 3. Leyden Institute for Law and Public Policy, 1976.

Shelling, Thomas. *Choice and Consequence: Perspectives of an Errant Economist*. Cambridge: Harvard University Press, 1984.

———. *Micromotives and Macrobehavior*. New York: W. W. Norton, 1978.

———. , ed. *Incentives for Environmental Protection*. Cambridge: MIT Press, 1983.

Schultze, Charles. *Pollution, Prices and Policy*. Washington, D.C.: Brookings Institute, 1975.

Schumacher, E. F. "Buddhist Economics". In *Economics, Ecology, Ethics: Essays Toward a Steady-State Economy*, Edited by Herman E. Daly. San Francisco: W. H. Freeman, 1980.

Stokey, Edith, and Richard Zeckhauser. *Primer for Policy Analysis*. New York: W.W. Norton, 1978.

Stone, Deborah. *Policy Paradoxes and Political Reason*. Boston: Scott, Foresman and Co, 1988.

Tribe, Lawrence. "Policy Science: Analysis or Ideology?" *Philosophy and Public Affairs* 2 (1982): 66–110.

Tribe, Lawrence, Corinne Schelling, and John Voss. *When Values Conflict: Environmental Analysis, Discourse and Decision*. Cambridge: Ballinger, 1976.

Vogel, David. *National Styles of Regulation: Environmental Policy in Great Britain and the United States*. Ithaca: Cornell University Press, 1982.

Wildavsky, Aaron. *Speaking Truth to Power: The Art and Craft of Policy Analysis*. New York: Little, Brown and Co, 1979.

Zeigler, L. Harmon, and G. Wayne Peak. *Interest Groups in American Society*. Englewood Cliffs, N.J.: Prentice-Hall, 1972.

PUBLIC POLICY AND PLANNING IN DEVELOPING COUNTRIES

Andrain, Charles F. *Political Change in the Third World*. Boston: Allen and Unwin, 1988.

Bartelmus, Peter. *Environment and Development*. Boston: Allen and Unwin, 1986.

Centre for Development Planning, Projections and Policies. "Implementation of Development Plans: The Experience of Developing Countries in the First Half of the 1970s." *Journal of Development Planning*, (1977).

Chapin, Mac. "The Silent Jungle: Ecotourism Among the Kuna Indians of Panama." *Cultural Survival Quarterly* 14 (May 1990): .

Chenery, Hollis B., et al., eds. *Studies in Development Planning*. Harvard Economic Studies, vol. 136. Cambridge: Harvard University Press, 1971.

Clark, Robert, C. *Power and Policy in the Third World*. New York: McMillan, 1986.

Colchester, Marcus. "Unity and Diversity: Indonesian Policy Towards Tribal People." *The Ecologist* 16 (1986).

Cook, Wade D., and Tillo E. Kuhn. *Planning Processes in Developing Countries: Techniques and Achievements*. New York: North Holland, 1982.

Grindlee, Merliee. "Anticipating Failure: The Implementation of Rural Development Programs." *Public Policy* (Winter 1981).

———. *Politics and Policy Implementation in the Third World*. Princeton, N.J.: Princeton University Press, 1981.

Grindlee, Merliee, and John Thomas. *The Political Economy of Policy Change in Developing Countries*. Employment and Enterprise Analysis Discussion Paper No. 10, Washington, D.C.: USAID, 1987.

Hirschman, Albert O. *Development Projects Observed*. Washington, D.C.: Brookings Institute, 1967.

————. *Foreign Aid: A Critique and Proposal.* Princeton, N.J.: Princeton University Press, 1969.

————. *Toward a New Strategy for Development.* New York: Pergamon, 1979.

Hoben, Allan. "Agriculture Decision Making in Foreign Assistance." In *Agricultural Decision Making,* Edited by Bartlett. New York: Academic Press, 1981.

Horberry, John. "The Accountability of Development Assistance Agencies: The Case of Environmental Policy." *Environmental Law Quarterly,* 12 (1985).

Leonard, Jeffrey H., ed. *Divesting Nature's Capital: The Political Economy of Environmental Abuse in the Third World.* New York: Holmes and Meier, 1985.

Lewis, W. Arthur. *Development Planning: The Essentials of Economic Policy.* New York: Harper and Row, 1966.

McNeeley, Jeffrey A. *Economics and Biological Diversity: Developing and Using Economic Incentives to Conserve Biological Resources.* Gland, Switzerland: International Union for Conservation of Nature and Natural Resources, 1988.

May, Peter J. "Hints for Crafting Alternative Policies." *Policy Analysis,* vol. no. (Spring 1981): .

Morell, David. "Rhetoric and Reality: Environmental Politics and Administration in Developing Countries." In *Divesting Nature's Capital,* Edited by H. Jeffrey Leonard. New York: Holmes and Meier, 1985.

Moris, Jon. "The Transferability of the Western Management Tradition to the Non-Western Public Sectors: An East African Perspective." *Philippine Journal of Public Administration* 20 (1986).

Nube, Kenneth, and Rajan Sampath. *Issues in Third World Development.* Boulder: Westview Press, 1983.

Palmer, Monte. *Dilemmas of Political Development: An Introduction to the Politics of Developing Countries.* Itasca, Ill.: Peacock, 1985.

Ray, David. "The Dependency Model of Latin American Underdevelopment: Three Basic Fallacies." *Journal of Interamerican Studies and World Affairs* 15 (1973).

Redcliff, Michael. *Sustainable Development: Exploring the Contradictions.* New York: Methuen, 1987.

Rich, Bruce. "The Multilateral Development Banks, Environmental Policy and the United States." *Ecology Law Quarterly* 12 (1985).

Roemer, Michael, and Joseph Stern. *The Appraisal of Development Projects.* New York: Praeger, 1979.

Sachs, Ignacy. *Development and Planning.* New York: Pergamon, 1987.

————. "Developing in Harmony with Nature: Consumption Patterns, Time and Space Uses, Resource Profiles and Technological Choice." In *Ecodevelopment: Concepts, Projects, Strategies,* Edited by Glaeser. Frankfurt: Pergamon, 1984.

————. *The Discovery of the Third World.* Cambridge: MIT Press, 1976.

————. *Studies in the Political Economy of Development.* New York: Pergamon, 1980.

Smith, Tony. "The Underdevelopment of Development Literature: The Case of Dependency Theory." *World Politics* 31 (January 1979).

Tendler, Judith. "Rural Projects Through Urban Eyes." World Bank Working Paper 532, 1982.

Todaro, Michael. *Economic Development in the Third World.* New York: Longman, 1985.

Uri, Piere. *Development without Dependence.* New York, Praeger, 1976.

Environmental Policy and Management

Asian Development Bank. *Environmental Planning and Management: Regional Symposium on Environmental and Nature Resources Planning.* Manila, Philippines: Asian Development Bank, 1986.

Badaracco, Joseph. *Loading the Dice: A Five Country Study of Vinyl Choride Regulation.* Boston: Harvard Business School Press, 1985.

Barbira-Scazzocchio, Francoise. *Land, People and Planning in Contemporary Amazonia.* Cambridge: Cambridge University Press, 1980.

Barbour, Ian. *Western Man and Environmental Ethics.* Reading, MA: Addison-Wesley, 1975.

Brandt, W. *North-South: A Program for Survival.* Cambridge, MIT Press, 1980.

Brickman, Ronald, Shiela Jasonoff, and Thomas Ilgen. *Controlling Chemicals: The Politics of Regulation in Europe and the United States.* New York: Cornell University Press, 1985.

Bromley, Daniel. *The Development of Natural Resource Economics and Their Relevance to Developing Countries.* Madison: University of Wisconsin Press, 1987.

Brown, Lester R. *State of the World: A Worldwatch Institute Report on Progress Toward a Sustainable Society.* New York: W.W. Norton. The World Institute has published these reports annually since 1985.

Caldwell, Lynton K. *International Environmental Policy: Emergence and Dimensions.* Durham, Duke University Press, 1990.

Caufield, Catherine. *Tropical Moist Forests: The Resource, the People, the Threat.* London: Earthscan, 1982.

Clay, Jason. *Indigenous Peoples and Tropical Forests: Models of Land Use and Management from Latin America.* Cambridge, MA: Cultural Survival Inc., 1988.

Cooper, Charles. *Economic Evaluation and the Environment.* New York: United Nations Environment Programme, 1981.

Dixon, John, and Maynard Hufschmidt. *Economic Valuation Techniques for the Environment: A Case Study Workbook.* Baltimore: Johns Hopkins University Press, 1986.

Glaeser, B., and Vyasulu, 1984. "The Obsolescence of Ecodevelopment?" In *Ecodevelopment: Concepts, Projects and Strategies.* Edited by Glaeser. New York: Pergamon, 1984.

Goudie, Andrew. *The Human Impact on the Natural Environment.* Cambridge: MIT Press, 1986.

Haig, Nigel. *European Economic Community Environmental Policy and Britain.* London: International Union for Conservation of Nature and Natural Resources, 1984.

Hardin, Garrett. "The Tragedy of the Commons." *Science* 162(1968): 1243–1248.

Horberry, John. *Environmental Guidelines Survey: An Analysis of Environmental Procedures and Guidelines Governing Development Aid.* Washington, D.C.: International Institute for Environment and Development, 1983.

Jasanoff, Sheila. *Resource Management and Political Culture.* Beverly Hills: Sage, 1986.

Jordan, C. F., ed. *Amazonian Rain Forests: Ecosystem Disturbance and Recovery.* New York: Springer-Verlag, 1987.

Lewis, C. S. "The Abolition of Man." In *Economics, Ecology, Ethics,* Edited by Daly. San Francisco: W. H. Freeman, 1980.

Lim, Gil Chin. "Implementation of Environmental Impact Assessment in Developing Countries." Research Program in Development Studies, Woodrow Wilson School of Public Policy, Princeton University, 1984.

Lowry, Kem, and Richard Carpenter. *Holistic Nature and Fragmented Bu-reaucracies: A Study of Government Organizations for Natural Systems Management.* Honolulu: East-West Center, 1984.

Lundquist, Lennot. "Do Political Structures Matter in Environmental Policies? The Case of Air Pollution Control in Canada, Sweden and the United States." *Canadian Public Affairs* 17:(1974).

Mayda, Jaro. "Environmental Legislation in Developing Countries: Some Parameters and Constraints." *Ecology Law Quarterly,* 12(1985): .

Myers, Norman, ed. *GAIA: An Atlas of Planetary Management.* New York: Anchor Press, 1984.

Otway, Harry, and Malcolm Peltu, eds. *Regulating Industrial Risk.* London: Butterworth, 1985.

Repetto, Robert, ed. *The Global Possible: Resources, Development and the New Century.* New Haven: Yale University Press, 1985.

Solesbury, William. "Issues and Innovations in Environmental Planning in Britain, West Germany and California." *Policy Analysis* 2(1976).

Szekely, Francisco. "The Environmental Impact of Large Hygroelectric Projects on Tropical Countries." *Water Supply and Management* 5(1983).

Thibodeau, Francis R., and Hermann H. Field. *Sustaining Tomorrow: A Strategy for World Conservation and Development.* London: University Press of New England, 1984.

Wandesforde-Smith, Geoffrey. "Environmental Impact Assessment and the Politics of Development in Europe." In *Progress in Resource Management and Environmental Planning* Edited by O'Riordan and Turner. New York: Wiley and Sons, 1980.

Wijkman, Anders, and Lloyd Timberlake. *Natural Disasters: Acts of God or Man?* London: Earthscan, 1985.

World Commission on Environment and Development. *Our Common Future.* New York: Oxford University Press, 1987.

NEGOTIATION AND CONFLICT RESOLUTION

Amy, Douglas. *The Politics of Environmental Mediation.* New York: Columbia University Press, 1987.

Axelrod, Robert. *The Evolution of Cooperation.* New York: Basic Books, 1984.

Bacow, Lawrence, and Michael Wheeler. *Environmental Dispute Resolution.* New York: Plenum, 1983.

Bingham, Gail. *Resolving Environmental Disputes: A Decade of Experience.* Washington, D.C.: The Conservation Foundation, 1985.

Boulding, Kenneth. *Conflict and Defense.* New York: Harper and Bros., 1962.

Brown, L. David. *Managing Conflict at Organization Interfaces.* London: Addison-Wesley, 1983.

Carpenter, Susan, and W. J. D. Kennedy. *Managing Public Disputes: A Practial Guide for Handling Conflict and Reaching Agreements.* San Francisco: Jossey-Bass, 1988.

Fisher, Roger, and William Ury. *Getting to Yes: Negotiating Agreement Without Giving In.* New York: Penguin Books, 1981.

———. *International Mediation: A Working Guide, Ideas for the Practitioner.* Cambridge: Harvard Negotiation Project, 1978.

Forester, John. "Planning in the Face of Conflict: Mediated-Negotiating Strategies in Local Land Use Permitting Processes." Paper prepared for the Lincoln Institute of Land Policy, Cambridge, MA, 1984.

———. *Planning in the Face of Power.* Berkeley: University of California Press, 1989.

Goldberg, Stephen, Eric Green, and Frank Sander. *Dispute Resolution.* Boston: Little, Brown and Co, 1985.

Lax, David, and Jim Sebenius. *The Manager as Negotiator.* New York: Free Press, 1986.

Lewicki, Roy, and Joseph Litterer. *Negotiation.* Homewood, Ill.: Richard Irwin, 1985.

McCreary, Scott T., and Francisco Szekely. "Applying the Principles of Environmental Dispute Resolution to International Transboundary Conflicts: The Case of a U.S.–Mexico Border Dispute." The Program on the Processes of International Negotiation, American Academy of Arts and Sciences. Working Paper No. 5, 1987.

Ozawa, Connie, and Lawrence Susskind. "Mediating Science-Intensive Policy Disputes." *Journal of Policy Analysis and Management* 5(1985).
Pruitt, Dean, and Jeffrey Rubin. *Social Conflict: Escalation, Stalemate and Settlement.* New York: Random House, 1986.

Raiffa, Howard. *The Art and Science of Negotiation.* Cambridge: Harvard University Press, 1982.

Sachs, Andy. "Nationwide Study Identifies Barriers to Environmental Negotiation." *EIA Review* 3(1982).

Schelling, Thomas. *The Strategy of Conflict*. Cambridge: Harvard University Press, 1960.

Susskind, Lawrence. "Environmental Mediation and the Accountability Problem." *Vermont Law Review* 6(1981).

Susskind, Lawrence, and Jeffrey Cruikshank. *Breaking the Impasse: Consensual Approaches to Resolving Public Disputes*. New York: Basic Books, 1987.

Susskind, Lawrence, and Scott McCreary. "Techniques for Resolving Coastal Zone Management Disputes." *Journal of the American Planning Association* 51.

Susskind, Lawrence, and Gerald McMahon. "The Theory and Practice of Negotiated Rulemaking." *Yale Journal of Regulation* 3(1985).

Susskind, Lawrence, and Michael Wheeler. *Resolving Environmental Regulatory Disputes*. Cambridge: Schenckman, 1983.

CULTURE AND COMMUNICATION

Barrett, Richard A. *Culture and Conduct: An Excursion in Anthropology*. Belmont, CA: Wadsworth, 1984.

Basso, Keith. *Portraits of "The Whiteman": Linguistic Play and Cultural Symbols Among the Western Apache*. London: Cambridge University Press, 1979.

Casse, Pierre. *Training for the Cross-Cultural Mind*. Washington, D.C.: The Society for Intercultural Education, 1981.

Condon, John C. *Communicating Across Cultures for What?*. Tokyo: Simul Press, 1983.

Darrow, Ken, and Brad Palmquist, eds. *Transcultural Study Guide*. Stanford, CA: Volunteers in Asia, 1975.

Fisher, Glen. *International Negotiation*. Yarmouth, Maine: Intercultural Press, 1980.

Gluckman, Max. *Politics, Law and Ritual in Tribal Society*. Oxford: Basil Blackwell, 1965.

Goodwin, Glenville. *Myths and Tales of the White Mountain Apache*. Syracuse: Syracuse University Press, 1939.

Gulliver, P. H. *Disputes and Negotiations: A Cross-Cultural Perspective*. New York: Academic Press, 1979.

Hall, Edward. *Beyond Culture*. Garden City, N.Y.: Anchor, 1976.

Harris, Philip, and Robert Moran. *Managing Cultural Differences*. New York: Gulf, 1987.

Hultkrantz, Ake. *Belief and Worship in Native North America*. Syracuse: Syracuse University Press, 1981.

Kohn, Alfie. *No Contest: The Case Against Competition*. Boston: Houghton Mifflin, 1986.

Merry, Sally Engle. "Cultural Frameworks of Mediation." Paper presented at the Workshop on Transcultural Issues in Dispute Resolution, University of Hawaii, June 1987.

Nader, Laura, and Harry F. Todd, Jr., eds. *The Disputing Process: Law in Ten Societies*. New York: Columbia University Press, 1978.

Scollon, Ron, and Suzanne Scollon. *Narrative, Literacy and Face in Interethnic Communication*. New York: Columbia University Press, 1981.

Smith, Watson, and John Smith, 1954. *Zuni Law: A Field of Values*. Santa Fe: University of New Mexico Press, 1954.

Taylor, Lynda, et al. "The Importance of Cross-Cultural Communication between Environmentalists and Land-Based People." *The Workbook* 13(1988).

Tiewul, Sylvanus. "Law Without Institutions: An Introduction to the Regulation of Order and Conflict in African Society." Submitted for L.L.M. Degree at Harvard Law School, Cambridge, MA, 1973.

Zimmerman, Mark. *How to Do Business with the Japanese*. New York: Random House, 1983.

THE CARIBBEAN

Alleyne, Mervyn C. "A Linguistic Perspective on the Caribbean." In *Caribbean Contours*. Edited by Sidney W. Mintz and Sally Price. Baltimore: Johns Hopkins University Press, 1985.

Axline, W. Andrew. *Caribbean Integration: The Politics of Regional Negotiation*. New York: Nichols, 1979.

Bell, Wendell. "The Invasion of Grenada: A Note on False Prophecy." *Yale Review* 1986:564–86.

Dash, Michael J. "Marvelous Realism: The Way Out of Negritude." *Caribbean Studies* 14(January 1974).

Duncan, Neville. *Movements and Subculture: A Preliminary Examination of Social and Political Protests in the Anglophone Caribbean.* Bridgetown, Barbados: Institute of Social and Economic Research, University of the West Indies, 1983.

Emmanuel, Patrick, 1987. *Political Competition and Public Policy in the Eastern Caribbean.* Bridgetown, Barbados: Institute of Social and Economic Research, University of the West Indies, 1987.

Erisman, H. Michael. *The Caribbean Challenge: U.S. Policy in a Volatile Region.* Boulder, CO: Westview Press, 1984.

Guillén, Nicolás. *Man-Making Words.* Boston: University of Massachusetts Press, 1972.

Henry, Paget, and Carl Stone, 1983. *The Newer Caribbean: Decolonialization, Democracy and Development.* Philadelphia: Institute for the Study of Human Issues, 1983.

Hoetink. H. " 'Race' and Color in the Caribbean." In *Caribbean Contours.* Edited by Sidney W. Mintz and Sally Price. Baltimore: Johns Hopkins University Press, 1985.

Izevbaye, D. S. "The Exile and the Prodigal: Derek Walcott as West Indian Poet." *Caribbean Quarterly* 26(1980).

Kahn, Jamal. *Public Management: The Eastern Caribbean Experience.* Providence, R.I.: Foris, 1987.

Koester, Stephen. "From Plantation Agriculture to Oil Storage: Economic Development ane Social Transformation." Ph.D. diss., University of Colorado–Boulder, 1986.

Lewis, Gordon K. *Growth of the Modern West Indies.* New York: Monthly Review Press, 1968.

MacDonald, Vincent R. *The Caribbean Economies: Perspectives on Social, Political and Economic Conditions.* New York: MSS Information Corp., 1985.

Metraux, Alfred. *Voodoo in Haiti.* New York: Schocken Books, 1972.

Mintz, Sidney. "The Caribbean as a Socio-Cultural Area." *Journal of World History* 9(1966).

Parry, J. H., and Philip Sherlock. *A Short History of the West Indies.* London: McMillan Caribbean, 1971.

Pastor, Robert, and Sergio Diz-Briquets. "The Caribbean: More People and Fewer Resources." In *Bordering on Trouble.* Edited by Maguire and Brown. New York: Adler and Adler, 1985.

Patterson, Orlando. *The Sociology of Slavery: An Analysis of the Origins, Development and Structure of Negro Slave Society in Jamaica.* Cranbury, N.J.: Associated University Presses, 1969.

Payne, Anthony, and Paul Sutton. *Dependency Under Challenge: The Political Economy of the Commonwealth Caribbean.* Dover, N.H.: Manchester Press, 1984.

Ramchand, Kenneth. *Best West Indian Short Stories.* London: Nelson Caribbean, 1984.

Renard, Yves, ed. *Perceptions of the Environment: A Selection of Interpretative Essays.* Bridgetown, Barbados: Caribbean Conservation Association, 1979.

Richardson, Bonhan C. *Caribbean Migrants: Environment and Survival on St. Kitts and Nevis.* Austin: University of Texas Press, 1983.

Simpson, George E. "Afro-American Religions and Religious Behavior." *Caribbean Studies* 12(July 1972).

Stephens, Evelyn Huber, and John D. Stephens. *Democratic Socialism in Jamaica: The Political Movement and Social Transformation in Dependent Capitalism.* Princeton, N.J.: Princeton University Press, 1986.

Stone, Carl. "A Political Profile of the Caribbean." In *Caribbean Contours.* Edited by Sidney W. Mintz and Sally Price. Baltimore: Johns Hopkins University Press, 1985.

U.S. Congress, Office of Technology Assessment. "Integrated Renewable Resource Management for U.S. Insular Areas." Washington, D.C.: U.S. Government Printing Office, 1987.

Valenzuela, Samuel, and Arturo Valenzuela. "Modernizations and Dependency: Alternate Perspectives in the Study of Latin American Underdevelopment." *Comparative Politics* 10(July 1978): .

Walcott, Derek. *Collected Poems 1948–1984.* New York: Farrar, Straus and Giroux, 1986.

Watson, Hilbourne Alban. "The Political Economy of Investment in the Commonwealth Since World War II." Ph.D. diss., Howard University, 1975.

Williams, Eric. *From Columbus to Castro: The History of the Caribbean 1492–1969.* New York: Vintage Books, 1984.

Index